THE CYMBAL BOOK

BY HUGO PINKSTERBOER

EDITED BY RICK MATTINGLY

To Hedy, who knows more about cymbals
than anyone who never wanted to know about cymbals
will ever know about cymbals, a symbol of my love

ISBN 0-7935-1920-9

HAL•LEONARD®
CORPORATION
7777 W. BLUEMOUND RD. P.O. BOX 13819 MILWAUKEE, WI 53213

ACKNOWLEDGEMENTS

Special thanks to:
Rick Mattingly, for his introduction, his editing, and for cleaning up my Dutch-American/English.
Stephen Rauch at HLP, for everything he did to help.
Erk Willemsen, for starting *Slagwerkkrant*, proofreading and advice.

Ronald Willemsen, for his illustrations and his mouse-hammered cymbals.
Bas Westerweel, for his studio photos.
Ulbo de Sitter, for his B/W printing and photographic advice.
Piet Klaassen Drum Service, for supplying me with experience, and for his (broken) cymbals.
Henk Wijngaard, for editing the last-minute changes.
Jim Gordon and Simon Goodwin, for helping me out with the intricacies of the English language.
Behnan Göçmez, for helping me out with my Turkish.
Peter Tax and Alexander van den Eijnde, for helping my computer understand Macintosh, and vice versa.
Fred van Vloten, for his help and his enthusiasm.
Steve Clover, for being there, whenever.

And
For inviting me out at their companies, for sharing their knowledge with me, and for making cymbals:
At Zildjian: Armand Zildjian, Ian Croft, Lennie DiMuzio, Colin Schofield, Robert Seeley, Charlie Yanizzi
At Sabian: Robert Zildjian, Dan Barker, Wayne Blanchard, Nort Hargrove, Dave McAllister, Gabe and Kerope Zilcan
At Paiste: Robert, Toomas and Michael Paiste, Fredy Studer, Marc Smitt
At Meinl: Reinhold Meinl, Wolfgang Wunder, Stefan Hänisch
At UFIP: Luigi Tronci, Carlo Biasei, Alex Mühlbauer, the late Giovanni Spadacini
At Zilciler Kollektif Sirketi (Istanbul): Mehmet Tamdeger, Agop Tomurcuk, Nusret Özevin and Roberto Spizzichino

And
The Dutch cymbal distributors BMI, Drum Partner, JIC, PPP, Serlui and Weerts for supplying the 125 cymbals on the cover.

And
James Blades, for his information and approval
Grace Frary, *The Music Trades*
Herb Brochstein (Pro-Mark)
Vic Firth (Vic Firth)
Roger Horrobin (Premier), for information on Zyn cymbals
Mitsuo Yanagisawa, President of Pearl Musical Instrument Co., Japan
Karl-Heinz Menzel, Sonor, for information on Tyrko, Zymbor and Trowa cymbals
Michael Ranta, Asian Sound, Cologne, Germany, for information on Chinese cymbal making
Paul Real, Paul Real Sales/PR Percussion, Pasadena, for information on Wuhan
Lou Dias, British Historical Drum Society.
Dr. Thomas Rossing, Northern Illinois University, Department of Physics, for the beautiful hologram interferograms.
Alan Buckley of the Classic Drum Museum, England, for supplying me with historic photos and historic catalogs.

And
Everyone else, who ever, in one way or another, said or wrote meaningful things about them.

THE CYMBAL BOOK

by HUGO PINKSTERBOER

edited by Rick Mattingly

design and layout by
Keijser 18 Mediaprodukties, Amsterdam.

Cover photo by Bas Westerweel

TABLE OF CONTENTS

INTRODUCTION

How is it that something made of metal, which is considered a "cold" substance, can evoke such strong emotions? That is certainly the case when the metal is used to make a cymbal.

It is cymbals that are most often mentioned when drummers talk of self-expression. It is the cymbals that drummers work to develop a "touch" on. It is cymbals that drummers constantly check out, always looking for a new one, a better one, a different one.

And it is cymbals that provoke the most heated arguments. Ask two drummers to discuss whether or not cymbals should be cleaned, or ask them to compare the merits of a cymbal that was manufactured using ancient traditions vs. one that was the result of the latest technology, and you might end up with a fistfight. Different philosophies of cymbal making not only provoke violent disagreements, they have actually divided families. It's hard to imagine anyone getting that upset over the differences between two snare drums.

Part of the fascination with cymbals is that they are shrouded in mystery: they are made from "secret" formulas that have been handed down from generation to generation. Metallurgists tell us that, given the materials from which cymbals are made, they should shatter like glass when struck. The fact that they don't is part of their magic.

And no one can really tell you what a cymbal sounds like. They have fundamentals, overtones, undertones, sweet spots, trash, ping, sustain, definition, wash, decay. And then there are the hidden sounds. To the uninitiated, a cymbal is a loud, crashing, brash-sounding instrument that should only be heard from a distance. But what drummer's eyes haven't widened in amazement upon first holding an ear next to a cymbal whose recent crash had appeared to die out only to find that the instrument has an internal hum that sounds like the purring of a kitten.

Cymbals have been analyzed from every angle: their composition, size, weight, profile, taper, hammering, lathing. Still, no one can tell you the best way to make one. It is quite possible to find two cymbals that were made the same way with the same specifications that sound very different. It is also possible to find two cymbals that were made two very different ways that sound very much alike.

It seems that every drummer has at least one cymbal that he or she feels is very special, that can't be replaced, that is the perfect cymbal for this musician. But that doesn't keep them from looking for another one, and another one after that. A drummer looking for a new cymbal probably has a wider choice than any other instrumentalist looking for any other instrument. But still they want even more choices, more sounds.

So the companies keep coming up with new ones. And new companies get started to fill the insatiable need for even more cymbals.

Hugo Pinksterboer has explored cymbals every possible way: from the people who make them to the people who play them to the instruments themselves. There is information here that will settle some old arguments and start a few new ones. From reading this book I know at least twice as much about cymbals as I knew before. And they are now twice as mysterious to me.

Anyone who would go to the lengths Hugo went to for the sake of round metal disks that people hit with sticks would have to be a bit crazy. Or he'd have to be a drummer.

Rick Mattingly

PREFACE

During the years I spent working on this project, I was repeatedly asked if it were really possible to devote an entire book to the subject of cymbals. The answer, obviously, is yes. The result ended up being a lot bigger than I had dared think.

My visits to the six Western cymbal factories contributed a lot to the quality of the book. It was given a solid base by the knowledge shared by presidents, research & development teams, testers, lathemen, hammerers and all the other employees with those companies—something that I will always be grateful for. Many of the insights, ideas, comments, information, tips and remarks also originated from numerous interviews and discussions with drummers of all kinds, and from a wide collection of magazines and books. My personal experience as drummer, editor of drum- and music magazines, drum-mechanic and cymbal salesman did the rest.

However simple and straightforward cymbals may look, they are most complex instruments, their sound being determined by innumerable different, interrelated factors. Because of their complexity and personal character, there are hardly any uniform opinions about which cymbal is the best for which purpose, about how to clean them, about why they sound the way they do, and about lots of other things. The many contradictory quotations that you'll find throughout these pages clearly indicate this. Consequently, these quotes do not always represent the opinion of the author.

The Cymbal Book offers in-depth information about the different ways in which cymbals are made, as well as a wealth of knowledge about such topics as repairs, cymbal selection, the creation of cymbal sounds, the composition of setups and all other related subjects.

Cymbals are quite unique instruments, considering that they are—as almost no other instrument—used in virtually every kind of music you can think of: from marching band to symphony orchestra, and from avant-garde jazz to heavy-metal rock. Yet, as indicated in the title, this book is mainly dedicated to drummers. To experienced drummers, beginners and pros. To inquisitive drummers in any style, from any background. It is also written for salesmen, distributors and others who want to know more about the subject. Of course, percussionists will find tons of useful material on these pages, too.

Types, series and brands of cymbals are mentioned with a certain frequency as examples of the information being conveyed. I did not strive to be complete in that regard. Mentioning every single cymbal every place where it should have been appropriate would have made this book twice as thick, but certainly not twice as interesting. Objectivity, at the same time, has been one of the main goals.

In writing *The Cymbal Book* I have also tried to be as complete as possible, which in itself is an impossible goal. Of course, I would be happy to receive any remarks, comments or ideas for a next edition.

It should be stressed that this book doesn't contain any reviews of specific cymbals, or any prescriptions. *The Cymbal Book* should be seen as a recipe that you may prepare according to your own taste. It contains a wealth of information, creating every chance to form an opinion of your own. I thank all of those who have shared their opinions with me, giving me the opportunity to write this book.

Hugo Pinksterboer
September 1992

1. HISTORY

The characteristic tendency of drummers to try out any given object that might possibly produce a musical sound dates from a long time ago. From the very first moment mankind began experimenting with metals and alloys, people have tested them for their sound.

Bronze, the material that has always been used for cymbals, is the oldest alloy known. In Asia it was first used around 3000 B.C. The earliest forefathers of cymbals, therefore, may go back some 5,000 years. This chapter describes the main lines of that extensive history: from the first ancestors, through the birth of the modern types of cymbals, up to and beyond the cymbal boom of the 1980s.

...extensive history...
Bronze cymbal from Nimrud (Tigris-Euphrates Valley; Middle East), 9th-8th century B.C.
Courtesy of The British Museum

1.1. CYMBALS FROM ANCIENT TIMES

James Blades, in his profound work *Percussion Instruments and Their History*, has delved intensely into the history of cymbals.[1] Most of the information in the first section of this chapter is derived from his work. Blades mentions many striking examples of the use of cymbals in ancient times. One of the oldest stories dates back to 1200 B.C. when the goddess Cybele was worshipped in Asia Minor. This ritual was always accompanied by the sound of cymbals.

Beggars and vagrants tried to better their chances for charitable gifts in this manner. Cymbals were often used to add luster to the exaltation of the numerous gods from antiquity. One of the gods mentioned by Blades is Dionysus, the Greek god of wine, who is largely known for the numerous orgies organized on his behalf.

In 1050 B.C., cymbals are mentioned in the Bible for the first time. When David transferred the Ark of God to Jerusalem, at his arrival he "and all the house of Israel played before the Lord on all manner of instruments made of Firrewood, even on harpes, and on psalteries, and on timbrels, and on cornets, and on cimbels."[2]

A Babylonian picture from 700 B.C. depicts cymbals that clearly show a similarity with instruments in use today: they are rather flat and have cups. Apart from this type there were also spherical cymbals and other models. Some of these very early cymbals already showed tonal grooves.

Bo. Pair of 14 3/4+ Chinese cymbals; age unknown. Collection Haags Gemeentemuseum, The Hague. The text on the outside says "Eternal friendship." On the inside there are three double columns of text: "The city gate of the city of Suzhou. Wang Dong Wen (owner)," "Percussion that has left the premises will under no circumstances be exchanged," and "Finely polished on both sides." Translation courtesy of Haags Gemeentemuseum.

Drinking Bowls

China is often regarded as the first country where cymbals were manufactured. However, the bible of Chinese Musical Instruments, the Yo Shu (1101), says that at first they were imported from Tibet. India and Turkey were sometimes mentioned as possible places of origin of the cymbal as well. The art of casting, tempering and hammering bronze was known in these countries at a very early stage. Israel and Egypt also have long traditions in this field.

Nothing definite is known about the alloy used in those days. Unlike some pictures and stories, the instruments themselves have not survived. It is commonly assumed that the alloy of the ancient "holy" cymbals consisted of about 80% copper and 20% tin. As far back as history records, church bells were cast from this alloy, and it has remained one of the principal alloys from which cymbals are made.

In the various ancient cultures, cymbals did not only function in the worship of gods. They were also used at funerals, orgies and other ceremonies and parties. Witches utilized cymbals to counter lunar eclipses. In the second century, Pliny wrote of bee-keepers luring their swarms with "the sound of bronze." The Romans used cymbal-like instruments as drinking bowls, or vice versa. In ancient Greece these pleasant uses were also combined.

Etymology

The origin of the word cymbal has much to do with these old habits. It is derived from the Greek word *kymbos* (κψμβοσ) and the Latin equivalent *cymbalum,* meaning "cistern" or "beaker." The Dutch word for cymbal, *bekken,* and the German word *Becken* also stand for a "round, spherical, wide (drinking) bowl." These words are derived from the Latin word *baccinum,* meaning "basin" or "tray." The Italian word for cymbal is *piatto,* meaning "plate" or "tray." To distinguish them from the more domestic objects, in Italian cymbals are sometimes indicated by the term *piatti musicali.*

Percussion = War

For centuries, cymbals have been used by the military. They played an important part in the Turkish Mehter music (marching music, during the Ottoman Empire). In those days they were always played in pairs. The European military marching bands have used cymbals from the eighteenth century on.

Chinese cymbals, thin, with large cups. The smaller cups are shaped as handles, similar to the modern Chinese cymbals; age unknown. Collection Haags Gemeentemuseum, The Hague
Photo by the author

Apart from the musical use, cymbals often served to strike terror into the hearts of the enemy. As far back as 2,500 years ago, the Chinese scared the living daylights out of their adversaries with a cacophony of clashing cymbals, a technique that appears to have been used in Korea as recently as 1950. It is hardly surprising that the Chinese word for percussion also means "war."

In the Middle Ages the use of cymbals was largely limited to processions and other ritual events. In those days cymbals still looked a lot like the instruments the ancient Greeks and the Romans used. They were very thick and spherical, so they probably had a clearly distinguishable pitch.

The cymbal of that time mostly looked like an oversized, high cup with a very narrow edge. UFIP's Icebells resemble these forerunners quite closely. Their sizes ranged from 6 inches to 10 inches. Through the ages, the edge of those cymbals has grown into what is now the bow of the cymbal. The cup became relatively small. Not all Medieval cymbals were of the type just described. James Blades has found evidence indicating that a thinner cymbal with a diameter of about 12 inches also existed in that period.

Dancing Monkeys

Strungh was the first composer to make use of cymbals in the Opera orchestra *(Esther, 1680).* In 1794, Haydn required cymbals for his *Military Symphony,* in which he included elements from the Turkish military Janissary music. In the opera *Il Seraglio,* Mozart also enters this field.[3]

It was, however, not until the latter half of the nineteenth century that the cymbal started to be used widely as a serious musical instrument. The extensive cymbal parts that composers like Berlioz and Wagner prescribed were of great influence on this process. Berlioz (1803-1869) is also known as the first composer who required the playing of a single "suspended" cymbal with sticks. Before that, cymbals were always used in pairs. As progressive as Berlioz was, in other aspects he remained stoutly conservative. The sound of a cymbal combined with a stroke on a bass drum was, to him, only fit "to have monkeys dance to." Verdi and Rossini did not let this worry them too much and gladly made use of this effect, which was to become the most widely used way of playing accents.

Zildjian

Up to the first half of the nineteenth century, the Zildjian Company was a modest little enterprise that mainly sold its products to the military and the Church. As the orchestral use of cymbals increased the company grew rapidly. In 1851, Avedis Zildjian II built a schooner and sailed with his cymbals to exhibitions in Marseille, London and Paris, opening up a larger market for Turkish cymbals. The classification "Turkish" for today's regular ride, crash and similar cymbals, as opposed to the Chinese types with their flanged edges, can be traced back to Avedis' predecessors.

1.2. THE TWENTIES AND THIRTIES

The history of the present-day drumset, which has always incorporated cymbals, begins with the invention of the bass drum pedal. Until that time, there were always two drummers in a band: one playing snare drum, the other playing bass drum and cymbals. The invention of the bass drum pedal, at first believed to have put half of the drummers out of work, has often been ascribed to William F. Ludwig (1894). Others also mention the name Dee Dee Chandler (1894) in this context.

The first bass drum pedals were primitive wooden affairs, played with the heel. In 1909, Ludwig introduced the toe-operated bass drum pedal.

Back then, the choice in cymbals was largely limited to Zildjians and Chinese specimens. The fact that Chinese cymbals were used more often than Turkish cymbals was not so much due to preference as to availability. Only the big-time orchestras could afford Zildjians. The interest in Chinese cymbals eventually died out in the late twenties. Some four decades later jazz-rock players like Billy Cobham and Alphonse Mouzon inspired the comeback of that sound.

The first set drummers made far less use of their cymbals than their successors did in later decades. They primarily used them for single choked accents. The timekeeping focus was on the bass drum—four on the floor—and on the snare drum, playing accentuated press rolls. Baby Dodds and Chick Webb were two of the major practitioners of this style.

The hi-hat had not yet been invented. Instead, there was a device that could best be described as a bass drum pedal extension. Straight cymbal stands with tilters did not exist then. The relatively small (10" to 12") cymbals from the first part of this century were suspended from a leather strap. With the introduction of rack systems in the second half of the 1980s, the idea of mounting cymbals from above was re-introduced—be it with a different look.

Fine Effects

Initially, jazz drummers mostly used cymbals that were made for classical and military orchestras. Why? Simply because there was no such thing as a cymbal made especially for drumset players. A letter from the Avedis Zildjian Company to the Tronci Brothers (UFIP), dated December 8, 1930, documents the sizes that were popular at that time. In this letter Zildjian requests a list of the purchase prices of 10" to 15" UFIP cymbals, "...as we are considering to handle a lower priced cymbals...." There are no records showing that such a deal was ever realized.

The 1930s book *Max on Swing*, also leaves no room for doubt about the most common sizes of that time: "If, as I say, you can afford only one cymbal, then buy a 12" one. This should not be of the thick type, nor should they be, in my opinion, of the extreme 'paper thin' kind.... If your pocket allows you to run to more than one cymbal, then you should next posses yourself of an 11" cymbal, slightly thinner than your first,

...suspended from a leather strap...
John Grey Kit and Console, with
low-hat pedal, 1920s
Photo by Alan Buckley
Collection Classic Drum Museum,
Alan Buckley, England

...re-introduced—be it with another
look...
Tama Power Tower System, 1988
Courtesy of Hoshino, Japan

When the jazz era started out people couldn't afford many cymbals. You always had to get the maximum out of the minimum number.
—Ed Thigpen

Zildjian request for UFIP prices, December 8, 1930 "...therefore we must have your lowest prices..." Courtesy of UFIP

...jazz was, so to say, developing on his doorstep... Avedis Zildjian III Courtesy of Zildjian

and of a little higher pitch.... If you can still go to another, then you may indulge in the extra luxury of a 10" or 11" paper thin instrument; there are many fine effects possible with cymbals of this nature."[4] In 1933, Zildjian's wholesale price for a 10" cymbal was $3.00.

Made In USA

Some years before, two cymbal companies were established. Avedis Zildjian III, who started his career in the USA as a candy maker, produced the first American Zildjian cymbals in 1929. Despite the initial distrust of cymbals bearing the legend "Made in USA" and a growing loss of jobs among musicians caused by the introduction of talking films, he had no problem keeping his head amply above water. Among other things, this was probably due to the convenient location of Avedis' factory. Jazz was, so to speak, developing on his doorstep.

For the first time in history there was an opportunity for direct communication between the consumers and the producer. These contacts soon proved to be of enormous importance to a rapid evolution of the cymbal.

Five Italian cymbal-makers from the town of Pistoia, who in 1931 united in the *Unione Fabbricanti Italiani Piatti* (UFIP), were considerably less fortunate.[5] The fascist leader Mussolini simply declared jazz to be taboo. Despite that fact, the Italians were very active. This is clearly illustrated by a remark in a book from that time, written by C. Sachs: "...the so-called Turkish cymbals, originating, by the way, for the main part from the Italian village of Pistoia...."[6] Whether through ignorance or intent, Mr. Sachs obviously tried to rewrite history in just a few words. Around this same period Paiste started to export cymbals from Estonia, first to England, later to the USA.

1.3. ORIGINS OF HI-HATS, RIDES AND CRASHES

Few realize how new the classification of hi-hats, rides and crash cymbals is. Up to the late forties these terms were unheard of. The Zildjian catalog of 1948 listed just 20 sizes, ranging incrementally per inch from 7" to 26". One year later 27" and 28" models were added. At that time a 20" cymbal cost $49.50. All sizes were available in the weights Paper Thin, Thin, Medium Thin, Medium, Medium Heavy, and Heavy. The words "ride" and "crash," so familiar now, had not been coined yet—let alone onomatopoeic terms such as Ping, Pang, Smash and Splash. A remark in the same catalog gives some insight into the way cymbals were made in those days: "Sizes cannot be guaranteed to be accurate." Much has changed since then. How did the three main classifications of cymbals actually come about?

1.3.1. HI-HATS

The intriguing history of the hi-hat goes back to the so-called "clanger." A second beater, attached to the shaft of the bass drum pedal, simultaneously struck a small cymbal that was mounted vertically to the bass drum. Sonor featured such an item in their 1907 catalog.

The snow-shoe, also written as snoe-shoe, was the successor of this rather primitive invention. It consisted of two hinged, flat wooden boards, each the size of a large shoe. Two small cymbals were attached to the ends. Some versions featured a strap on the top board, that prevented the foot from sliding off. At the same time this strap relieved the

Wooden snowshoe
Photo by Alan Buckley
Collection Classic Drum Museum, Alan Buckley, England

Premier Low-hat, 1926
Photo by Alan Buckley
Collection Classic Drum Museum, Alan Buckley, England

task of the built-in spring; the top board and cymbal could be more or less lifted with the foot. This was quite a troublesome process.

The snow-shoe was also known as the Crocodile Foot Cymbal Pedal, and as the Charleston pedal, after a well-know dance of the time. In French a hi-hat pedal is still called *Pédale Charleston*. A metal version of the wooden snow-shoe, the Bobby Salmons Foot-cymbals Pedal, was made by Boosey and Hawkes. It featured an adjusting device for the cymbals.

Other companies also have made a metal Foot Cymbal Pedal. The Premier 1926-1928 catalog praised its "swiveling cymbals for instant adjustment to the correct angle," its new heel rest and its four spurs. In 1927 a Ludwig Charleston listed for $5.00— including two cymbals.

Low-hat

Things were looking up when the low-hat, low-sock or low-boy was introduced. According to legend, this device was conceived around 1925 by drummer Vic Berton. The low-sock, as it was produced by the Massachusetts company Walberg & Auge, showed remarkable similarity with the hi-hat, yet it was only about 15" high. Luxury features such as spurs and adjustable spring tension were unheard of. The cymbals usually had a diameter of 10" and a relatively large cup.

The term "sock" is derived from the characteristic sound brought forth by these cymbals, although some people attribute the name to the fact that the instrument was physically located next to the drummer's cotton footwear. Variations on this theme were the 1928 Slingerland WOW Sock Pedal and the 1935 Ludwig Duncan pedal. Both these pedals featured vertically mounted cymbals.[7]

Hi-hat

Eventually, it was only a small step from the original low- to the modern hi-hat. Simply lengthening the tube allowed the possibility of playing the sock cymbals not only with the foot, but with the sticks as well. A world of new techniques, effects and completely different styles of playing opened up. This influential invention is ascribed by Art Blakey and Panama Francis to Kaiser Marshall.

The late "Papa" Jo Jones, however, stated that he saw Cuba Austin play with McKinney's Cotton Pickers in 1926: "And he had this little sock cymbal that you used to slide your foot into. It was through necessity that I went and got a pipe. I couldn't go down and play the sock cymbal on the floor."[8]

In those days we drummers didn't know much about foot cymbals—we were just flabbin' them. I switched over to the upstairs pedal because the new beat was takin' things by storm. It's the greatest thing ever invented... You can hold everything together with that snap.
—Jimmy Crawford

The first hi-hat I played was a floor model. It was made with two pieces of two-by-four, with a spring in the middle and two cymbals on the ends. Those cymbals were so thick you could hear them two blocks away.
—Panama Francis

*Trail-blazers: Papa Jo Jones and
Chick Webb.
Courtesy of Zildjian*

Jo Jones was one of the first drummers to use the hi-hat as the main timekeeper, instead of the snare and the bass drum. Chick Webb and Zutty Singleton were also considered trail-blazers in this field.

The small large-cupped cymbals that stemmed from the low-hat were, of course, hardly suited for playing a ride beat with sticks. The ride area simply was too small. With the introduction of the hi-hat, the cymbals were soon replaced by larger (11" and 12") and thinner ones, having a much smaller cup. In the mid and late forties the switch to larger cymbals was made. A suggested bebop setup of that time contained 15" hi-hats, a 22" medium ride and a 15" thin cymbal. Sonny Greer used a pair of 16" hi-hats in that period.[9]

The first hi-hats were made by Walberg & Auge and also marketed by Leedy, Slingerland and Ludwig in 1928. In a 1930s catalog Ludwig calls this pedal the High-Hat Sock Pedal, and it is listed next to the Low Sock Pedal. The forerunner of the remote hi-hat was invented by Billy Gladstone, as early as 1939.[7]

1.3.2. RIDE AND CRASH CYMBALS

Gene Krupa and Dave Tough were two influential drummers who, in the late twenties, debuted doing full justice to the sound of their cymbals; they let the sound die out, instead of choking them right after the stroke. The choked cymbal sound started to lose ground. Slowly, cymbals—especially the hi-hat, which had reached its maturity by now—began to grow more important to timekeeping. Their sizes were still quite modest.

In the latter part of the thirties, Gene Krupa accompanied the first swing bands with an 8" Splash, 14" and 16" medium cymbals, a 13" thin and a pair of 11" hi-hats. In the setups of the leading swing drummers, 14" and 16" cymbals were used arbitrarily as ride or crash. It was not until after World War II that the development of a specific ride cymbal started to gain momentum. Before that time, indications like Ride and Crash just did not exist.

Especially in the big bands, drummers were developing a need for cymbals with sufficient power and definition to cope with the volume of the brass. They started asking for bigger cymbals. This caused a number of problems. Even the production of a 16" cymbal, some years before, was not without difficulty at first.

Armand Zildjian recalls: "So rides had to get bigger. I remember Krupa wanted a 16". Jesus! Our rolling mills weren't strong enough to get all that metal through. We were still using leather belts to drive the mills back then."[10]

This must have been in the earliest days of the company, as Zildjian offered 17" cymbals in 1933. The Turkish K. Zildjian factory featured 11" to 18" cymbals, in whole and half inch sizes, as early as 1924.

*"...pencil your requirements in the
left hand corner of this letter..."
Zildjian pamphlet, 1933
Courtesy of UFIP*

Riding the Ride

Kenny Clarke became a trendsetter by transferring the jazz beat from the hi-hats to the ride cymbal. "I just moved over from the hi-hat to the ride and played the same thing that I'd been playing on the hi-hat. The hi-hat became another instrument I could play with my left hand. It opened up the whole set, you know," he explained.[11] At first, Clarke's new way of playing was not received with much enthusiasm ("I was always getting fired"), but fortunately he persisted. The results are well-known.

In classic bebop, as pioneered by Max Roach and Art Blakey, the time is kept by the ride cymbal. The bass drum and snare drum are used to play syncopated figures around it; the hi-hat takes care of the afterbeat.

Around 1950 the first cymbal stand with a tilting mechanism was introduced, to facilitate the playing of the ride cymbal. Zildjian reacted to bebop by producing heavier and clearer sounding cymbals such as the Bop ride and the Ping ride. Big band drummers like Louie Bellson and Ed Shaughnessy were very happy with these new types. Bellson used 16" Bounce (Medium) and 22" Bounce (Heavy) cymbals in the late forties, combined with 14" hi-hats and 15" and 18" crash cymbals. This complete cymbal set had a retail price of $215.60.[9]

In that same period, Buddy Rich still used smaller cymbals. His five cymbals, including 12" hi-hats, the tiny splash he never parted from, and a 15" bounce cymbal, retailed for $144.10.[9] Bop and Bounce ride cymbals eventually disappeared.

28" Rides

In this period the bass drums grew smaller and smaller. From the original 26" monsters they gradually went down to 20" and 18". The fact that drumsets were moved around in cabs most of the time played an important part in this development. At the same time, the sizes of the cymbals expanded enormously. Stan Kenton wanted to hear 24" ride and 22" crash cymbals in his big band. Later on, 18" hi-hats and 28" rides were being made—and sold, supposedly.

Obviously there is not much to add about the history of the crash cymbal: as soon as a specific ride cymbal was developed, drummers needed a lighter, faster type of sound to play the accents. Still, it was not until the early fifties that the term "crash cymbal" became more or less common.

1.4. THE SIXTIES AND SEVENTIES

In the following period, the ride remained the main timekeeper. At first, the cymbals themselves didn't change too much. Numerous new musical trends developed, but the music industry hardly seemed to respond. The ride cymbals used at first in groups like The Beatles, The Rolling Stones, The Who and other major bands from the sixties were quite thin; *too* thin for that type of music, actually. On most records from that period the ride beat could hardly be distinguished. When it could be heard at all, it sounded more like a continuous shshshh-sound than as a rhythmical series of pings. Robert and Toomas Paiste, who had settled in Switzerland in 1957, began to satisfy the need for more volume with their Giant Beats.

Power

In 1966 The Beatles decided to give up live performances. The hysterical crowds just screamed too loud, and the musicians couldn't hear themselves playing anymore. But technology won out. Amplifiers became more powerful by the day. Slowly it became clear that the rather thin 16" and 18" medium-thin crashes of that time did not have enough power to project under these circumstances. Their place was soon taken over by heavier types like rock crashes. Timekeeping became more audible through the use of heavier ride cymbals. The beat musicians of the sixties then started to play pop and rock. Rock and soul gave birth to funk; bebop and rock lead to fusion. Punk, new wave, hard rock, heavy metal, speed metal and thrash metal were crowding the doorstep.

An end to the increase of the average volume of live performances was not yet in

...the Turkish K. Zildjian factory featured 11" to 18" cymbals as early as 1924...
Early 1920s Ludwig catalog
Courtesy of Ludwig

...and the 8" splash he never parted from...
Buddy Rich (late 1980s)
photo by the author

sight. There was a demand for cymbals that were even louder. The first unlathed cymbals entered the market. Zildjian introduced the Earth Ride, which was soon followed by Paiste's Rude series.

The counterpart of these powerful cymbals had then been on the market for quite some time; in 1964 Paiste introduced the first flat ride, a very controlled sounding cymbal without a cup. In the years that followed, P.A. systems were introduced and improved up to a level that even the smallest, softest sounding cymbals could be used in the loudest bands, and be audible.

Clearly Defined

In the latter half of the seventies the sound of the ride cymbal started to disappear from rock 'n' roll and other, related styles. Drummers of pop, rock, funk and disco rediscovered the hi-hat as a basic timekeeping instrument. The way of playing in those kinds of music demanded this clearly defined beat.

Especially in disco the playing style seemed to go back to the beginning of drumming history. The bass drum is again limited to four on the floor, with a solid two and four from the snare drum. In these styles the role of the ride cymbal is quite minimal, as can be clearly heard in the majority of the hits from the seventies and eighties. In the exceptional cases in which a ride cymbal is preferred, it is usually of the heavy, power or rock type.

The drumming generation of that time had grown up with a solid, clearly defined hi-hat beat. When it came to picking ride cymbals, they went for a cymbal with a very definite "ping." As a result of this, crash cymbals and hi-hats got heavier too. This trend is also noticeable in other styles. During all those developments, jazz drummers complained that their wishes were largely ignored.

> They have forgotten how to make ride cymbals with color. They're all too heavy. They don't know what a dark sound is.
> —Mel Lewis

...eight or more cymbals...
Mark Brzezicki
Courtesy of Zildjian

Creativity

Obviously, it was not just volume that counted. More and more drummers started searching for new ways to express their creativity. In the late sixties rock drummer Ginger Baker started using double-decker combinations of pang and crash cymbals, foreshadowing what Terry Bozzio and many others picked up later on.

Stewart Copeland, in the early seventies, highlighted the reggae rhythms of The Police's new wave with a collection of splashes. Phil Gould of Level 42 played funk on hand-hammered cymbals that, up till then, seemed to be reserved for bebop drummers. Phillip Wilson is one of the many jazz drummers that was known for using Rudes, meant for rock drummers.

These and other musical developments led to wider applications of the available cymbals. It also showed the industry the need for a greater variety in sizes, shapes and sounds. Cymbal setups started growing accordingly. A Dutch survey in 1987 showed that amateur drummers used an average of almost five cymbals each.[12] Later, setups consisting of eight or more cymbals became quite common in certain styles. This increase co-initiated the cymbal-boom of the eighties.

1.5. 1980 AND ONWARD

The one word to characterize the 1980s is multiformity. There was no such thing as a dominant style. Everything could be done. Possibly even more was being done. From a multitude of different musical styles new avenues were explored and fusions with other

...drummers who go for the ancient handwork... Sarkis Tomurcuk, son of one of the presidents of the company, finishing the edges of an Istanbul splash. Photo by the author

styles came about. Combined with major technological developments in cymbal making, the arrival of new brands and the expansion of existing brands, this made the eighties the most turbulent decade in the cymbal industry.

In 1980 professional drummers had a very limited number of series to choose from. Paiste provided the 2002, Formula 602 and Sound Creation cymbals, while Zildjian's catalog was—temporarily—limited to the Avedis series. Next to these four series two Italian companies made a small contribution to the market. In the years that followed, Sabian, Istanbul and Spizz were founded, while Meinl and Pearl modestly set feet in the higher price ranges.

The result: within twelve years these eight companies launched no less than *thirty* new professional series. The number of available ride cymbals from the three major brands went up to 250 in the same period. Amazing, especially when considering that the other brands offered substantial supplies as well.

Part of this quantity could, of course, be categorized as more of the same, especially in the lower and medium budget ranges. On the other hand, new technologies gave way to better control over the parameters that influence the sound of a cymbal, leading to meaningful alternatives. More room was also created for off-the-wall specialties.

The quality of lower-priced ranges notably benefitted from these developments. These ranges were largely expanded in terms of available models as well.

The Future

Drummers, contrary to shopkeepers, never seemed to be hampered by having such large quantities to choose from. The variety that had been created stimulated a growth towards even more types of cymbals, rather than bringing such developments to an end. "And it's going to go on, I guarantee you. Drumming will be changing all the time," commented a president of one of the leading cymbal companies, when asked for his idea of the future.

The aforementioned industrial evolution and the increase in competition in the field of cymbal making also played their roles. "As things progress you have got to be right there. If you are not out there leading this, then you won't be there at all," according to a president of another company, "and drummers that were once happy with the available types and series will be even happier with the latest additions."

The other extreme has always been formed by the drummers who go for the ancient handwork: cymbals that sound different not because of new manufacturing techniques,

Competition in the cymbal market nearly doubled the market over the past five years.
—The Music Trades (April 1992)

but because of old inconsistencies.

No matter what choices were being made, the world of cymbals was fully alive when these pages were written.[13] Its future will invariably be determined by the interplay of what the industry supplies, and what drummers want. "You may have a perfect marketing plan, but if the market decides otherwise, you will have to change accordingly," commented a third president.

In the past, these two forces have proven to be able to cooperate and to stimulate one another to great heights. They probably will continue doing so, though the idea that a better cymbal than the instruments that have been available so far, will ever be made, can be safely rejected.

Notes:

...the total retail value of cymbals sold in the USA in 1991 was $28,000,000...
Courtesy of Meinl

1. *Percussion Instruments and Their History*, by James Blades, Faber and Faber Ltd., London, England, 1975. Revised and updated 4th edition: Bold Strummer Ltd., Westport, CT, USA, 1992.
2. II Samuel, 6, 5; *The Holy Bible*, The Authorized Version, 1611. Oxford University Press, by Samuel Collingwood & Co, 1833. *In The New English Bible*, by Oxford University Press / Cambridge University Press, 1970, it says: "David and all Israel danced for joy before the Lord without restraint to the sound of singing, of harps and lutes, of tambourines and castanets and cymbals."
3. *Il Seraglio*, original title *Das Entführung aus dem Serail*, by W.A. Mozart, 1782.
4. *Max on Swing*, by Max Bacon, The Premier Drum Company Ltd., London, England, 1934.
5. *Unione Fabbricanti Italiani Piatti* = Italian Association of Cymbal Makers.
6. *Handbuch Der Musikinstrumente*, by C. Sachs, 1930
7. "The Evolution of the Hi-hat," by Chet Falzerano, *Modern Drummer*, vol. 14, no. 9, Modern Drummer Publications, Inc., New Jersey, USA, 1990.
8. "Papa Jo Jones," by Chip Stern, *Modern Drummer*, vol. 8, no. 1, Modern Drummer Publications, Inc., New Jersey, USA, 1984.
9. Avedis Zildjian catalog, 1948.
10. "Armand Zildjian," by Richard Egart, *Modern Drummer*, vol. 10, no. 5, Modern Drummer Publications, Inc., New Jersey, USA, 1986.
11. "Kenny Clarke, Jazz Pioneer," by Ed Thigpen, *Modern Drummer*, vol. 8, no. 2, Modern Drummer Publications, Inc., New Jersey, USA, 1984.
12. Bekken-enquête (Cymbal Survey), by the author, 1987.
13. In the years 1989-1991 annual cymbal sales in the USA had a total retail value of $26,0000,000, $29,000,000 and $28,000,000 respectively. The number of drumset units that were sold decreased from 70,500 to 46,750 in the same period. Source: *The Music Trades*, Volume 140, No. 3, April 1992, New Jersey, USA.

2. TYPES OF CYMBALS

Application, characteristics, sound and sizes of the various types of cymbals are the main issues of this chapter. Crash/rides and special effect cymbals are dealt with separately from the three basic types. Apart from the large variety of sounds that can be found in the first five sections, there are types of cymbals that were not specifically made for drummers, as well as other types of "instruments" that can be used as such. These are dealt with in the last section.

Photo by Tineke van Brederode

Designations such as *ride* and *crash* are meant as guidelines and not as some kind of rule. Typologies are indispensable for easy communication, but they also tend to generalize, or even to mislead. Crashes, for instance, are generally supposed to be thinner than rides. Yet an 18" power crash may well be heavier than an 18" light ride from the same series. The ride cymbal in the setup of a dinner-dance drummer may easily be thinner than the crash of his heavy metal colleague. Luckily, nobody will ever be criticized for playing a soft, subtle groove on a rock crash. In the end, it is the drummer who decides what kind of cymbal it is.

Please be aware that some of the statements in this chapter may have a generalizing character. Mentioning every exception would have made this book twice as thick.

2.1. RIDE CYMBALS

Ride cymbals were given this designation since people started to play—what else?—rides on them: rhythmical patterns that support the time of the music. The ride cymbal as such came to life after 1945, when it started taking the role of main timekeeper over from the hi-hat. In later decades there has been a reversal in some styles, such as rock and funk, and many types of music derived from those styles. Wherever music asked for a very well-defined beat, the hi-hats were usually used as the main timekeeping device.

The ride cymbal, however, stayed fully alive. Especially drummers in electric jazz and fusion have displayed an unremitting urge to renovate. Their ride cymbals have been played beyond their role as mere time keepers, being crashed, splashed, popped and played in every conceivable way.

The right ride has to have good definition and a clear ping. At the same time, it has to spread and shimmer, it has to have a bright sounding cup that is not too harsh, sufficient crash qualities without being too thin, a certain dryness, a taste of darkness....

Obviously these and many other demands have led to the development of many new types of ride cymbals, from extremely bright to extremely dark and everything in between. On the other hand, a strong need for cutting, yet musical cymbals developed—and was replied to.

Personal Cymbal

The ride cymbal is considered to be your most personal cymbal. First, it is very sensitive to the way it is being played. Second, it is at least as sensitive to the type of stick that is being used. Third, the ride cymbal reacts to your playing more than any other type of cymbal. The rebound of one ride or the other may differ anywhere from an anvil-like hardness to a soft, giving, flexible feeling. In turn, your way of playing is affected by way the cymbal feels. This kind of interaction is present with any type of cymbal, but mostly with the ride.

Ride cymbals are, in comparison to crashes of the same setup, usually larger in

When I was coming up, everyone told me these preconceived things, like on cymbals it says "ride." Hey man, that's a *cymbal.* Don't tell me... You can use a cymbal any way you want, but the company stamps them "ride" or "crash."
—Tony Williams

I wouldn't dare say that the Raker series are more rock-like cymbals. And you know why? People never do what you expect them to do: I've seen so many jazz drummers playing Rude cymbals!
—Reinhold Meinl

I like to look at my ride cymbal sound as a wave on the ocean; it doesn't have to be loud. It just coats the entire area. It surrounds you.
—Marvin "Smitty" Smith

A different ride cymbal makes you play different.
—Steve Smith

Hunt Sales: "The way I use my ride cymbal is definitely from the jazz vein. Getting tones out of the cymbal, bringing it up and down as far as volume and intensity—I've got a 26" ride cymbal with rivets in it, and that kind of becomes its own entity; it creates its own tone."
Photo by Lissa Wales

Somebody may explain a sound like a heavy feeling or a fresh breeze. Others use colors, like "a green sound, but a little more on the blue side." There is no logical determination.
—Robert Paiste

...their names suggest what they sound like...
Paiste Sound Formula Full Ride
Courtesy of Paiste

The type of music modern drummers are playing encompasses so many different styles of music. Just look at Dave Weckl; he's playing straight ahead trio-jazz as well as real heavy electronic stuff in one show. These people *need* versatile cymbals.
—Colin Schofield

diameter and heavier in weight. Furthermore, they have a higher profile. These factors largely account for the relatively limited amount of overtones in the sound.

A ride cymbal has to be able to produce an identifiable ping. Too many harmonics would conceal definition. The ratio of overtones and ping may be very different from type to type, ranging from a very clear and high cutting ping on a heavy ride to a dry, low throaty tick that is surrounded by washing—but modest—harmonics on a dark jazz ride.

In the majority of musical settings a 20" is most popular. Next is 22", followed at some distance by 18". Larger ride cymbals are seldom used anymore. The same goes for smaller ride cymbals, like the 16" or the very occasional 14". Yet there are always exceptions: In the early 1990's Hunt Sales accompanied David Bowie's Tin Machine using a 26" ride cymbal.

From Dark to Bright

The number of ride cymbals to choose from is incredibly large. Their names usually suggest what they sound like. Deep, Power, Light, Medium, Rock, Dark, Jazz, Bright, Full, Studio, Rough, Metal and Dry are just some of them. Interestingly, the ideas that manufacturers have about, for instance, the term "dry" are not really identical. Neither are their cymbals. The characterizations that are supplied in most catalogs come closer to reality. Still, they are just words.

Ride cymbals strongly differ in the extent to which they can be deployed in various styles of music. There are ride cymbals that are concentrated on giving as much definition and power as possible, versus cymbals that mainly seem to strive for versatility.

It is hardly possible to put all these characteristics together in one cymbal. This implies that for drummers who play many different styles, a small number of rides to choose from is not that much of a luxury. On the other hand, some drummers have succeeded in finding a single ride cymbal that satisfies them both in acoustic trio and heavy metal settings, though not without the help of a good P.A. system.

The industry has concentrated mainly on the louder types of ride cymbals for a long period of time. The first unlathed and power cymbals seemingly started a battle for the loudest ride cymbal of all time. Complaints about too heavy and shallow sounding ride cymbals were heard frequently, especially—yet not alone—among jazz drummers in that period.

Later, the scope started to broaden substantially. Darker, warmer and more complex sounding cymbals came in to the picture again, not just in jazz drummers' setups but also in those of rock drummers. It wasn't simply that rockers discovered the charm of the dark, warm sound as opposed to the cutting pings they were used to. It was also a matter of modern descendants of the "old K" sound getting brighter, or becoming available in heavier weights as well.

2.2. CRASH CYMBALS

Crash cymbals are supposed to do exactly what their name sounds like. Contrary to rides, crash cymbals respond quickly with an overabundance of harmonics, and die out shortly afterwards. They are generally thinner and smaller than rides within the same setup. Their bow is less pronounced. Where ride cymbals are meant to propel the beat, crashes are there to accent, to color and to phrase.

Crash cymbals are available in sizes ranging from 12" to an occasional 22". The combination of a 16" and an 18" has been widely used in most styles of music for the past decades. Towards the end of the eighties, smaller crashes became increasingly popular. The smallest crashes, from 8" up to 12", are usually referred to as splashes (see 5.2.).

Modern Drummer's Buyer's Guide of 1991 contained about 350 different crash cymbals.[1] Compared to the number of rides available (250), it may not seem that much, especially since most drummers use several crashes and just one ride. The ride cymbal, however, is generally subjected to more specific demands and therefore needs more diversification.

Wide ranges

Crashes are often designated by their weights, ranging from paper thin or extra thin through thin and medium-thin to medium. Power and rock crashes, which may be heavier than a medium ride of the same series, are obviously meant for drummers who need more volume. Terms such as bright, dark, full, mellow and fast speak for themselves, yet no word can completely cover the character of sound of a crash—or any other cymbal.

Within wide ranges of volume and pitch, a large choice can be made between crashes for short, fast accents or punctuation marks, crashes for a sustaining sound, or anything in between. Thanks to the fast developments in the cymbal industry, contemporary crash sounds may be short and low, long and high, short and high, loud and short.... The boundaries, set by acoustical laws of vibrational patterns within circular convex plates, sometimes seem to be surpassed by today's instruments.

As with ride cymbals, crashes of the "dark and warm" type have found their way into the setups of rock drummers in the eighties. This phenomenon has been explained by the need drummers feel to balance out the multitude of electronic sounds, which in most cases cannot really be characterized as being warm and dark at all.

2.3. HI-HATS

The role of the hi-hat very much depends on the style of music it is being used in. In most popular styles it is the main timekeeper. Kept close and played by sticks most of the time, it punctuates the beat very clearly.

Traditional bebop drummers use the hi-hat on two and four, closing it with the foot. In electric jazz, fusion and other, more improvisational types of music, the hi-hat has gained a much more versatile function. It has become more of an independent, equal voice of the set, instead of merely being used as a foundation for the beat.

Along with drummers who have signature ride sounds, players like Omar Hakim, Jack DeJohnette and Sonny Emory have made their mark by the way they treat their hi-hats. Many of these techniques involve intricate combinations of hands and foot, figures that wouldn't have been possible on the hi-hat pedals of the past.

As is the cymbal industry, the hardware industry is frequently challenged to come up with new equipment that can handle, simplify and aid new techniques. These products, in turn, inspire drummers to go another step further.

Cross Matching

Next to common labels such as light, medium, heavy and power hi-hats, there are lots of other designations from which the character of sound can, and sometimes cannot, be derived. Fusion, Power and Dark Crisp speak for themselves, while one can only guess what Dyno Beats, New Beats, or Flat Hats would do for you. Most hi-hat combinations

Everyone seems to be solving the problem of breakage by making the cymbals too heavy. Cats make them so indestructible that you can forget about all the good qualities of sound.
—Pheeroan ak Laff

...to accent, to color and to phrase...
18" Zildjian crashes
Courtesy of Zildjian

To me, the hi-hat is another ride cymbal. Every cymbal I use is a ride cymbal. Every one of my cymbals is also a crash cymbal. I only use three. Three is enough.
—Mel Lewis

I don't use the ride cymbal a lot because there's so much more definition in the hi-hat as far as keeping a rhythm section locked into something. If I do play the ride cymbal, I very rarely play in the middle or on the edge. I always play on the bell, because the bell cuts through.
—Andy Newmark

...10" and 12" hi-hats came into the picture again...
Zildjian Studio Recording hi-hats
Courtesy of Zildjian

A heavy cymbal underneath and a medium on top is a classic combination for hi-hats. It's like snare drums: most drummers tune their bottom head higher than the top head, because that helps carrying the attack. The higher pitched bottom cymbal actually gives you the "chick."
— Pete York

(about using a 13" top and a 14" bottom cymbal)
If you get the same size top and bottom hi-hit cymbals, sometimes you get a crunch, rather than a crisp sound.
—Billy Higgins

consist of a medium-heavy to heavy bottom and a medium to medium-thin top, in various weight categories. Some drummers go for an even lighter top, using medium-thin crash cymbals.

Even a small collection of hi-hat cymbals provides the owner with numerous sound combinations. Having two different bottom cymbals and one top, for instance, will make two quite different pairs of hi-hats. Combining hi-hats from different series or brands is called "cross matching." Zildjian's K/Z combination was the first factory-made cross-matched pair, featuring an extremely heavy Z series bottom and a considerably (about 40%) lighter K top. This type of combination has become very popular.

Most manufacturers now offer hi-hats with similar weight ratios. Another way of cross matching is simply using the top for the bottom. Pairs of hi-hat cymbals of different sizes have been used to prevent air-lock (see below), and for other reasons as well. Max Roach, for instance, used a 15" top and a 14" bottom in the late forties. Combinations with a smaller top cymbal have also been used.

Most traditional setups include a 20" ride, 16" and/or 18" crashes and a pair of 14" hi-hats. As with crashes, around the late eighties a tendency towards smaller cymbals and 10" and 12" hi-hats came into the picture again. These sizes had been out of use for a couple of decades. In 1992 almost every manufacturer featured such hi-hats again. Most drummers used them as an additional pair (on an X-hat or remote pedal), but some used them as their main hi-hats, especially for recording (see Chapter 4).

Air-Lock
In the past decades manufacturers have found various solutions for the air-lock or air-pocket phenomenon. When closing the hi-hats, most of the air between the two cymbals is forced out. This underpressure between the two cymbals results in a dull sound as opposed to a clear chick.[2] To prevent air-lock, Paiste introduced their patented Sound Edge hi-hats (1967), of which the bottom cymbal has a corrugated edge. As soon as the patent ran out, Meinl and UFIP started producing similar cymbals.

Other manufacturers simply drilled a couple of holes in the bottom cymbal. Many of them claim to be the first one to have done that, but supposedly drummers had applied the same trick long before pre-drilled cymbals hit the market. When Meinl first tried to sell such cymbals, they were all returned to the factory; shopkeepers were convinced that some terrible mistake had been made.

Sabian and Istanbul drilled smaller holes and applied rivets to them, in the bottom and top cymbal respectively. Zildjian had yet another idea. They cut eight small semi-circles out of the edge of their (now discontinued) Amir and Impulse series bottom hi-hats. Sabian applied a similar approach to the first edition of their 1991 EQ-Hats (see 9.3.2.).

Still, the majority of hi-hat cymbals do not have any of these modifications. Slightly tilting the bottom cymbal works well enough in most cases.

Paiste Sound Edge Hi-Hats
Courtesy of Paiste

Sabian EQ Hats
Courtesy of Sabian

2.4. CRASH/RIDE CYMBALS
The statement that every cymbal is a crash/ride cymbal is at least in some form

justifiable. Yet there have been reasons to give a cymbal that has been specifically designed for fulfilling both purposes a name of its own. In a typical setup a crash/ride cymbal, most often 18" or 20", will be in between the crash and the ride in size, weight and shape. Depending on the brand, a crash/ride of a certain size may, however, be lighter than a medium crash of that size.

Crash/rides have the advantage of being very versatile. Given the right cymbal in the right situation, it can produce a clear enough ping as well as a full-bodied and reasonably explosive crash. On the other hand, a crash/ride will never have the definition of a ride, nor the fast response and decay of the average crash cymbal.

As cymbals have to obey certain physical laws, it is impossible to unify the best of both worlds in just one solid piece of bronze.

Especially with crash/rides it is the drummer who decides which type of cymbal it will be. Jazz drummers, more often than others, use crash/rides both ways. Heavier drummers might use them as crash exclusively, while a club drummer in an unamplified piano trio is bound to loose his job when doing so just once.

Most catalogs put crash/rides in the ride section. Paiste has been the only major company to distinguish between crash/rides (up to 19") and ride/crashes, from 20" to 24" (Rude series). Some minor brands have used the indication ride/crash too. Another variation on the crash/ride theme is the Sabian El Sabor (1992), a multi-functional cymbal that was specifically designed for Latin percussionists.

Vader ride/crash, made in Germany
Courtesy of Vader

Medium

Medium cymbals are often thought to be about the same as crash/ride cymbals: a sound in the middle of two extremes. Generally, medium cymbals are heavier than crash/rides. In the design of the crash/ride there's more attention paid to the crash qualities. The taper of a crash/ride is stronger. It has a relatively thin edge, resulting in a faster response.

Medium cymbals, on the other hand, are basically meant as medium-weight ride cymbals. Yet there are numerous rock drummers using medium cymbals for crashes. They are heavier, so they sound higher and louder, and they cut better. Most of the sustain, which is quite long, disappears in the volume of the music. And what about legendary bebop drummer Art Blakey? He often used just three medium cymbals, 20", 21", and 22", and, yes, he crashed the hell out of them.

My preference is the 20" medium for a crash. It has the sustain, it has the instant attack and it has durability. I've tried lighter cymbals and they fall apart. Not everybody uses 3S sticks...
—Alex Van Halen

2.5. SPECIAL EFFECTS

In the latter decades of the twentieth century special effect cymbals have become so popular that they hardly deserve the name any more. The category contains Chinese cymbals (and their Western counterparts), splashes, and a series of instruments that can only be labeled under the collective indication "Thick and Small."

2.5.1. CHINESE CYMBALS AND CHINA-TYPES

Chinese cymbals were popular with drummers in the first decades of this century, when they mainly served as an additional ride sound. A few Western variations also date back from a long time ago, such as the Pang and the Swish (Zilco, 1939). Jazz-rock drummers in the early seventies repopularized these and similar cymbals, mainly using them as additional crashes.

From that time on, Western manufacturers have devoted a great deal of research to a large variety of cymbals with names such as China-type, Chinese or China Boy. Actually, almost every cymbal with a visible flanged edge is named that way, though the differences sometimes surpass the similarities.[3]

Nowadays drummers sometimes take interest in sounds that were originally used by the old drummers, even if they don't know where it came from.
—Pete York

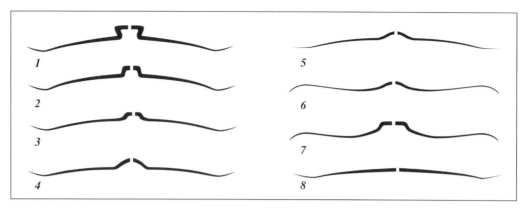

Approximate profiles of authentic Chinese Lion cymbals and some Western descendants
1. Chinese Lion cymbal (e.g. Wuhan) 2. China Type (Paiste) 3. China Boy (Zildjian)
4. Swish (Zildjian) / Chinese (Sabian) 5. Pang / Power Smash (Zildjian) / Flat Chinese (Sabian)
6. Novo China (Paiste) 7. Reversed China (UFIP) 8. Flat China (UFIP). Sketches by Ronald Willemsen

Idris Muhammad: "One guy asked
me why I don't have a China. Well, I
like China cymbals, but I could play
a China in the cymbals that I use. I
don't need another cymbal just to
make one sound."
Photo by the author

Rancan Sheung cymbal, with a
raised blade and a spherical cup
Courtesy of Latin Percussion

The Flange

The only characteristic that the authentic Chinese "Lion" cymbals and pseudo-Chinas or China-types have in common is the flanged edge. The original Chinese cymbals all have a conical cup, which was originally used as a handle. Their Western descendants, depending on the brand, have a more or less square bell or a small Turkish (regular) one. Square cups in most cases have flat tops. This prevents the cymbal, being mounted upside-down as it often is, from getting into a rocking motion.

Western-made flanged cymbals usually sound less "garbage can-liddish" than their authentic ancestors, though there are some notable exceptions. Cymbals with a moderate flange, such as the Pang, the Mellow China and the Flat Chinese, sound much warmer and more harmonic. They also sustain longer than cymbals with a sharper flange.

Chinas and related types are mainly used for short, punctuated accents with an exotic atmosphere. Depending on size, weight and shape they are also used for ride patterns and anything in between. Because of the flange, such cymbals can be played in many different ways. The edge, the flanged part, the actual flange and the ride area all produce their own sounds. Besides, depending on the specific type of cymbal, there can be considerable differences between playing the cymbal face up or flipped over.

Inverted and Reversed

The cup, in most cases, cannot be used because of the common upside-down position of these cymbals. Paiste solved that problem with the 2002 Novo type, a cymbal with an inverted cup (1983). UFIP introduced the comparable Reversed Chinas in the early nineties. Other notable cymbals in this pseudo-Chinese category include Zildjian's Z China Boy, as well as Sabian's Jack DeJohnette China type. These extremely heavy cymbals really have little more than the flanged edge in common with their Eastern ancestors. China types are made in virtually every size and shape. The smallest cymbals in this category are 8" (Istanbul, with a Turkish cup); the largest are up to 27" (Wuhan).

Chinese Turkish Cymbals

Chinese cymbalsmiths, by the way, do not only produce cymbals of the type discussed above. Chinese splashes and Bell cymbals, such as Swatow, Peking and Sheung cymbals, have a spherical cup and a raised blade.

Because of the fact that Western products are hardly available in China, Turkish-type cymbals are also made there. These cymbals have been available under their own name (e.g. Wuhan), but also from Meinl (Single Dragon and Cobra, discontinued), Latin Percussion (Rancan Chinese Crash) and other companies.

Slingerland listed such cymbals as Chinese Jazz cymbals as early as the 1930s, as having "that peculiar hiss-tone that is high, sharp and piercing." Due to the production process, the alloy and the irregular way of hammering, they usually sound extremely dark and complex.

UFIP China Splash
Courtesy of UFIP

2.5.2. SPLASHES

Splashes can be considered small crash cymbals as well as special effects. They are fast and bright, they have short sustain, and are most popular in 10". Other sizes are 6", 8" and 12", and uneven sizes also exist.

Splashes may vary from Istanbul's cigaret paper-thin ones to the hefty Sabian Rock Splashes that feature extremely large bells. Lighter cymbals of the category Thick and Small (2.5.3.) may be employed as splashes also.

Other variations are Samba Splashes and China Splashes, which are made by different companies and in various shapes. Some feature a square cup and a regular bow, others have a regular Turkish cup and an inverted bow. Besides being used for accenting, coloring and quick embellishments of ride patterns, splashes are being mounted on top of, or inside the cup of, another cymbal.

I had Zildjian make some little band cymbals that I think are cut from marching band cymbals. They're anywhere from little 6" to 14"'s. I use them for bell sounds.
—Gregg Bissonette

2.5.3. THICK AND SMALL

For high, penetrating and sustaining sounds most manufacturers offer a wide choice in Bell and Accent cymbals (e.g. Paiste), Icebells (UFIP), EFX #1's (Zildjian), Cup Chimes, the aforementioned Chinese Bell cymbals and lots more. Apart from being used for occasional accents, some of these instruments can easily be used to ride on, especially for drummers who go for the cup of their ride cymbal anyhow. The thinner this type of cymbal is—or the harder you hit—the better it can be used as a splashy type of sound. A pair of cymbals from this category may also be used as auxiliary hi-hats, producing very well-defined and clear cutting sounds. These effect cymbals are not purposely tuned, but as their dimensions cause them to have more of a predominant pitch, they may sound terribly out of tune when used at the wrong moment.

Sabian "CD" Cymbal Discs
Courtesy of Sabian

Also fitting this category, yet not cymbals in the authentic sense of the word, are instruments such as Burma Bells, Crotales, Sound Discs, Sound Plates and "CD" Cymbal Discs. They may be pitched or tuned—there *is* a slight difference—and have small sizes. Their sounds are very focussed and bell-like. A single one can be used to create occasional effects. Complete sets may be used to perform melodic lines.

2.6. "IMPROPER" CYMBALS

The category of "improper cymbals" basically contains every type of cymbal or cymbal-like instrument that has not been mentioned in earlier sections. Most of them were not specifically made for drumset players. Still, there are a lot of such sounds that deserve at least some attention from drummers. The same goes for almost every kind of metal object.

...I had one of those splash cymbals that is cut out of a hi-hat so it sounded real thick.
—Vinnie Colaiuta

2.6.1. CONCERT BAND/MARCHING CYMBALS

The major manufacturers all produce one or more series that are designed to meet the demands of marching percussionists. These cymbals are usually quite heavy and loud, as they must be able to project in open air. Cymbals of this type can perfectly act as hi-hat cymbals, or, in bigger sizes, as crashes or rides. Tommy Lee is just one drummer who is known to have used two 20" marching cymbals as crashes: "Because they're super-loud and don't crack too easily," so said his drum tech.[4] This type of cymbal 's generally available in sizes from 12" to 22".

2.6.2. SYMPHONIC CYMBALS

Other cymbals are specifically made for symphonic applications. Suspended cymbals, for instance, usually played with mallets, are of a modest weight and have a lower profile than the average drummer's crash. Their pitch is therefore quite low, yet they sustain long, offering good contrast to the faster crashes drummers mostly use.

The name "Suspended" has an historic background. In the past, cymbals were played in pairs exclusively. The introduction of the single, mounted or suspended cymbal required a specific type of instrument. It was simply given this designation to discern it from the others. The name of Zildjian's Thin Suspended La Mer cymbal, by the way, also has a historic background: it was invented for Debussy's suite of that name.

The pairs of cymbals that are made for symphony orchestras (hand cymbals) can be split up and used by drummers as well. These cymbals measure 16" and upward. Three major types can be distinguished.

The French style cymbals generally are medium thin, producing a bright and splashy sound. The Viennese hand cymbals, the most all-around type, are of medium weight and sustain. The German type weighs somewhere between medium heavy and heavy. There are, by the way, no exact specifications on how much a "medium" or a "medium-thin" cymbal of a certain size should weigh. Each factory seems to have its own ideas about these measures.

2.6.3. GONGS

Actually, gongs shouldn't be mentioned in a book about cymbals—the only relationship being that both are round, made of metal, and belong to the family of metallic idiophones. Yet there was a time that a drumset hardly seemed complete without an impressive gong in the background. The sixties' setups of Pink Floyd drummer Nick Mason, ELP's Carl Palmer and the late John Bonham of Led Zeppelin were the most striking examples. Cozy Powell and Nicko McBrain were still using such large gongs in the 1990s.

...still using such large gongs in the 1990s...
Nicko McBrain
photo by Peer Rede

The size and price of such gongs prohibited a more widespread use. Therefore, and apart from large arrays of gongs for symphonic and orchestral use, several cymbal companies feature smaller and more affordable types. Examples are Zildjian's and Sabian's China Gongs, that easily fit in a cymbal bag. Paiste, having made the world's largest gong (80"!), and UFIP also make gongs that are suitable for use by drummers and percussionists. Some companies import gongs from their native region, the East, in addition to their own products. The diversity amongst gongs is enormous—not only in size and shape, but also in character.

Even among specific drummer's types of gongs almost any kind of effect can be found, ranging from huge, warm and rich explosive sounds to the weird raising pitch of the small Chinese Opera Gongs. Some basic types are Symphonic, Turkish, Gamelan, China, Taiwan, Gong Chimes and Flat Gongs, each having its own characteristics and applications, with or without a boss (as the cup of a gong is called), being either pitched, tuned to a specific note or not tuned at all.

Some series are available in tuned sets of a chromatic octave or more, which usually isn't the kind of thing drummers will be after. Larger types of non-pitched flat gongs, without flange or cup, are officially referred to as tam tams.

"...and then I said 'garbage-can lids'..."
Omar Hakim
Photo by Mark van Schaick

2.6.4. AND FURTHERMORE...

The scale of sounds and objects that can be added to the drumset is only limited by the borders of your imagination. One well-known example, which was frequently used in avant-garde and jazz setups in the mid-eighties, is the garbage-can lid. Omar Hakim, at one time, was looking for an instrument that could acoustically simulate the handclaps sound of a drum computer: "We banged on everything in Joe Zawinul's house and his backyard, and then I said 'garbage-can lids.' To his wife's dismay, Joe got the garbage-can lid out of his backyard. He drilled a hole in it, we put in on a stand, and I used it on that tune. I've gone through a few since then. They bend up and then they're dead. The 'trash' goes away...."[5] A company by the name of Drum Vision even tried to market garbage can lids for drummers. Their ad appeared only once.[6]

In 1988 Remo introduced the Spoxe, basically the frame of a Roto-Tom, to be used as a single effect "cymbal" or mounted in a bell tree fashion. Drummers such as Michael Blair and Terry Bozzio have used Spoxes as hi-hats, producing more of a "snap" than the usual "chick."

Of course, almost any metal percussion instrument can be used instead of a regular cymbal. The Pete Engelhart Metal Percussion collection contains some good examples, such as the Crashers and Ribbon Crashers. Other objects that have been applied are circular saws, car fenders, hubcaps, circular brakes, pressure cookers, pan lids, cash register bells and numerous other pieces of hardware. All of them can produce astonishing sounds. They are also relatively cheap and, on top of that, virtually indestructible.

I've always used a wide variety of metal things that go "clank" and "shank"...Drummers always used to flip out when they saw me use my cookie-sheet, which I mounted over my ride cymbal, playing paradiddles between that and the snare. The sound of the one I found was very electric, biting and bright; others would have more of a clunk-sound...
—Paul Wertico

Notes:

1   MD's Buyer's Guide, vol. 15, no. 10, Modern Drummer Publications, Inc., New Jersey, USA, 1991.

2   The term air-lock, according to this explanation, is therefore theoretically not correct. Due to its widespread use it will be indicated as such in this book nevertheless. This phenomenon has also been indicated as "catching-a-crab."

3   This is with the exception of Sabian's Sound Control cymbals and UFIP's Fast Crashes, where the very small and slightly flanged edge serves another purpose.

4   Drum tech Clyde Duncan, Tommy Lee interview, *Modern Drummer*, vol. 10, no. 9, Modern Drummer Publications. Inc., New Jersey, USA, 1986.

5   "Omar Hakim," by Robin Tolleson, *Modern Drummer*, vol. 8, no. 12, Modern Drummer Publications. Inc., New Jersey, USA, 1984.

6   Drum Vision Enterprises, ad in *Modern Drummer*, vol. 8, no. 10, Modern Drummer Publications, Inc., New Jersey, USA, 1984.

SELECTION AND TESTING
...finding the right cymbal...
Photo Messe Frankfurt

3. SELECTION AND TESTING

Sometimes people just stroll into a music shop, hit the first cymbal in sight, fall in love, pay for it and are happy for the rest of their life. Usually, finding the right cymbal takes a lot more time. Some preparation might be worthwhile, too. The second section of this chapter contains general tips for selecting any type of cymbal: what to look and listen for when testing. As a ride cymbal is not played the same way as a crash, there are specific tips for each type. These are described in separate sections. The last section deals with informative hints concerning the technical qualities of cymbals, and what to pay attention to when buying used cymbals.

As it mainly consists of a list of tips, this is not the chapter to sit down with for some cosy reading. Its form was chosen to make it as informative and organized as possible, sacrificing readability to some degree. It will rarely happen that somebody is actually going to painstakingly follow each and every tip that is given here. I wouldn't consider doing that, either.

3.1. TIPS IN ADVANCE

There are people who simply enter a drumshop, say: "I'd like a cymbal," and remain silent ever after. Supposedly, they do not read books like this one, but just in case: get an idea of what you want before you go out. What to think of, what to consider, what to load into your car, and which drumshop to drive to are some of the subjects of this section.

3.1.1. CONSIDERATIONS

Even the most unbiased author will confront you with one more subjective, personal opinion: his. So inform yourself by reading reviews, catalogs, newsletters and other relevant publications. Every subjective opinion that you encounter will help to shape your own. Besides, such documents will make you familiar with the typical jargon.

Setups

Study setups of drummers in any style. Chapter 4 offers such information. If you are just starting out or if you are in a limited financial position, it might be hard to translate the sounds of professional cymbals into more affordable items. You might just have to read this entire book.

Bottom of the List

When buying a new stereo set, the loudspeakers often come at the bottom of the list. In the case of first-time drummers it is usually the cymbals. Consider that it is much harder to influence the sound of a cymbal than it is to alter the sound of a drum. Any drumset can be made to sound at least acceptable. A cymbal basically sounds the way it sounds.

Differences in Price

What exactly causes the considerable differences in price in cymbals? First and foremost, it is the amount of work that is put into the instrument. The price of the alloy is a second—but less important—factor. A major aspect that is often overlooked is the number of different cymbals available within a series. Most low-budget series consist of one or two rides, a few crashes, one type and size of hi-hats and sometimes a China-type or a splash. Most professional series contain numerous variations in every type. This implies more tools, more research, a larger number of more exclusive, less sellable types of cymbals and more stockroom. Promotion, percentages and publicity are price-determining factors also.

After all is said and done, a Cymbal—to fulfill its true mission in the band or jazz orchestra—must be more than tinkling brass. It must have a Tonal Individuality that lends itself readily to the conductor's and the cymbalist's interpretation of the music.
—Zildjian pamphlet (1933)

For a beginner, it is very difficult to choose a cymbal. You have to know what you are after or be able to make correct decisions.
—Simon Phillips

I once got a letter about a cymbal we made: "This cymbal is not too far away, but lacks a 'whoosh.' It has a large sound... a little aggressive... has a nice attack and will probably cut. I'm missing a full-bodied sense. The cymbal doesn't spread after it reaches its pinnacle. It doesn't have an umbrella effect; the sound is one-dimensional." I had to read that five times. I speak German and a little English, but no "Cymbalese"!
—Reinhold Meinl

3.1.2. LUGGAGE

Your Cymbals

If you go out to buy a cymbal, take your other cymbals with you. Any purchase is supposed to become part of a set, and not just another addition to a randomly gathered collection.

Apart from that, you wouldn't be the first one to come home with a new cymbal that is identical to one you already had. Apart from proving that you know what you like, this a quite a useless experience. The acoustic properties of the shop will be somewhat neutralized when you can compare new cymbals with the ones you are familiar with. If a friend owns the kind of cymbal you are after, take that cymbal with you as well. Nothing is harder than remembering sounds accurately.

Names of Types of Cymbals

If you happen to hear the cymbal you are after at a concert, try to buy it straightaway. If the drummer shows no immediate signs of cooperation, write down brand, type and size. Don't just order that cymbal at your local store. Consider, for one, that amplified cymbals usually do not sound the same acoustically.

Another Drummer

To judge a cymbal correctly you have to step away from it. The audience is at some distance also and what they perceive has top priority. Volume, definition, pitch, sustain and response—every detail of the sound—can be appraised more accurately from a distance. Your assistant should be a drummer; anybody can hit a cymbal, but it takes more to *play* it. In case there is no one around, try playing the cymbal while keeping the ear that is pointing in its direction closed. It works.

Music

Another way to help you form an opinion about cymbals is to play them while listening to the music you play. Preferably use a tape without drums. A cassette player with headphones will do for this purpose. This way you imitate, to some extent, what the cymbals will sound like in the context of a band. Always try out cymbals in combination with a drumset, for the same reason. Hearing the drums in interplay with the cymbals may open up your ears to certain—positive or negative—characteristics that you would not perceive otherwise.

Your Sticks

Take your own sticks, especially if you are looking for a ride cymbal. The sound of such cymbals largely depends on what they are played with. You can also use a medium general-purpose stick like a 5A, next to a type similar to what you use. Some people take along their hi-hat and cymbal stands, as they might influence the sound.

3.1.3. THE IDEAL SHOP

Since selecting cymbals basically comes down to comparing cymbals, the drumshop should have an acceptable stock. A small inventory makes choosing easier, but increases the chance of buying the wrong one. Manufacturers, distributors and importers may allow you to select cymbals at their place, the retailer being the intermediate—and the one you pay. This gives you a wealth of cymbals to choose from, be it from one brand at the time.

For me, a ride cymbal has to be heard in relation to the entire kit, not as something separate. I hear a lot of cats who play the drums, then play the cymbals, and it sounds like two different kits.

—Tony Thompson

If I do a special selection of cymbals I always pick up my 5A's, because they tell me every tattle-tale story about them. To me, it's a sort of point-of-reference stick.

—Nort Hargrove

"Identical" Cymbals

Having found the cymbal of your choice, compare a few species of that type of cymbal. There are no two cymbals exactly alike. Computer-made cymbals are, of course, "more identical" than hand-hammered cymbals will ever be. Yet you've got to take the very cymbal that you picked, and not merely one of the same type and size.

Proficiency

A proficient salesperson is worth his or her weight in bronze. Good shops offer time, advice and patience. Your ears can stand only so much at one time. Take a break in between. It is better not to buy an entire set of cymbals at the same time for this reason.

Second-hand

Have a look at the second-hand cymbals around. Sometimes people really do not know what they are selling.

...computer-made cymbals are, of course, "more identical" than hand-hammered cymbals will ever be.... Courtesy of Zildjian

For Starters

A number of brands offer so-called "cymbal packs," usually consisting of a 20" ride, an 18" crash and a pair of 14" hi-hats. This is an easy way out. Listen to other brands as well. They might offer a faster crash than the one in the pack, or a more harmonious sounding ride or a better pair of hi-hat cymbals. You might leave with less money but with a more satisfying set, composed of two or three brands.

And Furthermore

Price, brand name[1] and indication of the type of cymbal are less important than what you hear. There are numerous pros around who incorporate lower-budget cymbals in their setups. They have their—priceless—reasons. Use your ears, not your eyes.

3.2. TESTING ONE, TWO

Should you go out to buy an entire set of cymbals on one day, concentrate first on a ride cymbal. Then pick a pair of complementary hi-hats and go for the rest at the end.

Comparing

Comparing cymbals is the main thing to do. When you have to choose from a number of different types of cymbals, set a number of stands at equal heights and mount the cymbals at equal angles in a semi-circle in front of you. Cymbal-tree displays may affect the sound of the cymbal you are listening to. Imitate your own style of setting up cymbals (flat, steep, tight, loose) as closely as you can, to create as much of a "live" situation as possible. Also, play the cymbals the same way and at the same volume as you play them in real life.

Eliminating

After you have made your basic decisions, a good way to pick the right one is to handle just two at the time. Put them on stands and pick out the best one. Pick a third cymbal and repeat this procedure until you have tried them all. It is a matter of gradually eliminating— making the pile smaller and smaller until you end up with just one cymbal: yours.

Serial Numbers

Some cymbals have serial numbers. This offers a nice possibility to test your hearing.

What kills me is that a lot of the jazz drummers at clinics will say, "If you hit the cymbals there, you get a real tingy sounding...." And I think, "Yeah, sure!" That's because the music I play with this band is a bit louder than what you're going to hear at the cymbal demonstrations.
—Vinny Appice

Write down the number of the cymbal you selected first, put it back in the stack and try to find it again—by ear, that is. If you manage to do that, buy the cymbal. Go home and jot down the number again, this time for insurance reasons.

3.3. WHAT TO LISTEN FOR

Professional cymbal testers do not listen for what's there in a cymbal. They mainly concentrate on what's not. This demands a 100% clear and true image of the supposed, factory-prescribed sound of the cymbal in question—which is the main reason to do it the other way around when you are buying cymbals. What to listen for in a cymbal varies from type to type. Yet there are a number of general things to pay attention to.

Harmony and Frequency Specter

The sound of a cymbal should be harmonic and even, excluding most Chinas and other specialty sounds. Wavering frequencies, interfering overtones and any other kind of disturbing effects, as well as the entire beauty and potential of the cymbal, can be discovered by playing it in various ways. A blow or a roll with a timpani mallet or yarn marimba mallet will cause the entire frequency range come to life, without the influence of the sound of the harsh tip of a drumstick. The lowest partials will become audible when using the same mallet softly near the edge of the cymbal. The cymbal can be made to build up by increasing the force of your strikes. Be aware of the blending of the harmonics.

The higher frequencies can be triggered by playing near the cup, preferably using a nylon-tip stick. The interval between the notes you hear up there should be in harmony with the low note that you will find near the edge.

Eccentrics can also trigger the higher frequencies and harmonics by blowing softly along the edge of the cymbal. It works, so don't be concerned with anyone who might be staring at you.

Pitch (Tessitura)

Cymbals are non-pitched instruments. Whether a cymbal is judged as being high, medium, or low sounding depends on the predominant frequency-range or tessitura. A good cymbal produces frequencies in each of those three areas. They all have a certain function in the sound. The proportions between them determine the character of the cymbal to a great degree.

Volume

Volume is very hard to judge in a shop. Besides the size of the shop as compared to the size of your average stage, all kinds of things may influence your perception of the actual loudness of the cymbal. A ride cymbal with a very defined ping will seem louder than a ride that builds up very strongly. The same goes for high versus low sounding crashes. Comparing cymbals with the ones you know is the best way to get a realistic idea.

Response

Response is the time it takes the cymbal to react to your stick-attack. Crashes demand a quick response, while ride cymbals should respond more slowly in order to avoid too much build-up of the overtones. Generally, thinner cymbals respond quicker than heavier ones. The most critical way to judge response is by playing softly. With plenty of force, any cymbal responds.

Selecting a cymbal is very much like being in a perfume factory. One particular fragrance may work beautifully for one person's skin where the same brand won't work for someone else.
—Ed Thigpen

When I select cymbals, I listen for tonality because some cymbals have overtones going on that I don't like. I also listen for rise times: some cymbals are sort of up there from the start, while others come up and then explode. Then I listen to the decay time.
—Jerry Speiser

...volume is very hard to judge in a shop...
Gregg Bissonette
Photo by the author

Papa Jo Jones never picked a cymbal with a drumstick. He did it all with his hands, snapping them with his fingers, just like that. Maybe for half an hour or so, listening to their cleanness, looking for certain notes.
—Lennie DiMuzio

Sustain

The sustain of a cymbal largely depends on the decay of the high frequencies. The highs are the first to cut out; the lows will go on for quite a long time. This can easily be detected with your ear close to the edge of the instrument.

An audience will not perceive the lowest frequencies. They will mainly hear the highs. Those frequencies are responsible for the effective sustain.

Dynamic Range

Try each cymbal at different volume levels in order to find out about the dynamic range. Some cymbals only sound good when played very hard, others are more effective in low-volume situations. Few can do both.

Dynamic Sensitivity

Dynamic sensitivity mainly has to do with the way the cymbal responds to variations in the force of your strokes. The more sensitive a cymbal is, the more versatile it will be. Such cymbals require more control to make them sound even when riding them. Cymbals also differ in the way they respond to different sticks, grips, playing angles, etc. Of course, this goes mainly for ride cymbals.

Do it All

Play each cymbal in every way you can think of. Ride crashes, crash rides, play hi-hats open, closed, half-open, on the side, on top, use the cup and play with butt-ends if you are used to doing so. Just do it all.

3.4. TIPS PER TYPE OF CYMBAL

While rides may be crashed and crashes may be ridden, generally their purposes and the way they arc played are quite dissimilar. And so should they be tested, in order to find what you're looking for. Hi-hats and Chinas ask for an individual approach as well.

3.4.1. RIDE CYMBALS

A ride cymbal needs more of a predominant note than a crash cymbal. It has to be able to speak at a certain range. This goes for the cup as well. At the same time, the sound has to be able to blend in with any identifiable pitch, with any chord. Therefore, a full scale of harmonics is needed. A ride cymbal without any spread and shimmer will sound flat, shallow and one-dimensional. A metal ashtray would do the same for less money.

Overtones

A good ride cymbal has to produce a fine blend of ping and shimmer. The ratio between these two aspects may differ strongly, depending on your taste and the style of music you play. In a music shop the build-up of overtones will seem much stronger than it will actually be on stage. Stepping away from it may work well in making a better judgment.

If you are worried about loss of definition because of all these overtones, try crashing the cymbal with considerable power; play a ride pattern on it immediately afterwards. If the ping can be clearly distinguished from the first stroke, things should be okay. The one-ear-closed trick may help as well.

Discern between the buildup of undertones and overtones. The lower harmonics help the sound to sustain and give it its body, the higher ones increase projection. The best way to judge the building up of overtones is by riding the cymbal in a slow crescendo,

When jazz cats pull out a ride cymbal, you can really tell they spent some time on it.
—Tony Thompson

To be honest, I'm not into all the technicalities of what cymbals sound like– I just hit them. If you're into jazz and that sort of gear then you're talking about the vibes on the this and the ping of the that. Honestly, *I* just hit them.
—Simon Wright

going from very soft to the point where the overtones cover up the ping completely. On very heavy cymbals the latter may never occur.

Pitch

More than one pitch can be distinguished: the pitch of the ping (the attack) and the pitches of the dominating ranges of harmonics. Generally, a high-pitched ping will be combined with mostly higher harmonics, but there are also ride cymbals with a fairly high ping and dominating low undertones, or vice versa.

Response and Feel

Ride cymbals basically should have a slow response. If the response is too quick—the entire cymbal responding at once to your strokes—there will be no definition, no ping. Next to response, in the sense of how fast the cymbal speaks, ride cymbals differ in the way they react to your stick. The feel or rebound may vary from harsh and sturdy on unlathed, heavy rides, to flexible and supple on thin hand-hammered types.

Sustain

Ride cymbals usually are expected to be able to fill the silence between two beats, even at slow tempos. Listen for the sustain, especially of the highs. Play the cymbal at slow and fast tempos at various volume levels.

Attack

Listen for the type of sound of the attack—what you hear at the moment the stick touches the cymbal. This may vary from the sound that commonly is described as ping, being quite bright, to an extremely dry or throaty tick.

Cup

Play the cup as well as the rest of the cymbal, both with the shoulder of the stick and with the tip. The sound should be clear without excessive overtones, it needs some body and should not produce any disturbing frequencies. Find out if the character and the loudness of the bell match the characteristics of the cymbal itself.

Sweet Spot

Ride cymbals may have a "sweet spot." This is the spot, or a place anywhere in an imaginary circle, where it sounds best. It is the spot where the cymbal gives you good definition with harmonic and helpful undertones and overtones, which color the sound but do not get in the way. Finding the sweet spot on a ride cymbal may take months. The same goes for really learning how to play it.

Position

Even the slightest variation in the thickness of a cymbal or a hole that is just off-center will cause the cymbal to return to the same position every time you play it. Try to find out if this is the case with the cymbal you intend to buy. Spin it around a few times and see if it always comes to rest in the same place. If so, test the cymbal in that position.

Versatility

Besides all the different ways there are to play any cymbal, it's good to find out if your future ride cymbal is suited for occasional crash effects as well. Some types will lend themselves to this purpose better than others. A cymbal with a high bow and of

When you have picked out a good cymbal, you have to get accustomed to each other. It really takes time to learn how to play a cymbal. It has its own personality. It's an object, but it still has certain characteristics. You have to learn how to work with those characteristics, sort of get acquainted with them, and learn how they're going to respond.
—Ed Thigpen

"That cymbal that I got up there I gave away five times to five different drummers. I told them: 'I'm going to let you have this for a month. You learn how to play this, you can have it.' They ain't learned to play it yet."
—Papa Jo Jones
Photo by Rick Mattingly

considerable weight won't do for subtle crashes, nor for loud ones. Also try "crashing" the cymbal with the shoulder of the stick in the ride area and see how it responds to dead-sticking.

3.4.2. HI-HATS

Selecting hi-hat cymbals may take a lot of time. You have to deal with two different cymbals that may be combined in numerous ways, and a number of different playing techniques. Have two or three hi-hat stands and a number of spare clutches at hand. That will save you a lot of time changing top cymbals. Within one series and size, bottom cymbals, due to their heavier weight, tend to sound more similar to each other than top cymbals.

Pitch

Having two cymbals means having two pitches to deal with. Usually the top cymbal has a lower pitch than the heavier bottom cymbal. Together they produce the pitch of your hi-hat.

Distinguish between the pitch, sustain, response and volume produced by playing the hi-hat with sticks versus playing it by foot. The interval between the two cymbals affects both volume and projection. A larger interval implies more presence, everything else being equal.

Sustain and Response

The sustain and the response time of a pair of hi-hats mostly depends on the top cymbal, but the bottom one plays a role also. Splash the cymbals with a quick motion of your foot and listen carefully. Also play patterns with your sticks, opening and closing the hi-hats frequently.

Combinations

Each pair of hi-hats has its own character of sound, which may vary from extremely focussed to wide and large, from high to low, from gentle to harsh. The combination of the cymbals has a lot to do with this. Try different combinations, played by foot as well as by sticks.

Hollow

In closed position, hi-hats should not sound hollow. Varying the pressure of your foot when playing them in closed position may display such effects.

Sabian's Fusion Hats: AA or HH top with hand-hammered unlathed Leopard bottom
Courtesy of Sabian

Sweep

Hi-hat cymbals that are too thin and/or too flat may produce a sweeping sound when being closed, right after the initial chick. Exchange tops and bottoms to find the guilty one.

Cross Matching

Cross matching is making combinations of hi-hat cymbals from different series or brands. This is not always appreciated by shopkeepers. Some manufacturers list cross matched pairs. Usually these are combinations of very heavy bottom cymbals and relatively light top cymbals. Examples are Zildjian's K/Z hi-hats and Sabian's Fusion Hats, which combine an AA or HH top with a Leopard series bottom.

Single Cymbals
With one extra bottom or top cymbal you may be able to get a completely different sound out of your hi-hats. It's much cheaper than buying a second pair, too. UFIP used to sell packages of three hi-hat cymbals in the late eighties. These "Tri-hats" consisted of one bottom and two top cymbals. Zildjian listed similar packages in the mid-eighties.

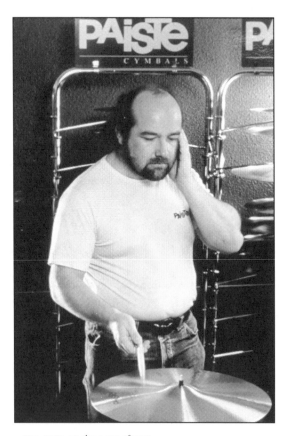

...step away, or close one of your ears...
Courtesy of Paiste

I always hit a crash cymbal quickly two or three times, to make sure that I'm going to get an attack from each successive hit. Some cymbals sound like a mess by the second or third time you hit them.
—Jerry Speiser

Warped Hi-hat Cymbals
Warped hi-hat cymbals somewhat reduce the risk of air-lock, but will not sound tight when played softly. They will sound like they are forced together over a very short period of time, which is exactly what is happening. Some people go for slightly warped hi-hats because they feel that they respond better to pitch-bend effects by varying the pressure on the pedal. Apart from these variations, it is better to find a pair of flat ones. You will then be able to control air-lock and any other effects yourself.

3.4.3. CRASH CYMBALS
Just like rides, crashes have a certain predominant pitch. The overtones, however, are much more present. Try a crash cymbal at various volumes and with various playing techniques (glancing, popping, dead-sticking) and find out whether it sounds in harmony with itself, without any disturbing frequencies.

Pitch
Thin crashes may seem to sound higher than medium crashes of the same size and series, while the opposite is true. Higher frequencies simply respond faster. That may be very misleading, especially in test situations. Step away, or close one of your ears.

Sustain, Attack and Response
The same goes for sustain. When listening to crashes in a music store, they always seem to ring longer than you would like them to. Apart from the by-now-familiar hints to find out about these things, sustain, attack and response time can be checked by giving the cymbal a few quick blows. If each blow is clearly audible, the sustain will not be overwhelming and the response will be quite quick.

Response
A good crash cymbal gives you a quick spread of both high and low overtones. Contrary to a ride cymbal, a crash has to respond quickly. Play the cymbal at various volume levels and find the level of power it needs to start vibrating entirely. That is the minimum amount of power to make it work as a crash. If you hear highs emerging some time after the blow, response is bound to be slow. Also try crashes for ride and cup sounds, and do not decide after having heard them only in combination with a bass drum.

Rumble
By holding your ear close to the edge, slight traces of rumble may be detected. A soft

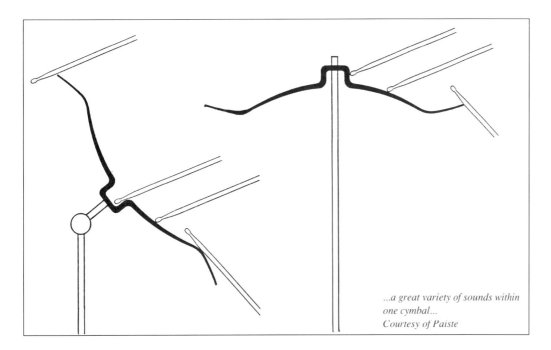

...a great variety of sounds within one cymbal...
Courtesy of Paiste

Oftentimes, perfectly good crashes will exhibit a sort of "drone" in the lows and mids—something like a small engine humming or a cat purring. This doesn't invalidate them as crash cymbals. Just don't use them in the studio.
—T. Bruce Wittet

blow will trigger it. In the studio, especially when close-miking, these low frequencies can be picked up.

Seasoned drummers always say: "There are at least three sounds on a cymbal." However, you see a lot of younger drummers who have eight cymbals, and four or five sound identical. Because they haven't taken the time to get that stuff together.
—Carl Allen

Contrast

Differences in the sound of crash cymbals will be much more evident in a shop than they will be on stage. Especially if you are playing with a P.A., quite dissimilar crash cymbals will tend to sound very much alike once they reach the audience. Try to find strongly contrasting sounds if you want them to hear some nuances as well.

3.4.4. SPECIAL EFFECTS

The character of sound of authentic Chinese cymbals and their Western counterparts varies from garbage can lid-like noises to a mixture of sweet, swelling Oriental harmonics. The sustain may be anywhere between a sharp cutoff of sound to long, slowly decaying vibrations. One important similarity is the flanged edge they all have, some sharp, some flat. This flange leads to a great variety of sounds within one cymbal. When testing, play the ride area, the edge, the flange and—if possible—the cup. Try out the difference in sound when the cymbal is mounted upside-down. Be sure to test the cymbal the same way you intend to use it: as an additional ride or as a crash, as both, or any other way.

Special "EFX", by Zildjian
Courtesy of Zildjian

The tolerance in weight of the China-types of some of the Western factories is larger than of their other types. The sound of "identical" cymbals, therefore, may vary considerably more than with rides and crashes of the same brand.

For testing splashes, refer to the section on crash cymbals. Heavier splashes may seem not to splash at all when played in a shop. Try them out in one of the ways mentioned earlier.

Information in the previous sections can also be applied to any other types of special effect cymbals.

3.5. TECHNICAL TIPS

The quality of manufacturing processes and quality control have considerably increased over the past few decades. Most modern cymbals will gloriously pass the following tests. Yet it is good to know how to judge the technical quality of a cymbal. Do not attempt any of these tips on authentic Chinese cymbals. Being made the way they are, all of them will fail these tests, which by no means says that you shouldn't buy them. The same goes for old, handmade cymbals with their sometimes oblique cups, warped edges, off-center holes or thin spots. Such "flaws" can make them most repulsive—or extremely charming. The sound of a technically perfect cymbal may not be what you are looking for, either.

...oblique cups and off-center holes... Note the pattern of the grooves around the cup
Photo by Bas Westerweel

Circles

Play the cymbal evenly in a number of circles at various distances from the cup. The sound should be the same within each circle. Variations in sound may be caused by uneven thickness.

Lines

Play the cymbal in straight lines, from the cup to the edge. If everything is okay you will hear an even change from high to low. There should not be any "dead" spots in the sound. Cymbals that sound higher in the middle of the ride area may be thinner around the cup. This could result in unwanted sound effects and, eventually, in cracking. While the edge seems to vibrate most intensely, it is actually the cup area that does.

Warpage

Check cymbals for warpage. Warped cymbals are likely to produce warped sounds. Hi-hat cymbals should especially be flat, although warped ones are be favored by some (see 3.4.2.).

Trademark

On very thin cymbals the trademark sometimes can be felt and seen as a dent on the bottom side. This may be a weak spot, caused by the force of the machine that is used to produce the logo. Round trademarks, such as the famous crescent moon, have—very—exceptionally been known to drop out of the cymbal, leaving a perfectly round hole, and a baffled drummer. Later the trademark was rolled in, rather than pressed, preventing such events.

Pit Marks

Pit marks or pit dents are small dark spots, originating from the manufacturing process. Occasionally they indicate weak spots, when situated close to the edge of a crash cymbal. Overall they can't do much harm. Due to improved techniques, pit marks are rare with new cymbals of most brands.

Dents

Check each cymbal for dents around the edge. It may have been dropped, causing stress at the point of impact. This enhances the chance of cracking.

Second-hand

Used cymbals should especially be checked for dents and other—even minor—damage. Check for cracks, mainly around the edge, at the base of the cup and around the hole. Playing the cymbal softly with a timpani mallet can disclose hairline cracks in the cymbal.

Listen carefully, with your ears very close to the cymbal. Hairline cracks cannot be seen, but may be detected this way. Avoid cracked cymbals, even if they are offered at moderate prices and even if you are charmed by that slight sizzling sound. It will start sizzling more by the day. For repairing broken cymbals refer to 7.5.

Note:

1   When drummers were asked for the most important considerations in buying cymbals, the brand name came last (11.4%), after sound (27%), price, solidity, versatility and volume (each around 15%). When asked for their ideal setup (regardless of the price), however, 70% of the respondents prefer to have cymbals of just one brand. This contradiction may speak for itself. Source: Survey by the author, 1987.

COMPOSING A SETUP
...fitting the musical context, the
hall, the soloist...
Lucas van Merwijk (l) and Martin
Verdonk (r)
Paradiso Van Slag, 1990
Photo by Bas Westerweel

4. COMPOSING A SETUP

Drummers have the possibility of actually composing their instrument, and of making arrangements of that composition each time they play. One of the most exciting—yet difficult—aspects is the composition of a set of cymbals. A good cymbal setup is more than the sum of a number of great sounding cymbals, just as a good choir is more than the sum of a number of great singers.

Composing a cymbal setup requires a concept: an idea of what you want to get across with your cymbals.

This concept has to blend with various demands, originating from the style of music, from the audience, and from anyone or anything in between. Developing such a concept also requires at least some knowledge of the criteria cymbals and cymbal setups can be distinguished by. These subjects are dealt with in the first section of this chapter. Next, some considerations about cymbals in the studio are shared. As it is impossible to give recipes on composing setups, most of this chapter consists of examples: drummers' statements about their ideas, combined with diagrams of their setups.

4.1. IN ADVANCE

Rick Van Horn, in an article about composing cymbal setups, distinguishes two basic concepts or schools.[1] In the individual/variety school every cymbal in the setup has its own, clearly discerning character. They don't mutually relate, you could say. Proponents of the ensemble school, on the other hand, select cymbals that have mostly a similar type of sound, easily matching up with each other. These two schools imply a third school: the mixed one.

This is just one way of classifying concepts. You could as easily talk about drummers that prefer high, bright sounds, versus those who spend their lives looking for the darkest and dirtiest cymbals on the face of this earth. You could distinguish between those who go for short, cool, and compact, or for broad, warm, and spreading sounds, etc.

Every type of setup can be enhanced by adding one or more cymbals that do not fit in the general character of sound of that set. Can a heavy power crash be combined with the thinnest splash around? Yes, as long as they are not treated as equivalent instruments.

Before something can be created, there must be at least a basic idea of what that creation will look or sound like. Start by trying to define what you think is beautiful, inspiring, or attractive. And what happens once you find out? Right. You feel like something else would be nice, for a change. Drummers can be quite persistent in this continuously lasting act, also know as Cymbalitis.

Demands

One of the most important requirements of a cymbal set is that it fits the musical context in which it is used. First, the style of music deserves some consideration. Different styles usually require different cymbals. It is not only the volume at which the group plays, but also the character of the music that should be taken into account.

Second, the instruments being used may discourage or suggest the use of certain types of cymbals. A large horn section calls for a different type of accents and a different ride sound than a guitar-oriented rock group does. Conscientious drummers may purposely play a different cymbal behind a trumpet solo than they'd use with a tenor sax. Third, there are band leaders, soloists and producers who all want to have their say.

For these reasons, studio drummers and those who play widely varying styles usually need more than one set of cymbals, or very versatile ones. The same goes for drummers who play in very different halls, or who otherwise have to deal with varying situations. The acoustic properties of each venue may dictate the need to change all or some of the

I choose my cymbals in the same fashion that I tune my drums. I try to get the cymbals to sound good together as a group—homogeneous as a group—but individually they also sound distinctive, so that you know which cymbal I'm hitting.
—Tony Williams

This is a very guitar-orientated band, it took some time to find cymbals that could compete with these higher frequencies. Music is a series of frequency ranges. I look for the one that isn't being saturated, so my cymbals stick out.
—Kenny Aronoff

I change my cymbals depending on the situation. I try to get an appropriate sound for each context.
—Marvin "Smitty" Smith

I don't use any ride cymbals. That's one of the Duran Duran house rules: no ride cymbals and no organs!
—Steve Ferrone

cymbals in order to get an optimal sound.

Of course, the aforementioned statements are not laws. As with sticks, some drummers like to do everything with one pair, others use a different type of stick for every tune. This may not only be a matter of preference; ability has much to do with it, too.

The use of a P.A. system allows more freedom to choose cymbals than one would have without such help. In the latter case, it is the drummer that has to adapt to the required volume, be it very low or extremely high. The right setup may help in that respect. On the other hand, cymbals tend to sound quite alike when heard through a P.A. This phenomenon has to always be kept in mind when composing a setup.

Criteria

Volume, solidity, versatility and character of sound are the most obvious criteria you have to think about when composing a setup. Volume and solidity are, moreso than the other two, determined by the way you play and the demands of the band. Versatility comes next in line, while the character of sound is the most personal choice. Within those ranges various drummers can opt for completely different setups within one and the same style of music. So there are rock drummers using very thin crashes, jazz drummers who prefer Rudes, and drummers who use only flat rides. Roland Meinl once said: "It really doesn't make any difference what label you give your cymbals, or what kind of drummers you aim a specific series towards. Drummers don't give a damn about those things."

4.2. THE STUDIO

Studios are the most clinical type of playing environment. Therefore, a lot is demanded of the quality of the instruments that are used. That goes for drums, and even more for cymbals. The sound of the drums, after all, can be drastically influenced by mufflers, various types of heads and all kinds of electronic devices. Cymbals offer far less options in that respect. You might, of course, cut off all lower and midrange frequencies, trying to turn a poor sounding cymbal into an acceptable sound on tape. That is not the most musical solution.

One of the main characteristics of a cymbal is that it produces each and every frequency there is, and basically you shouldn't limit any of them. Recording is, for the reasons mentioned above, also very picky when it comes to rattling stands and washers, consistency of playing and, basically, anything that may not be noticed in the heat of a live performance.

The Recording Cymbal

"The" recording cymbal does not exist. Some cymbals may be better suited for recording than others, but these instruments will usually work fine in live situations as well.

There are cymbals that are typically associated with recording. Sabian's Sound Control and AAX Studio series, Paiste's Formula 602 series and Zildjian's SR (Studio Recording) Hi-hats are just some examples. Meinl used to promote their Profile series with the slogan "Direct to disc."

As different as these cymbals may be, they have one thing in common. All of them have, in some way or another, a sound that is rather easily controllable and therefore ideal in recording. Controllability is the quintessence in this phrase; the examples that were given may be forgotten immediately. It is generally agreed that relatively small and light cymbals are easier to handle in recording than loud and heavy ones. This simply

If you use more than just a few cymbals, it's important that their pitches are quite different from each other, because otherwise the audience will experience them as having roughly one and the same pitch, especially if you play through a P.A.
—Mel Gaynor

Speaking as an engineer, I can make a bass drum from molded clay sound great. I can make a snare drum with heads made of old newspapers sound good. I can even make toms carved from solid blocks of shredded wheat sound passable. What I cannot do, however, is make cymbals hammered out of hubcaps and dustbin lids (and there's a lot of them about) sound fantastic.
—Dave Simpson

You can be sure that any stray overtone your hear in the music shop will be twice as obvious in the clinical recording environment.
—T. Bruce Wittet

People figure, "big crash, big sound," but it doesn't work that way. If you want a powerful crash, you're better off with smaller, lighter cymbals, because they're faster, they cut like glass breaking and then they're gone. Big crashes tend to be lower pitched, which means that most of the sound is going to get lost in the low frequencies of the electric guitar and bass, while in acoustic music it'll be too overpowering. But big crashes can be very effective in a controlled environment like the recording studio.
—Pheeroan Ak Laff

has to do with the fact that smaller and lighter cymbals are easier to control by the player, as well as by the engineer.

Besides, and at least as important, they tend to bleed less into the drum mic's. It is also good to note that heavy cymbals, however useful their cutting power might be on stage, are generally not needed in the studio: there's nothing to cut through, to put it simply.

4.3. SETUPS

The drummers on the following pages all have—or had, as some of them have passed away—their own personal opinion on the best way to compose a setup. Their demands, their ideas, their preferences, the circumstances in which they work and the styles they play are all different. Most of them possess additional cymbals, of course. The setup that is shown with each quotation is just one of the setups that the drummer in question was using at the time of the interview. Actuality is not that important in this context. It is mainly the translation of their statement into that specific combination of cymbals that counts. The same statement can, in most cases, be easily translated into newer types or series of cymbals. Whenever available, such translations have been provided. The dates refer to the year the interview was held.

All but one of the featured setups are composed of cymbals of one brand only. This might be misleading. Surveys show that most drummers without endorsements actually do use several brands in their setups, though not always voluntarily. Of course, limiting yourself to one series facilitates creating a matching set of "school ensemble" cymbals. But setups like that can also be created using various brands. By the same token, almost any type of ensemble can be picked from one catalog.

Cymbals can be a problem when it comes to recording, so I try to get cymbals that do not have too much mid-range, but which have a lot of nice, crisp highs to them that decay quickly.
—James Stroud

When recording, I always end up using one or two flat rides on records. Whenever there's an ethereal, esoteric, spaced out section I think, "Ah, Gottlieb," and I grab a flat ride. That's one of the most beautiful cymbal sounds there are.
—Rod Morgenstein

VINNY APPICE (Dio)

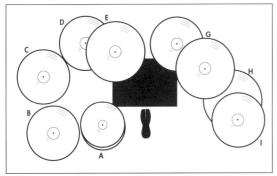

Sabian
1988
A: 15" HH Flat Hats
B: 18" AA Medium Crash
C: 18" AA Chinese
D: 18" AA Medium Thin Crash
E: 20" AA Medium Crash
F: 18" AA Chinese
G: 20" AA Rock Ride
H: 20" AA Medium Crash
I: 18" AA Medium Crash

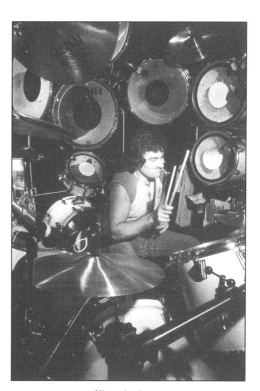

Vinny Appice
Photo by Niels van Iperen

All I want is a good crash. I use two 20" crashes and three 18" crashes, all medium weights. In the studio, I'll use smaller ones—an 18" or maybe a 16" because the big ones tend to ring a bit too much. Then you end up taping them and getting a real garbage-can sound out of it. I like to use smaller, lighter-weight cymbals in the studio, so I get more of a splash, and then it simmers down for the next crash I'm going to do. No gongs; I hate gongs. Years ago, with Derringer, I used all 22" heavy cymbals. They'd sound like mini-gongs. You can't actually stop those cymbals if you want to. I don't know why I did that.

HAN BENNINK (Instant Composers Pool, freelance)

I usually use just one cymbal; I guess it's very luxurious to have a lot of them around. So I go for the hard way. You do learn how to play a cymbal that way—to use the cup, the edge, the shoulder. Sometimes I use two, or even three cymbals. My father gave me an A

Han Bennink
Photo by the author

Art Blakey
Photo by the author

Zildjian, 32 years ago. Its sound still improves, each time I play it—or is it that I get to know it better?

The hi-hat cymbals, with their large cups, are very old cymbals from Tibet. They produce a lot of harmonics, which makes them unusable for an afterbeat.

ART BLAKEY (Jazz Messengers)

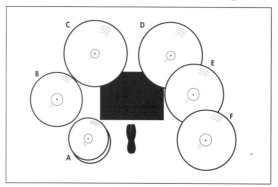

Zildjian
1988
A: 14" A New Beat Hi-hats
B: 18" A Medium Thin Crash
C: 22" K Ride
D: 22" A Medium Ride
E: 21" A Medium Ride
F: 20" A Medium Ride

Do I have a very special cymbal sound? I do? I don't know nothing about that. I play anything. Just do the best you can with what you have. It ain't the cymbal no way, it's the person who's playing it. Just give me a cymbal and I play it. I don't select them, I ain't got time for that.

VINNIE COLAIUTA (studio, freelance)

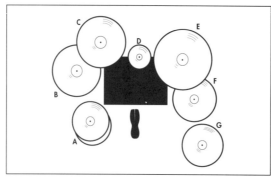

Zildjian
1990
Live setup
A: 13" K/Z Hi-hats
B: 14" or 17" China Boy
C: 17" K Dark Crash Brilliant
D: 8" K Splash Brilliant
E: 20" K Custom Ride
F: 15" K Dark Crash Brilliant
G: 14" New Beat Hi-hats Platinum

It's always a combination of selecting cymbals so that they sound good individually and sound good collectively as well. Next to that they have to be appropriate for the musical application that you choose. I like my cymbals to be crisp enough, without sacrificing the darker quality of the K's.

Vinnie Colaiuta
Photo by the author

I select different cymbals for different purposes. Sometimes I might use 16" and 14" paper-thin crashes that speak very quickly, even when I don't strike them hard. Light cymbals breathe better for me. I might use an Amir ride with these crashes, because it's a little dry and dies fast, as the paper-thin crashes do. These paper-thins are a little more fragile. There's two ways to look at that. Sometimes when you take a fragile instrument you just bash it and violate it, and then you can create a different vibe with it. But normally I wouldn't do that. I'd go to a heavier cymbal. I won't, however, use a cymbal that is too heavy, because it takes too long to speak.

The crashes that I use are applicable to a large variety of situations. They have the amount of cutting power that you need in contemporary music and at the same time they are musical sounding. Usually, when you wanted a musical cymbal, you had to go to a lighter cymbal that had more spread but it might not be loud enough to cut through.

I've been experimenting with different setups also, like using the 12" SR hi-hats for recording and live. They sound real crisp with a high-pitched snare drum. I just try to combine cymbals logically. Unless, of course, you want contrast for the sake of contrast, but that's another concept.

JACK DEJOHNETTE (Special Edition, freelance)

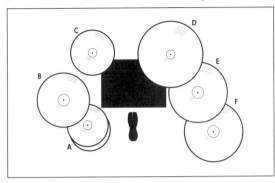

Sabian
1989
A: 14" Hi-hats
B: 18" Crash
C: 16" Crash
D: 22" Ride
E: 20" Ride
F: 20" Chinese
All cymbals: Jack DeJohnette Signature series

Jack DeJohnette
Photo by the author

I know that at some point in life, every drummer finds that special cymbal—an irreplaceable sound, a one and only. I know of drummers who wouldn't think about playing without that cymbal; it's their voice. I've spent years looking for such a cymbal, but when I finally got close, I realized that I didn't want "a" special cymbal—I wanted *all* my cymbals to be special. These cymbals are all about tonal control. Because the sound is so pure, it's harmonically pleasing. Their dynamic and tonal response is directly determined by the manner in which they are played. They give out exactly what I play into them, so I needn't concern myself with the possibility of the cymbal's sound or volume getting away from me. Because of their dry character, you can play them a lot heavier, dig in a lot more, without having to worry about going too loud, wiping out the singer, or the horn. A lot of times horn players complain about all they can hear is cymbals.... I sometimes fuse this little set with hand-hammered cymbals, which are brighter. The contrast between the two gives a nice mix-and-match.

SONNY EMORY (Earth, Wind & Fire)

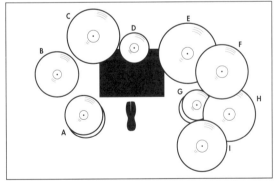

Sabian
1987
A: 13" HH Sizzle Hi-hats
B: 16" HH Thin Crash
C: 18" HH Medium Thin Crash
D: 10" HH Splash
E: 20" HH Heavy Ride
F: 18" HH Medium Thin Crash
G: 10" AA Mini-Hats
H: 18" HH Chinese
I: 17" HH Thin Crash
(all Brilliant finish)

Sonny Emory
Photo by the author

I use a big cymbal setup for the Earth Wind & Fire show. Normally I don't use this many cymbals. Usually I don't use the 17" crash, nor do I use the combination of the 14" China on top of the 16" crash. The reason for the extra 17" is just that I need two big power crash cymbals with this particular ensemble. It's like needing an extra crash cymbal when you start using a second floor tom. If you haven't got a crash cymbal in that area, it might take you quite some time to go from that particular drum to a crash on your left side; a lot of times the music won't wait for you that long.

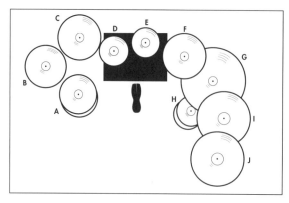

SONNY EMORY
Sabian
1990
A: 13" Sizzle Hi-hats
B: 14" HH Sound Control Crash
C: 15" HH Sound Control Crash
D: 10" HH Splash
E: 10" HH Splash
F: 16" HH Sound Control Crash
G: 22" HH Sound Control Ride
H: 10" Mini-Hi-hats
I: 18" HH Sound Control Crash
J: 18" Chinese

The 10" mini- hats are additions for this show as well. I decided to use them because Maurice [White, bandleader] is mostly on my right side during this show; playing a lot of hi-hats all the time, I couldn't really pay attention to what he was doing. The second hi-hat kind of opens me up. On top of that it allows the left hand freedom to do some other stuff on the drums.

The main reason I chose these cymbals is that I like the warm sound, which still is brilliant. The character of this type of cymbals brings a certain warmth to the electrified music that we're playing. With everything else being so much on the edge, these cymbals balance things out. I added the 12" and 14" AA for real tight, short accents, and they're a lot brighter sounding.

I've always used a 22" medium ride because it's real versatile. I can take it to a small club and it's not too overbearing; I can take it to a 16,000-seat hall—which is what we've been playing with Earth Wind & Fire—and it can really do the job.

DANNY GOTTLIEB (Elements, Blues Brothers, Mel Lewis Vanguard Orchestra)

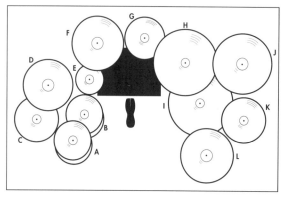

Paiste
1992
Elements (large setup)
A: 13" Sound Creation Hi-hats
B: 14" 3000 Heavy Hi-hats
C: 16" 3000 China Type
D: 17" 3000 Crash
E: 10" 3000 Splash
F: 18" 3000 Crash
G: 14" 3000 Crash
H: 22" 3000 Heavy Ride
I: 22" 602 Medium Flat Ride
J: 20" 3000 China Type
K: 16" Paiste Line Fast Crash
L: 18" Paiste Line Mellow Crash

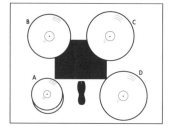

Blues Brothers setup
A: 14" Paiste Line Heavy Hi-hats
B: 18" Paiste Line Fast Crash
C: 21" Paiste Line Dry Heavy Ride
D: 18" Paiste Line Power Crash

Mel Lewis Orchestra setup
A: 14" Istanbul Hi-hats
B: 18" Istanbul Heavy Ride
C: 22" old K Zildjian Crash/Ride
D: 22" Zildjian Rock Knocker with 22 rivets

Cymbals have played a very big part in my musical development in terms of my role as a drummer/percussionist. I seem to gravitate to cymbal sounds, and I guess cymbals are more often dominating in my playing than the drums.

This is not something you develop overnight, or something that just happens by accident. It's been taking a long time. It kind of evolves.

The sounds that I use come from my exposure to the drumming greats, and their cymbal sounds. My first cymbal influence was, I guess, Buddy Rich—the dominant ping ride, the crashes flat on either side of the kit, and the small splash cymbal. Then I was influenced by my teacher, Joe Morello. Joe used Paiste 602 cymbals, and had a set manufactured to his specifications. They had a different texture than the Zildjians that

Buddy had. I liked both types of sounds.

Then I heard Mel Lewis on a Maynard Ferguson record, *The Blues Roar*, using a 20"
A Zildjian ride that had two chunks of metal cut out due to breakage. It sounded
amazing.

Additional cymbal sounds I have been exposed to were Tony Williams' dark K
sound—his ride sound with Miles Davis changed the face of cymbal playing
completely—and Elvin Jones and his bashing, but yet light K sound. Then Roy
Haynes with a Paiste Flat cymbal on Chick Corea's *Now He Sings*, and the
amazing variety of cymbal colors of Jack DeJohnette.

What makes these people so special? It's the conception of how they play
music, how they use the cymbals in the music, the choice of the sounds and the
type of cymbal that they pick, the way that they hit the cymbal and the stick that
they use. There's a lot more to it than just selecting a couple of good sounding
cymbals.

In 1976 I replaced Bobby Moses, who used Zildjian Flat cymbals, in Gary
Burton's band, and I tried to copy his sound, so I could keep the gig. This was
my first opportunity to use cymbals to develop a sound.

When the Pat Metheny Group started in 1977, Pat suggested I use a wide
variety of cymbals, as he wanted the group to sound different. He also felt that a
lot of drums got in the range of his guitar, and as a result I tended to play more
cymbals. I ended up using the 602 22" Flat Ride as a main sound, and as there
were so many sounds available, many others as well. At one time I think I had
28 cymbals at the kit. It was insane, but I always enjoyed having the perfect
sound for each spot.

With Elements I use a modified version of the basic Metheny setup. With
Mahavishnu (1984-1986) I used more of a rock setup, with very large cymbals.
With Gil Evans, I'd often just have a ride, a crash, and a pair of hi-hats. When I
needed a change of color, I could do it with dynamics, and changing back and
forth from wood-tip sticks to nylon-tip sticks.

Danny Gottlieb
Photo by Ulbo de Sitter

My Blues Bothers setup was a ride, and two crashes, in the R&B fashion. In the Mel
Lewis Orchestra (1992), that still continues after his passing, I use his special cymbals,
which so inspired me as a child.

All the bands I've played with have warranted different sounds, and I change all the time.
I'm trying to come up with just one cymbal setup, but I still haven't. I love the sounds of all
sizes, brand and types, and I hope I can continue to use them in a way that reflects my
influences and inspiration, and that is reflective of my musical personality as well.

RICK LATHAM (studio, freelance)

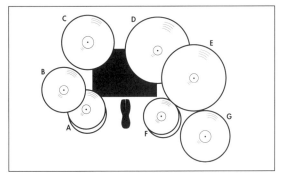

Sabian
1988
A: 14" HH Heavy Hi-hats
B: 16" HH Extra Thin Crash
C: 18" HH Thin Crash
D: 22" HH Heavy Ride
E: 22" HH Chinese
F: 12" or 13" Mini Hats
G: 17" HH Medium Crash

I prefer crash cymbals that die fast, just "psh" and that's it. All of my cymbals now are

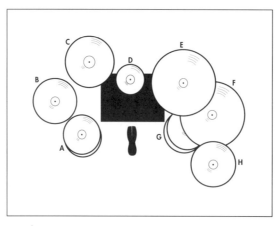

RICK LATHAM
1992
A: 13" HH Hi-hats
B: 16" HH Extra Thin Crash
C: 17" HH Thin Crash
D: 10" HH Splash
E: 22" HH Heavy Ride or 22" JJ Leopard Ride
F: 22" HH Chinese
G: 14" HH Hi-hats
H: 16" HH Thin Crash

Rick Latham
Photo by Tineke van Brederode

HH, which I find not only to be darker than AA's, but faster as well.

Because I play a lot between the left-hand hi-hat and the ride cymbal, these cymbals have to go with each other. I use very heavy hi-hats that really cut and have more definition to them, so I use a very heavy ride too. The HH Rock rides have a definite ping, which is darker than a Ping ride.

So if I go to pick out a ride cymbal, I always take my hi-hats with me. In fact, I take whatever cymbals I have with me, to complement them.

I have this 22" HH Chinese with a thin 16" mounted inside: you can vary the amount of rattle by changing the tension on the cymbals, or by changing the amount of felt between the cymbals.

MEL LEWIS (Mel Lewis Orchestra)

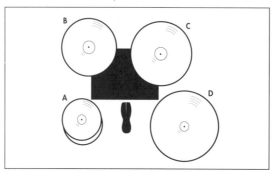

Istanbul
A: 14" Medium / Heavy Hi-hats
B: 20" Medium Ride
C: 19" Heavy Ride
D: 22" Medium China Ride (22 rivets) or Swish

Darker cymbals are more complementary to horns than any other kind of cymbal. High pitched cymbals have a tendency to obliterate high sounds. So when you hit a high crash cymbal with the brass section while they're up in that high register, you will knock out half their sound.

For riding a big band, I think the pingier a cymbal is and the less overtone and spread it has, the more empty everything will be. It's important that you have a good, full, fat sounding cymbal. Even in my dark sounds there is still a higher sound, a medium sound, and a lower sound. I'll use the high sound behind a piano. I'll also use the lowest sound behind a piano. But I won't use the middle sound behind a piano because it's too much in the piano's range.

To me, the hi-hat is another ride cymbal. Every cymbal I use is a ride cymbal. Every one of my cymbals is also a crash cymbal. I only use three. Three is enough.

To have more than two to four cymbals is totally unnecessary, because where are you

Mel Lewis
Photo by Camilla van Zuylen

going to put them anyway, and how are you going to reach them? They shouldn't be there just for looks.

I've been noticing that almost everyone has only one ride cymbal and a million crash cymbals. You don't need the crash cymbals. You need the ride cymbals, because that's where your whole thing is coming from. Crash cymbals are only for accents, so you can hit any cymbal for a crash.

NICKO McBRAIN (Iron Maiden)

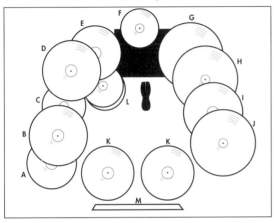

Paiste
1987
A: 17" 3000 Power Crash
B: 19" 3000 Power Crash
C: 16" 3000 Power Crash
D: 19" 3000 Power Crash
E: 17" 3000 Power Crash
F: 13" 602 Heavy Bell
G: 22" Sound Creation Bell Ride
H: 22" Sound Creation Bright Ride
I: 20" 3000 Rude
J: 24" 2002 Crash
K: 18" China, Color Sound Black (2)
L: 14" 602 Heavy Hi-hats
M: 40" Symphonic Gong
As of 1990, Nicko McBrain used Paiste Line cymbals exclusively, including five Power Crashes (16"-20"), a 22" prototype Crash, three Heavy Chinas and a 40" Symphonic Gong.

Nicko McBrain
Photo by Lissa Wales

It's taken me many years to formulate my cymbal setup. I like to have a lot of different sounds, as well as I do with my drums.

Cymbals are very, very personal for me. I always play a combination of different series. Basically it now consists of 3000's. One of my cymbals is a 20" Sound Creation Bright ride, which is primarily designed for jazz drummers. I use a Sound Creation China Type as well, whereas I should maybe use a 3000 or a Novo China. But it lasts, it's robust, and it sounds good. It's what you want to hear, not the way something is marketed. My hi-hats are Extra Heavy 602's, where I used to use Rudes.

See, it depends. I might get fed up with that same sound every night and change to 3000's or whatever. The band don't really notice that too much. I like that freedom.

Some of my cymbals are really more or less for show. You see, I got a couple of Color Sounds in the back, which are really just for visuals.

DOANE PERRY (Jethro Tull)

I probably play more of a variety of cymbals than your average rock drummer. They have a very particular purpose. Every job, every gig I do requires a different kind of cymbal setup. I like a great spectrum of sound no matter what I'm doing. If I'm doing a recording session I will have thin cymbals as well as heavy cymbals, small cymbals and big cymbals. I don't use them all from one series either. I'm mixing them up a lot.

Similarly in concert equipment, perhaps more so than in the studio, I have a great variety of cymbals because there are very particular things, especially in Tull's music, that require a very definite sound. I've always wanted to incorporate my cymbals in a very melodic and textural way, whether or not I play with Jethro Tull, where there's a lot of textural and an orchestral approach to playing. In studio work it's much the same, and I'm always finding more colors to add to the pallet.

Doane Perry
Photo by the author

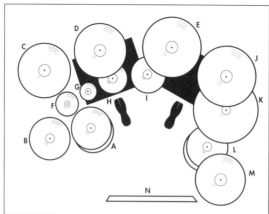

DOANE PERRY
Paiste
1990
A: 15" Paiste Line Heavy Hi-hats B: 14" Paiste
Line Full Crash
C: 18" Paiste Line Heavy China
D: 18" Paiste Line Heavy Crash
E: 20" Paiste Line Heavy Crash
F: 7 1/2" and 6 3/8" Cup Chimes
G: 5 7/8" and 4 7/8" Cup Chimes
H: 10" Paiste Line Splash
I: 2" Paiste Line Splash
J: 20" Paiste Line Heavy China
K: 22" Paiste Line Power Ride
L: 14" Paiste Line Heavy Hi-hats
M:16" Paiste Line Full Crash
N: 34" Symphonic Gong
Before, Doane Perry used a combination of 3000
and 2000 series cymbals, a Rude China and a
602 Heavy Bell

If I could I'd probably take thirty cymbals on every gig, but obviously that's not possible; my arms aren't long enough.

SIMON PHILLIPS (freelance)

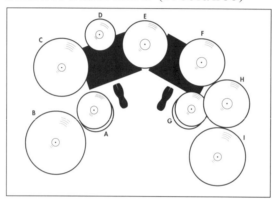

Zildjian
1992
A: 14" A Custom Hi-hats
B: 22" A Custom Swish
C: 22" A Custom Ride
D: 12" K Splash
E: 19" A Custom Crash
F: 18" A Custom Crash
G: 10" S.R. Hi-hats
H: 17" A Custom Crash
I: 22" Swish (no rivets)

Simon Phillips
Photo by James Cumpsty

Choosing cymbals is a very personal thing, and you do go through a lot of changes. You have to know what you're after to be able to make correct decisions. I used to use extremely heavy rock crash cymbals. I used to hurt my hand hitting them. Now I use incredibly thin crashes, because I like to hit them quietly and hear them.

No, I don't break them and that's because they're so thin: they give more than heavier cymbals do. I occasionally dent my cymbals, but they never crack. According to me, thin cymbals generally sound better than heavier ones. Of course, when the situation calls for it—for instance if you need the volume, while not having a P.A.—you have to make a concession and use heavier cymbals.

Jeff Porcaro
Photo by Lissa Wales

JEFF PORCARO (Toto, studio)

When I use a crash cymbal in the context of a song, such as on a verse where it's a softer dynamic, I like people to hear the cymbal's tone and sustain ring over a bar or two. To me, a lot of crash cymbals cut off too soon. They're there—splash!—and that's it. I have a couple of those for when I want that sort of thing, but basically, when I hit a crash cymbal, I like it to ring over the bar. Some I like to last two bars, and some I like to last four bars. And I like to be heard, that's why I have such big crash cymbals.

Over a loud band, either live or in the studio, I still like the cymbal to cut

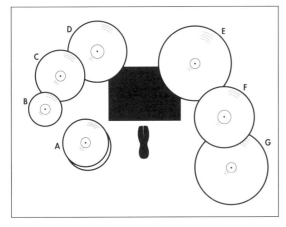

JEFF PORCARO
Paiste
1991
A: 13" Paiste Line Heavy Hi-hats
B: 10" Paiste Line Paiste Splash
C: 16" Paiste Line Fast Crash
D: 18" Paiste Line Fast Crash
E: 20" or 22" Paiste Line Full Ride
F: 18" Paiste Line Full Crash
G: 20" or 22" Paiste Line Thin Crash

through loud dynamics. The ring—the "overhang" of the cymbal—should be there.

Every time I sit behind my kit, my cymbals inspire my expression. Very often, the first cymbal crash on the downbeat of a tune will set the mood of my performance. Cymbals are that important.

JOHN "J.R." ROBINSON (studio)

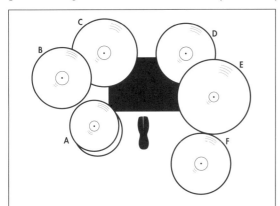

Zildjian
1987
A: 15" Quick Beat Hi-hats
B: 19" K China Boy
C: 20" Thin Crash
D: 20" K Custom Dry
E: 22" Swish
F: 18" Thin Crash

In 1992, John Robinson described his Zildjian setup to consist of 13" to 15" hi-hats of all series, crashes, mostly thin, of the K and A series, 20" to 22" rides of all series, and various chinas, splashes and gongs, depending on what the situation calls for.

I have drummers call me up and say, "I'm looking for a new cymbal," and they haven't even experienced an 18" thin crash. When I was first learning about cymbals, I got a 16" thin and an 18" thin, and those were the perfect crash cymbals for the gigs I was doing at that time.

When I got into heavier playing, I found that I had to go to 18" and 20" thins, with the same pitch difference. A lot of times, even on the lightest of gigs, I can still get away with that 20". But if I feel that it is too heavy for a particular situation, then I'll go back to a 16" and 18". I always carry an array of cymbals. Even on the road–a different hall can require different cymbals.

I'm still partial to A's because of the variety. They tend to be able to cut any situation. I use bigger hi-hats than most people–15" Quick Beats. I find that I can cover all of the bases with those, whether it's a light jazz thing or real hard, bashing rock 'n' roll.

John Robinson
Photo by Lissa Wales

MICKEY ROKER (freelance)
Dizzy Gillespie has just one cymbal, a Swish, that he likes you to play. When he's soloing, he likes that cushion under him. I don't mind using it. I never asked him the

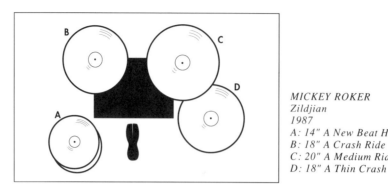

MICKEY ROKER
Zildjian
1987
A: 14" A New Beat Hi-hats
B: 18" A Crash Ride
C: 20" A Medium Ride
D: 18" A Thin Crash

Mickey Roker
Photo by Veryl Oakland

reason. All I know is that he liked the cymbal and I liked Dizzy, so it doesn't hurt me to play the cymbal. As long as I'm playing, I don't care.

Jeff Potter: This particular Swish had a dark sound, which may be the reason Dizzy liked it so much; a lot of trumpet players feel that bright, brassy cymbals can clash with their range.

STEVE SMITH (Vital Information, Steps Ahead)

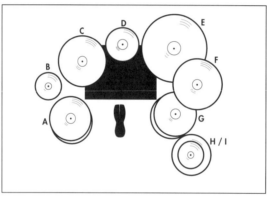

Zildjian
1989
A: 12" A SR Hi-hats
B: 8" K Splash Brilliant
C: 16" K Dark Crash
D: 10" K Splash Brilliant
E: 20" K Custom
F: 15" K Dark Crash
G: 13" K/Z Hi-hats
H: 8" A Splash (resting on top of I)
I: 12" EFX Piggyback

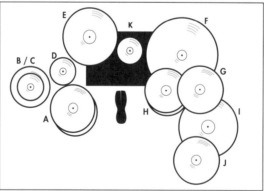

Zildjian
1992
A: 13" K/A Hi-hats
B: 12" EFX Piggy Back
C: 8" A Splash
D: 8" K Splash
E: 17" K Dark Crash, Brilliant
F: 8" K Splash, Brilliant
G: 22" K Custom
H: 14" K Dark Crash, Brilliant
I: 12" SR Hi-hats
J: 18" K Flat Ride, Brilliant
K: 14" K Mini-China (inverted)

I used the same ride cymbal for a trio gig with pianist Ahmed Jahmal (the only thing being amplified was his piano) as I did on Dweezil Zappa's hard rock album, that same week. It's also the cymbal that I used on Richie Kotzen's heavy metal album in 1989. It was a 20" K Custom with a real nice bell and a beautiful ride sound.

Of course, much has to do with the way you play the cymbal. I've worked a lot in getting the right angle of the tip of the stick on the cymbal, the right touch, the right volume. I can make almost any cymbal sound okay, but especially if it's a good one. It's good to have one ride cymbal that you can use for any kind of gig. You don't have to adapt your way of playing to the cymbal each time.

The same goes for my hi-hats. I've been using the 12" SR's for a while. They sounded so crisp in the studio that I have been using them as my main hi-hats sometimes, both live and in the studio. Yes, also on the heavy metal album. I know that I'm supposed to use 15" hi-hats for that type of music.

Technicians like these 12" hi-hats because they don't bleed into all the other mic's. Besides, I don't play them that hard, and I keep them closed most of the time. This gives me more definition and more feel on the hi-hat. Apart from that I get a bigger drum sound that way, because room mic's can be used.

If you play your hi-hats wide open and overplay your ride cymbal all the time, room mic's can't be used: the engineers end up retriggering toms and bass drum because the sound is just all cymbals. That's what Beau Hill, who produced Dweezil Zappa's record, told me, and he made a good point. There are so many drummers around who think they're burning because they can play their cymbals so loud, but all they're doing is destroying the drum sound.

Steve Smith
Photo by Tineke van Brederode

FREDY STUDER (freelance)

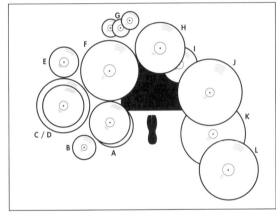

Paiste
1990
A: 14" Paiste Line Dark Crisp Hi-hats
B: 8" Paiste Line Bell
C: 14" Paiste Line Sound Edge bottom on top of
D: 18" Paiste Line Thin China
E: 10" Paiste Line Splash
F: 20" Paiste Line Mellow Crash/Ride (prototype)
G: Three bended 2002 Sound Discs (prototypes)
H: 16" Paiste Line Mellow Crash
I: 12" Paiste Line Bell
J: 22" Paiste Line Dry Rough Ride (prototypes)
K: 22" Paiste Line Gong Ride (prototypes)
L: 20" Paiste Line Thin China or 20"
*   Paiste Line Flat Ride*

My situation is like a paradox: on the one hand I play different styles of music, on the other hand I am very persistent about using the same basic cymbal setup in each situation, adding sounds if necessary.

That's why all my cymbals have to fully accomplish their characteristic purposes, they have to comply with my wishes soundwise, and they have to feel good. The in-between tension has to be as strong as possible.

Every cymbal responds to your sticks and to your playing in a different way. They're like people: You can feel comfortable with a large quantity of friends, but each friendship will be different.

Next to my ears and my feelings, I mainly use my intuition to combine the right sounds. As a consequence, a relationship with the cymbals is created: they return to me whatever I put in.

Fredy Studer
Photo by the author

ED THIGPEN (freelance)

Cymbals are very personal, let's face it. A lot of it has to do with the person's touch. What I'm looking for are sounds that stimulate one's thoughts. The cymbals should become an acoustic extension of the person. It's natural. That's one of the reasons that it takes people years to accomplish a final setup. Yes, and then that might change.

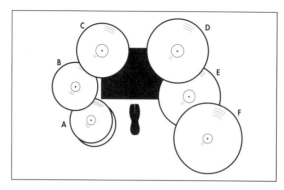

ED THIGPEN
Sabian
1989
A: 14" HH Hi-hat
B: 15" HH Sound Control Crash
C: 16" HH Medium Thin Crash
D: 21" HH Sound Control Ride
E: 21" HH Chinese
F: 22" HH Flat-Bell Ride

Particular groups will call for certain types of sounds. So you do that, because the situation will dictate what you need. Most of my work is with small groups and, ironically, I have some big cymbals. But they give me a wide spread, many tonalities. And that's basically what I'm looking for. My setup has a neutrality so it can blend in with any key changes.

The number of my cymbals may change depending on how big the stage is. Sometimes I can only use two cymbals, and that's also good. In those cases you need something that gives you a wide variety of sounds and a lot of imagination.

I have a sizzle that I use when I work with Milt Jackson. First thing when I come in: "Where's that sizzle cymbal? I want that sizzle." I also have an authentic Chinese cymbal with a real funky sound for big band. Horn players love it, and it works great behind reed ensembles. It's all a matter of blending the sound into the musical situation.

In picking out a set of cymbals the thing is consistency. Of course, you still can choose your cymbals from different factories. I like it when people are open to changes. You should have options to alternatives, that's a necessity.

With these cymbals I can almost create melodies, you know; "cymbolic" melodies, that is.

Ed Thigpen
Photo by Lissa Wales

TONY THOMPSON (Chic, Power Station, Madonna)

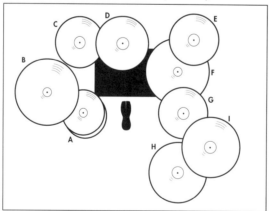

Zildjian
1987
A: 15" A Quick Beat Hi-hats
B: 22" A Swish
C: 16" Z Light Power Crash
D: 19" A Thin Crash
E: 17" K China Boy
F: 22" Z Light Power Ride
G: 17" A Paper Thin Crash
H: 18" A Thin Crash
I: 19" K China Boy

Tony Thompson
Photo by Lissa Wales

The choice of your ride cymbal identifies you. I'm always looking for a ride that is not too heavy, with a touch of spread and a bit of personality to it. Ultimately, it probably doesn't have anything to do with the cymbal make: It's the right cymbal and the right cat hitting it with the right touch in the right spot.

The ride cymbal always has to be heard in relationship to the entire kit, not as something separate. I hear a lot of cats who'll play the drums, then play the cymbals, and it sounds like two different kits. It's weird. After all, it's a percussion instrument—it's a kit—and everything is supposed to work together perfectly, like in an orchestra.

I switch around a lot. I might use K's sometimes, but I wouldn't use them on tour with Bowie, Chic, or Power Station.

CHAD WACKERMAN (Frank Zappa, Allan Holdsworth)

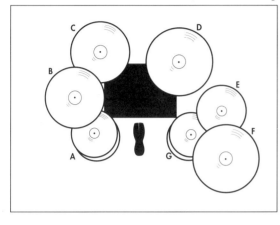

Paiste
1987
A: 14" 602 Heavy Hi-hat
B: 18" 2000 Mellow China
C: 18" 3000 Thin Crash
D: 20" 3000 Medium Ride
E: 16" 3000 Thin Crash
F: 20" Rude China
G: 13" Sound Creation Heavy Hi-hats

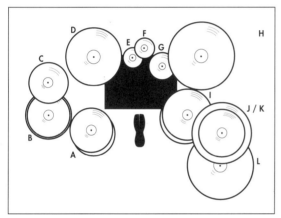

Paiste
1992
A: 13" Sound Creation Dark Hi-hats
B: 13" 2002 Crash directly on top of 14" Rude
*   Crash-Ride*
C: 12" Sound Formula Splash
D: 16" Paiste Line Fast Crash
E: #6 Cup Chime
F: #5 Cup Chime
G: 8" hi-hats (bottom: 2002 Bell / top: 8" Rude
*   Splash)*
H: 20" Paiste Line Dry Ride
I: 15" Rude Hi-hats
J: 18" Paiste Line Fast Crash
K: 14" Paiste Line Fast Crash
L: 20" Paiste Line Thin China

All my cymbal sounds are kind of separated, as are my toms. I Use 10", 12", 14" and 16" toms. No 13", because that might sound a little too close to my 12" or my 14". So I want each cymbal to have its own definite place, a couple of notes apart from each other.

There's very much a right and a left side in my setup. The two trashy sounds that I'm using, the very far left on the bottom stack, is a 14" Rude crash and a 13" 2002 crash sitting right on it. Loosely, so it's real trashy, real dark. The other trashy sound is my China, which is the exact opposite, on the right side.

The hi-hats work the same way. They are at the same height, so I can ride them either way, but they are extremes: the Dark Sound Creation Heavy hats in the left, and 15" hats on the right, very different. The two main crashes are 16" and 18". They are fairly related. Above those I have two fast sounding cymbals. They are kind of at the same level, for the same kind of effect, left and right. You have the trashy ones, the splashy ones, and below those the crashes.

I like the bell cymbals a lot so I have two cup chimes fairly close together. There is a third hi-hat source, the 8" hats, above the third rack tom. And then there is a 20" dry ride.

I think of it kind of like a mirror setup, in a way, which at the same time is very

Chad Wackerman
Courtesy of Paiste
Photo by Marlene Den Dekker

contrasting, like the China versus the stack. Both are very trashy, but they have a lot of contrast too.

This setup works well for everything: I can play very modern things because I have the bells and the trashy sounds. At the same time I can play very conventional because I have those sounds as well. I've used the same cymbals with Barbra Streisand as I did with Allan Holdsworth and Frank Zappa, live as well as in the studio.

If the engineer or the producer wants a specific kind of sound, say like a Tony Williams ride sound, then I pull another one out of the bag. But I hardly ever get asked to do so.

PAUL WERTICO (Pat Metheny)

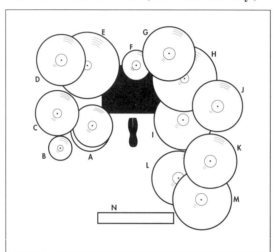

Paiste
1987
A: 14" 2000 Medium Hi-hats
B: 8" 2000 Sound Reflection Splash
C: 16" 2002 Crash
D: 17" 3000 Crash
E: 22" 602 Thin Flatride (2 rivets)
F: 11" 602 Splash
G: 22" Sound Creation Dark Flatride
H: 18" 3000 Crash
I: 21" 602 Heavy Ride
J: 17" 2002 Crash
K: 19" 602 Thin Crash (4 rivets)
L: 18" 2000 Mellow China
M: 20" 2000 China Type
N: Paiste Percussion Set

Paul Wertico's 1990 setup included, amongst others, Paiste Line Flat and Full Rides and four 2002 Sound Reflection cymbals. The Sound Creation ride remained, just as the mixture of 602 and 2002 cymbals, and the Percussion Set.

Paul Wertico
Photo by Lissa Wales

I try to get my cymbals in tune with each other, so I can play melodies; all the cymbals are matched, but still each one has a specific function.

I try to pick cymbals that are perfect for the tune. If we play an African type song I'll probably use a darker cymbal, but without too many low frequencies that might make everything kind of disappear.

I like different sounds for different reasons. If I'm playing bebop, for instance, I really like dark cymbals. So I have a great Sound Creation 22" Dark Ride with four rivets in it, that I combine with an 18" Short Crash, a flatride and hi-hats of the same series. Sometimes I'll use Rudes with that particular set, or Formula 602's. That's my jazz set, basically. In the studio I have been using the 2000 Sound Reflections, which record fantastic. I usually use the same cymbals for recording as I do on stage. On some albums, however, I might use different cymbals for different songs, and that's obviously something you can't do live.

I have always loved the "buttery" feel of the old K's. Paiste cymbals never give in that much. I grew up playing that way, so I really had to work on my attack when I started playing Paiste. I think they make you play more exact. That's fine.

DAVE WECKL (Chick Corea, studio)

It's very personal, it's emotional: I use the cymbals that I use because I like the way they sound. I listen for things that are pleasing to my ear. In a small room I might use a 15" and a 16" Dark Crash, but if I'm on a very loud and bombastic R&R gig I would probably use a 17" and an 18" instead. Crashes shouldn't be gongy or last too long.

In acoustic jazz I change my left-hand crash for a second ride, a very old 18" medium K. My other cymbals tend to get bigger in jazz. In those situations I don't need the quick

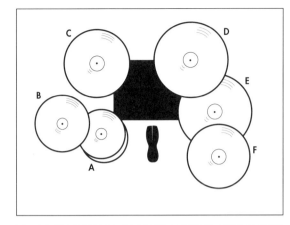

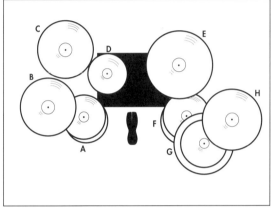

DAVE WECKL
Zildjian
Acoustic jazz setup (1987)
A: 14" K/Z Hi-hats
B: 15" K Dark Crash
C: 18" K Medium Thin Ride
D: 20" K Custom (Special, thin)
E: 20" A Swish (6 rivets)
F: 17" K Dark Crash Brilliant

Zildjian
1990
A: 13" K/Z Hi-hats
B: 17" K China Boy Brilliant
C: 17" K Dark Crash Brilliant
D: 12" K Splash Brilliant
E: 20" K Custom
F: 14" K/Z Hi-hats
G: 18" K Dark Crash Brilliant
H: 14" A Swish, on top of G
I: 7" K Dark Crash Brilliant

Dave Weckl later added a 6"
splash and changed to 13" and
14" K Hi-hats.

Dave Weckl
Photo by Ulbo de Sitter

crashes; I prefer to have more cymbals to ride on, which gives me different colors.

I usually like a small and thinner ride cymbal that blends more and doesn't ping. But that particular sound gets lost in Chick Corea's Elektric Band, which can be quite loud. So I cooperated in designing the K Custom: I needed a lot of definition so I could hear the stick attack without it being pingy. I hate pingy cymbals. It also had to have the ability to crash it, in a way that doesn't spread all over the place. The bell-sound had to be clean and very separate from the cymbal sound. Such a cymbal just didn't exist yet.

My hi-hats have to be very versatile as well. The heavy bottom gives it a very definite and cutting chick. At the same time the top is very splashy, which gives me the possibility to play very fast open/closed hi-hat patterns.

When I'm in the studio, I might change cymbals every tune, depending on the tune. It's still mostly K's, but the sizes change.

STEVE WHITE (Paul Weller/Style Council)

Like many other drummers I fell under the spell of the original Turkish sound. For me, that expressive warm tonality became the reference point for my cymbal setup. I combined that character and tone, found in the HH cymbals, with the AA series that give the necessary punch and crash to cut through today's highly amplified sounds.

I picture my cymbal setup as an ensemble to sound good in combination and succession. Usually, I select my cymbals starting with the ride and the hi-hats.

In my live work I'm mostly using a 20" hand-hammered Rock Ride. Stick definition from the ride is a more important factor live. Besides, the subtlety of a thinner cymbal is

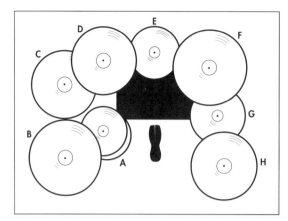

STEVE WHITE
1992
Sabian
LIVE:
A: 13" HH Regular Hi-hats or 12" Mini Hats
B: 20" HH Chinese (optional)
C: 18" AA Medium Crash
D: 19" AA Medium Crash
E: 14" HH Extra Thin Crash
F: 20" Classic Ride, 22" HH Classic Ride with
   3 rivets, or 20" HH Rock Ride (subject to
   requirement)
G: 16" HH Medium Crash
H: 18" HH Medium Crash

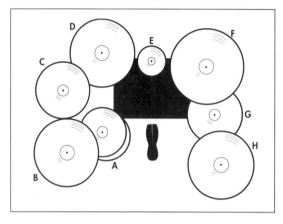

STUDIO
A: 13" HH Regular Hi-hats or 12" Mini Hats
B: 18" HH Chinese (optional)
C: 16" HH Medium Thin Crash
D: 18" HH Medium Thin Crash
E: 8" AA Splash (optional)
F: 20" Classic Ride, 22" HH Classic Ride with
   3 rivets, or 18" Crash/Ride (subject to
   requirement)
G: 16" HH Medium Crash
H: 18" HH Medium Crash

Steve White
Courtesy of Sabian

lost in an amplified situation. I always request fairly close miking live on the ride cymbal to ensure it cuts through loud and clear. I also use the brighter AA cymbals live.

In the studio I tend to go for a slightly thinner ride cymbal. I really like the shimmery overtones that build on a thinner ride. The very special 22" Classic Ride with three rivets I use to great effect in the more subtle tunes I may be required to play.

My choice of hi-hats is again from the hand-hammered series, in the studio and live, usually 13". I tend to be quite heavy on my hi-hat playing and the smaller cymbals, I find, are a little less inclined to step out of line. I don't go for heavy hi-hats as I really enjoy the sound of half closed hi-hats as an alternative to the ride cymbal. If the cymbals are too heavy that effect is lost. I tend to go for a slightly heavier crash than many drummers, usually for a 16" or 18" medium hand-hammered, that gives a warm full sound. I'm not really into the fast "All impact, no tone required" effect. Splash and Chinese cymbals are introduced to my setup as and when the music requires. My cymbal setup reflects the drum sound that I really like. I like to hear the sound of the snare drum rattling and the toms ringing a little bit. To me that's "live."

PETE YORK (Spencer Davis, Super Drumming, own band)

You shouldn't just think of the cymbals as a cymbal setup, but as a part of a drumset. The cymbals are the highest sound of the instrument, the bass drum has the lowest sound. Your ride cymbal should complement your bass drum sound.

One of the most important things in music is contrast. Contrasts surprise the listener.

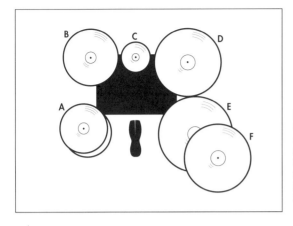

PETE YORK
Sabian
1992
A: 14" HH Regular Hi-hats
B: 6" HH Thin Crash
C: 8" HH Splash
D: 18" HH Thin Crash
E: 20" HH Heavy Ride

That's one of the reasons I use an 8" or a 10" splash instead of a 12": the smaller ones are so much faster, compared to my crashes.

Apart from the hi-hats and the ride I look for thin cymbals, both crashes and Chinas. I use a heavy 20" ride cymbal. I like that pingy sound for either jazz or rock things. It works well because it carries the rhythm and everybody can hear it. It works well with the bass as well, because they don't bother each other.

Other drummers would prefer not to use pingy cymbals. That depends on your particular style. For instance, Louie Bellson and the late Mel Lewis are well known for their big band work: the first plays a high pitched ride and accents mainly with his snare drum, the latter used to use dark sounding cymbals, playing accents mainly with his bass drum. For their way of playing, they're both right.

Pete York
Photo by Helmut Ölschlegel

Note:

1   "Cymbals for Club Drummers," by Rick Van Horn, *Modern Drummer*, vol. 8, no. 2, Modern Drummer Publications, Inc., New Jersey, USA, 1984.

CYMBAL ACOUSTICS
...the influence of factors like
diameter, weight and profile...
Courtesy of Paiste

5. CYMBAL ACOUSTICS

Why do cymbals sound the way they sound? Why will a cymbal of good quality never be out of tune? These kinds of questions cannot be answered in just a few words. As simple and basic as a cymbal seems to be, in reality it is one of the most complex instruments around. This chapter starts with some basic knowledge of cymbal acoustics. Armed with a dose of General Cymbalology, the next sections are easier to understand.

These sections give an in-depth view of the way cymbal sounds are created. The section Anatomy deals with the influence of factors like diameter, weight and profile on the sound of a cymbal. The effects of the alloy, different hammering methods, lathing, buffing and age are dealt with in the third section, Organizing the vibrations.

Questions, Answers, Questions
This multitude of information might lead to the conclusion that this chapter contains everything one can possibly know about cymbals. It does not.

Though nobody can deny the existence of certain acoustical laws, the sum total of sound determinants in a cymbal are so interrelated that it seems hardly possible to speak of unambiguous facts. It is no wonder that even the most knowledgeable people in this area tend to disagree on certain points. If, at one time, you have the idea of having found all the answers, they turn into questions again. That is when you really start getting there.

5.1. BASICS
Sound can be described as a "disruption of the balance in the air." If you position yourself directly in front of the loudspeakers of a group performing at full volume, you will feel that disruption pretty well. The way in which sound moves through the air can be compared with what you see when you throw a stone in a tub filled with water.

Starting from the point where the stone hits the surface, the waves move to the outer edges of the tub in concentric circles. It is hardly noticeable that, once these waves have reached the side of the tub, they continuously roll back to the center and out to the wall, again and again. The vibrations in a cymbal partly behave in a similar way. They bounce back and forth between the cup and the outer edge. The restrained sound of a flat ride is partly due to the fact that one of these obstacles—the cup—is missing.

Fifteen Patterns
Extensive research by Thomas D. Rossing and Richard W. Peterson, has shown that radial vibrational patterns (or modes) are most important in a cymbal.[1] The appearance and shape of vibrational patterns depend on the way the cymbal is played, the force that is being used and other variables. Besides, these patterns change a lot between the moment of the stroke and the moment that the cymbal is completely quiet again. The sound does too, of course.

There is a clear resemblance in the vibrational modes in membranes (drumheads), flat round discs and cymbals. The main difference between the latter two is caused by the saucerlike or convex shape of the cymbal. Rossing and Peterson distinguish fifteen different patterns, some of which are formed by combinations of others. In their research they have applied the technique of holographic interferometry, making these fascinating patterns visible.

Speed
Besides these different modes, there are also the speeds in which the various vibrations travel. This factor, not being a constant one either, depends on the way the cymbal is

"When I hear sounds I get images, sometimes. Cymbals are like pebbles, splashed in a pool of water. A big splash, a ripple. That's the kind of image I get from them. You can see the colors flow out like that, in circles..."
—Elvin Jones
Photo by Ulbo de Sitter

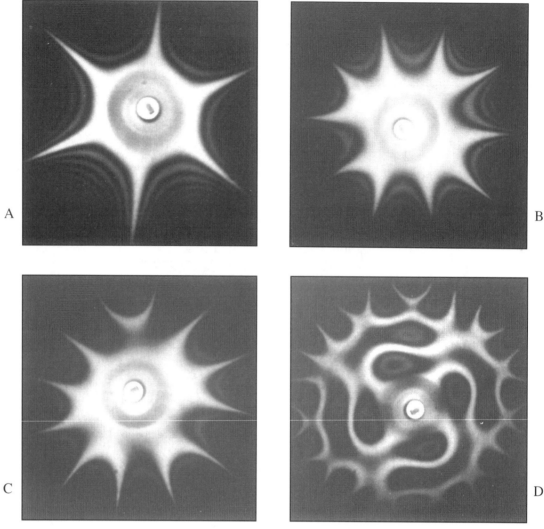

Hologram interferograms of four modes of vibrations in a 15" cymbal (in chronological order). The fourth interferogram shows a combination mode.
Courtesy of Thomas D. Rossing

being played and on many of the aforementioned variables in the cymbal itself. Cymbal makers control these variables by influencing the dimensions and other physical characteristics of their cymbals. Virtually each step in the production process has the goal to control the nature of the vibrations in the instrument, and thus the sound of the cymbal.

Overtones

Before going into this much deeper, a few of the specific characteristics of cymbals should be listed. Pitched instruments, such as a piano or a saxophone, generate clearly identifiable tones. This characteristic enables the player to perform a melody on them. At the same time, this property implies the disadvantage that they may sound terribly out of tune.

Each sound of this kind of instrument is always formed by a fundamental tone or frequency and a series of overtones or harmonics. Because of the differences in these series different instruments can be recognized. The timbre of an instrument depends on the specific series of overtones it brings forth. These series are connected to the shape of the periodic vibrations, which can be accounted for by the specific shape and size of the instrument and by the material(s) it was made of.

Noise-instruments

Cymbals, contrary to the instruments mentioned above, belong to the category of non-pitched instruments. In some languages they are also indicated with the term "noise-instruments." Not all metallic idiophones,[2] another category cymbals belong to, have that character. A vibraphone, for instance, is very much a melodic instrument. On non-pitched instruments you cannot play any recognizable song, but they can't be out of tune either. Why, in the case of cymbals?

Sympathetic Vibrations

A stroke on a cymbal does not produce just one, but a lot of fundamental frequencies. The main frequency of the tone of the cup is much higher than the frequencies you hear when playing the edge, and these are just the two extremes. Each of these frequencies has its own series of overtones. Because all of these frequencies mutually affect each other, even more frequencies appear. These sympathetic vibrations—and thus the complete sound of the cymbal—will be experienced differently by each person. Every pair of ears is as unique as a fingerprint. Obviously, the human ear is not capable of identifying "the" pitch of a cymbal. There is too much going on at the same time. The same phenomenon makes the cymbal one of the hardest instruments to sample.

Tessitura

The sound of a good quality cymbal always contains a full tonal scale with frequencies from high to low, that enhance and blend with each other harmonically. This characteristic guarantees that a good cymbal will always be consistently in tune with the other instruments in the band. Whether a cymbal is experienced as low, medium or high pitched depends on a dominating frequency scale within that complete range of pitches.

Actually, it is better to talk about a dominating tessitura (tonal range or scale) than about a dominating pitch. The term *pitch* is too strict for cymbals, indicating a definable note.

The narrower the dominating range is, the more focussed or tight the cymbal will sound. A cymbal that has a lot of spread has a wider dominating tessitura. A heavy ride cymbal, hammered in a regular pattern, sounds more focussed and compact than a thin hand-hammered crash cymbal. Large cymbals have more spread and sound fuller and fatter than comparable cymbals in smaller sizes.

Blend

A good cymbal always blends in with the harmonic context of the music. That goes for crashes, but heavy rides also have to meet that standard. A too-limited amount of harmonics makes the cymbal sound shallow and one-dimensional. A predominant pitch that is too strong will be irritating, and the cymbal will be out of tune at times. A ride cymbal with a predominant E does not work too well when playing a blues in F, for example. Drummers aren't always conscious of this, as many of them are not used to listening to pitches the same way other musicians do. Especially bass players—but not them alone—often have problems with ride cymbals that ring a certain note which interferes with the register they are playing in. A strong dominant frequency in a cymbal disturbs the harmony in the music, and may even sound out of tune in relationship to the total sound of the cymbal itself.

Cymbals that, on the contrary, only have spread and no dominating tessitura whatever

I was taught by Jo Jones that every good cymbal should have at least five distinct tonalities. At the same time it should not build one tone that could cause unattractive dissonance. Avoid fixed pitches: a good cymbal has a multi-tonality.

— Ed Thigpen

Every frequency you can have on a spectrum analyzer you can have in a cymbal, even in a bad one. It's the blending of all these different pitches that make for a good sound or a bad sound.

—Dan Barker

will sound undefined. They don't *speak,* but only produce undefinable noise.

High and Low

High notes sound shorter than low ones. If you hold your ear next to the edge of a cymbal half a minute after a stroke, you can hear some very low frequencies, which sometimes appears to be unlikely to ever stop. The highest frequencies die out right after the stroke. They also take care of the clearness and the projection of the sound, while the lower registers give the cymbal its body, blend and sustain.

The dominating tessitura will always be between those extremes. Generally speaking, medium-pitched cymbals are the most all-around types. They have plenty of definition and projection, while the sound will blend in most situations.

5.2. ANATOMY

Each type of cymbal has a very specific character and an individual sound. This sound is influenced by a great number of parameters. The influence of each of these factors is

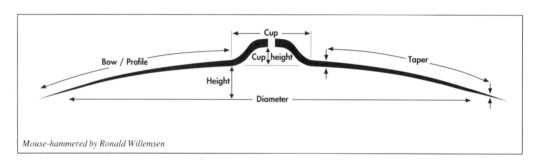

Mouse-hammered by Ronald Willemsen

always related to the other factors. If it were possible for you to install a different cup in a cymbal, you wouldn't have just another cup. The sound and character of the entire cymbal would change.

By the same token, every change in the dimensions or other variables of a cymbal can be compensated for by changing another parameter, to some extent. A rather flat cymbal, in principle, has a lower pitch than a convex one, but by hammering the first one a different way, it might sound higher in the end. In a nutshell: The final overall sound is formed by an entity of different factors that always work together with, and in relationship to, each other.

The terms used in the following sections have to be seen in context. It is assumed that in a given cymbal only the parameter that is being discussed is changed. All other parameters remain identical. When two cymbals are being compared, it is assumed they are from the same series, unless it is said to be otherwise. It should be mentioned that the words used to indicate effects of certain parameters on the sound will always be subjective.

5.2.1. DIAMETER

The larger a cymbal is, the more air can be moved and the more volume it is able to produce. At the same time, it takes more energy to get a larger quantity of metal to vibrate. Therefore, larger cymbals respond slower than smaller ones. They sustain longer also. It takes some time to get three kilos of solid metal to be quiet. This can present problems when choosing a cymbal.

Smaller cymbals respond faster, but produce less volume.
Courtesy of Paiste

Yes, an 18" crash cymbal will sound louder than a 14" version. However, if you want to use it for a short accent, you will wind up with the small one after all. This would imply making concessions as far as volume is concerned. Furthermore, the pitch of a larger cymbal is lower. The quantity of metal offers more room for long amplitudes or soundwaves.

To show the relativity of these remarks, a thick 8" bell cymbal could be compared with a thin 20" crash. The crash has more volume, but in certain circumstances you will be able to hear the Bell better because of its higher pitch.

5.2.2. WEIGHT

The influence of the weight of a cymbal is, on a number of points, comparable to the influence of the diameter. More metal means more volume, a slower response and a longer sustain. The pitch, on the contrary, rises as the weight increases. When comparing a ride and a crash of the same size and series this becomes clear. Comparing medium and thin crashes can be misleading. The thin one at first seems to sound higher, yet it does not. This is caused by the fact that the high frequencies in the thin one respond quicker, which tends to cheat the ears. When listening to the same cymbals from a distance (like the audience does) it is clearly audible that the medium is the one with the highest pitch.

...the pitch of a larger cymbal is lower... Collection Piet Klaassen Drumservice
Photo by Bas Westerweel

Overtones

The thickness of a cymbal also influences the amount of audible overtones and their character. Thicker cymbals produce less overtones and have a narrower frequency range. The overtones are limited by the large amount of material. A thin ride, therefore, has more spread and a broader, warmer sound than a heavy version of the same size and shape.

Most hi-hat combinations have a heavier bottom and a lighter top. The thick bottom cymbal gives volume and cutting power, while the top can respond fast. This makes the sound a little warmer at the same time.

Chart 1 (weights of cymbals) contains some random figures that clearly show within which ranges cymbals of various types are being made.

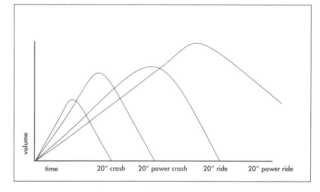

The cymbal's response and decay as influenced by the weight and the profile; the Power Ride has the most even attack/decay-line and provides the most volume.
Courtesy of Paiste

CHART 1: WEIGHTS OF CYMBALS in grams (1/1000 kilo)

12" splash UFIP Experience Samba *360* Avedis Zildjian **420** Sabian Rock Splash **600**	**20" ride** K Zildjian Pre-Aged Dry Light *2000* UFIP Natural **2750** Zildjian Earth **3400**
16" crash Sabian AA Sound Control *850* K Zildjian Dark **1050** Sabian Jack DeJohnette **1300**	**14" hi-hat** *top* Paiste 3000 medium *800* A Zildjian New Beat **900** Sabian Jack DeJohnette **1250**
18" crash UFIP Class Fast *1190* Paiste Sound Formula Full **1400** Sabian Jack DeJohnette **1650**	**14" hi-hat** *bottom* Paiste 1000 *950* A Zildjian New Beat **1200** Sabian Jack DeJohnette **1550**

Chart 1. Divergent weights of cymbals, per type. Note: These figures may vary slightly.

5.2.3. PROFILE

The profile or bow of a cymbal co-determines the pitch as well as the presence and the character of the harmonics. A relatively flat cymbal has a lower pitch, a darker character and more overtones than a high-profile cymbal. Realizing the fact that almost all cymbals originally have the shape of a flat disc, this is easy to understand.

The more convex a cymbal is made—by hammering, pressing and/or spinforming it—the greater the tension in the metal will be. Therefore, the pitch will rise.

The definition of the sound will increase when the cymbal is given a higher bow. The higher the bow, the less overtones, so the drier the sound will be. Like most other parameters, these characteristics can be compensated for in a number of ways. A high-profile cymbal may have an extra amount of overtones because of a low weight or because of certain hammering techniques.

Differences in the profile of cymbals can be quite substantial. Some clear examples are a 20" K Zildjian Ride with a bow of 11/16" (17 mm) and a 20" Istanbul Ottoman Ride measuring up to 9/8" (28.5 mm). These measurements excluded the height of the cup.

Thickness is sometimes said to be of greater importance than the profile. A 20" crash and a ride of the same size may have the same profile. The difference in weight will then make for the different characters. At the same time it can be assumed that even a heavy K Zildjian or Sabian HH (some types excluded) will never sound real high, because of the fact that they have a very low profile. The ride version of such cymbals, for the same reason, can be used as a crash much easier than more convex shaped ride cymbals.

Weight

Knowing this leads to the obvious conclusion that ride cymbals usually have a higher bow than crashes. Flatter cymbals respond faster than high ones. But there is more. On one hand the higher profile of the ride makes the ride sound more definite. There are less overtones. On the other hand, a high profile indicates a shorter sustain. Why then do ride cymbals sound so long? Because of their weight.

China cymbals and comparable types have a deviant profile. The sharp flange of the outer edge makes them very short and sharp in sound. The flange of Sabian's Sound Control series and UFIP's Fast Crashes is much smaller. It has a kind of a muffling effect on the harmonics as well as on the sustain, "controlling the sound that is allowed to come out of the cymbal," according to Sabian. This phenomenon can be understood by going back to the story of the stone and the tub.

5.2.4. TAPER

The taper of a cymbal is the change of thickness from the center of the cymbal to the edge. Crash cymbals usually have a larger or more gradual taper than rides. In other words, the difference between the thickest and the thinnest part of a crash cymbal is larger.

A gradual taper, resulting in a thin outer edge, will make a cymbal respond faster and sustain shorter. An even taper, resulting in a relatively thick outer edge, makes for a cleaner, less explosive sound and a longer decay. When reducing the size of a cracked crash cymbal, it will therefore sound less crashy after the operation than it did before. The relative taper has become more even (see 7.5.5.).

Due to mistakes at the lathing machine (however seldom occurring), a cymbal may have thinner spots towards the center. The sound of such a cymbal is likely to be somewhat hollow. For more information refer to the technical tips in 3.5.

...a much smaller flange...
UFIP Class Fast Crashes
Courtesy of UFIP

5.2.5. CUP

The size and shape of the cup mainly have an effect on volume, on the presence of overtones and on the response time. A larger cup will make a cymbal respond faster. It will give the cymbal more volume, more overtones and more of a full-bodied sound.

In other words, a larger cup enhances the crash qualities of a cymbal. Smaller cups make the sound tighter or more compact. The sound of a flat- or mini-bell ride makes that evident. Such cymbals have a limited volume, their sound is very defined and they hardly have the tendency to build up. Striking the edge on such cymbals is physically not impossible, but it will not result in *crashy* sounds.

Looking at crash and ride cymbals, it is notable that not all crashes have larger cups. In low- and medium-budget series there is often just one size of cup for all cymbals in a certain size-range. In the more expensive series, in most cases only the crashes in the larger sizes (18" and onwards) feature larger cups than the rides of the same size.

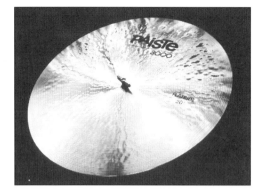

Paiste Flat Ride
Courtesy of Paiste

Flat or Heavy

Generally, the cup of power and rock crashes is one size larger than the cups on regular crash cymbals. You can find these large cups also on ride cymbals that are meant to supply a huge amount of volume. The surplus of overtones caused by the size of this cup is compensated for by the thickness of such cymbals.

It is interesting to note that a flat ride and a heavy or ping ride, having completely different dimensions as far as the cup is concerned, share a number of similarities in sound. Both hardly build up overtones and both have a positive stick definition. The difference, soundwise, is mainly the volume they produce.

Sabian HH Power Bell Ride
Courtesy of Sabian

Shape

When talking about cups, the term "size" actually is too limited. Cups also differ in shape. There are wide and flat cups, and smaller and high cups. Such different cups may have the same total surface, yet will produce a completely different effect on the sound of the instrument.

Traditional Chinese cymbals have a tapered cup, which enhances the fast decay and the raw sound. These sound characteristics were no point of consideration when the Chinese developed this type of cymbal. The cups acted as handles, the cymbals being played in pairs.

CHART 2: INFLUENCE OF DIMENSIONS ON THE SOUND OF CYMBALS									
dimension	SIZE		WEIGHT		PROFILE		CUP		TAPER	
infl. on	small	large	thin	heavy	low	high	small	large	even	gradual
pitch	high	low	low	high	low	high	—	—	high	low
volume	soft	loud	soft	loud	—	—	soft	loud	—	—
response	fast	slow	fast	slow	fast	slow	slow	fast	slow	fast
decay	short	long	short	long	—	—	short	long	long	short
overtones	—	—	more	less	more	less	less	more	less	more
ring	—	—	—	—	ringy	dry	—	—	tight clean	full explosive

Chart 2. Influence of dimensions on the sound of a cymbal
Note: It is assumed that one parameter at a time is changed, all others staying equal. Based on a Zildjian chart

5.3. ORGANIZING THE VIBRATIONS

Not only the dimensions and the weight of a cymbal influence the sound it will produce. Other factors are the material of which the cymbal is made, and how it is made and finished. Each step in the manufacturing process means an ongoing organization of the vibrations of the cymbal.

This section deals with the effects of those steps on the sound. Also the phenomenon of aging is dealt with. Not each step of every process will be described and explained in terms of sound. Yield and tensile strengths, temperatures, mixing procedures, and some other intimate factors are being skipped, regardless of how influential they may be to the final sound.

The limits of what is being discussed are given by the parameters that can be perceived when taking a close look at the instrument. These variables are also more obvious as far as their effect on the sound is concerned. Chapter 8 contains the technical details of the making of cymbals.

5.3.1. ALLOY

Up to the late eighties manufacturers mainly used two different bronze alloys for medium- and high-priced cymbals: B20, containing 80% copper and 20% tin, and B8, containing 92% copper and 8% tin. Small quantities of other metals may be added in both alloys.

A third bronze alloy, the Paiste Sound Alloy, was introduced by Paiste in 1988. This was first used for their Paiste Line series,[3] and later for their Sound Formula series. The exact ingredients of this alloy have not been revealed.

The B20 alloy is used for all professional Zildjian, Sabian and Istanbul series, for the Paiste Formula 602 and Sound Creation series and for most professional Italian cymbals.

B8 is being used for Paiste's professional 2002 and 3000 series, for their 2000 and Alpha series, for most of Meinl's cymbals and most of the other (medium- to low-priced) series.

The Cook

Every alloy can be prepared in many different ways. One cook will—with the same ingredients and recipe—make a different and maybe even tastier meal than his colleague.

Combined with the enormous amount of other parameters and the variety of cymbals available, this leads to one conclusion: it is a precarious enterprise to distill differences in sound just based on differences in alloys. The answers that the various manufacturers give on questions regarding this subject, therefore, have more to do with the characteristics of the cymbals they make than with the actual characteristics of the alloy itself.

Focus

The most objective description is that B8 has a more focussed blend of frequencies and accompanying overtones than B20 and the Paiste Sound Alloy. To put it simply, B8 cymbals sound more compact than cymbals made of one of the other two alloys. Sometimes this characteristic tends to suggest that B8 cymbals sound harder, or that they respond faster. Both these perceptions are caused by the narrower frequency-specter of the sound of B8.

This difference in character might have something to do with the different structures of the various alloys. In B8 metal, the grains run in a single direction. The B20 material is rolled in different directions, or cast in rotating molds (Italy), creating an interwoven

The difference in sound between B8 and B20? That's an easy question. I wish it was easy to answer.
—Robert Paiste

Future bronze: copper and tin at UFIP
Photo by the author

structure of the molecules. The resulting structures differ from each other.

About the Paiste Sound Alloy all that can be said is that it is cross rolled, more or less in the same way as B20. Also based on the sound and feel of these cymbals, this alloy is probably closer to (but still different from) B20 than B8.

"Identical" Cymbals

Another important difference between B20 and B8 cymbals is that the latter often are more consistent in sound than the former. The difference in sound between two "identical" B8 cymbals is, in most cases, smaller than it would be with two B20 cymbals of the same size, type and series.

This is not so much due to some basic difference in (sound) consistency between these alloys, but mainly to differences in the processes these alloys require. You can't do everything with B8 that you can with B20, while in other cases B8 will allow certain applications that are impossible with B20. The traditions of processing the alloys of some manufacturers have their consequences in this field as well (see Chapter 8).

Furthermore, the fact that B20 has a wider sound potential and frequency range than B8 indicates that even the smallest difference in the dimensions or the processing of a B20 cymbal will have larger influences than would be the case with a B8. In these matters the Paiste Sound Alloy is also more similar to B20.

Brass

Apart from the three aforementioned alloys, manufacturers use brass and nickel-silver. These alloys are mainly used for low-budget series. Their sound potential is smaller than that of bronze, giving them a more compact sound with shorter sustain and less brightness. Since the industrial applications of nickel-silver are decreasing—and its price is increasing—this material will be used less for the production of cymbals.

5.3.2. HAMMERING

The most important step in manufacturing cymbals is the shaping. For that purpose a multitude of different hammering techniques, presses, spinforming machines, rotating molds and combinations of these techniques are being applied. The more automatic machines and computers are part of the production process, the smaller the mutual differences between "identical" cymbals generally will be.

If the first of two identical flat discs is pressed into shape and the second one is hammered into that same shape, it is a logical assumption that each disc will sound different. They will, indeed. Hammering gives an additional tension to the metal. Pressing basically does not differ from bending the metal into the desired shape

When hammering a cymbal, the shape grows with every stroke and the metal is being compressed on certain spots only. Therefore the sound does not depend solely on the shape, but also on the way this shape has been obtained. Spinforming, a method to spin cymbals into shape, is applied for the manufacturing of low- and some medium-budget series. This method will not be discussed in this chapter.

Bonk or Wobble

A few very-low-budget series left aside, every cymbal is hammered one way or another. With some of the least expensive cymbals this happens mainly for cosmetic reasons. With all other cymbals the hammering is an essential part of giving the cymbal its sound. Hammering gives the cymbal its shape, and the sound is largely made by that shape. The application of hammers also compresses the metal. It becomes more dense at the points

...irregular patterns...
Hammering at Istanbul
Photo by the author

...regular patterns...
Hammering at Paiste
Courtesy of Paiste

of impact and the cymbal becomes stiffer and more resilient. The tension on the metal increases, the pitch gets higher, the frequency range is enhanced, the playback gets better, the sustain increases and the sound starts to open up.

A cymbal that has been hammered too little or too weakly will wobble; a cymbal that has been hammered too heavily will be too stiff. The latter will "bonk," as someone once expressed this sound.

Only a few professional cymbals are not hammered at all. Examples are the Zildjian Earth Ride and Sabian's Jack DeJohnette Signature series.

Hammering Methods

There are basically three different hammering methods. Hammering can be computer-controlled or automatic, mechanical, and by hand. Each method has its own characteristics that, on a number of other points in the process, may be enhanced, partially compensated for, or eliminated. The most important thing is not so much the method in itself, but the way the method is being applied. In Chapter 8 these differences are dealt with extensively.

Sound differences may originate from variations in the shape of the hammer(s), the distribution of the strokes, the number and the power of the strokes and other variables. Cymbals can be hammered on one or both sides, which also will affect the sound.

In the context of this chapter the major distinction is the difference between cymbals that have a regular hammering pattern, versus cymbals with an irregular pattern. The Istanbul, Sabian HH, and K Zildjian cymbals are the most well-known representatives of the latter kind. Paiste (Paiste Line and others), UFIP, Spizz and the Chinese companies also make cymbals in this fashion. In daily life these cymbals are referred to as "hand-hammered." It should be noted that mechanical hammers are being used for this type of cymbals also, instead of or in addition to a hand-held one (see Chapter 8).

"Irregular" Sound

The irregularity of the hammering pattern of this type of cymbals results—how obvious—in irregular vibrational patterns, and therefore in an "irregular" sound. On their journey through the body of the cymbal, the vibrations will be hindered by these irregularities and erratic alternations of hard and soft spots. The sound of a hand-hammered cymbal, therefore, is more complex, darker, drier and less smooth than the sound of a cymbal with a regular hammering pattern.

Of course, not every hand-hammered cymbal has these specific sound qualities. The Sabian HH Power Bell Ride, because of its respectable weight and its huge bell, can hardly be expected to sound similar to a "traditional" hand-hammered cymbal. Another exception are Zildjian's K Custom cymbals, which are treated both by an automatic hammer and a hand-hammering process, giving it both regular and irregular patterns.

Cymbals with a regular hammering pattern can generally be described as having a more even and brighter character of sound. They sustain longer and have a faster attack in comparison to cymbals with an irregular pattern.

Different Hammers

The differences in sound caused by hammering a cymbal with more or less power, more or less frequently, or with or without the additional help of a (pressing) machine, are very complex. The amount of variations and implications are numerous, and every factor is always interrelated with all other factors. No wonder that there is hardly any uniformity regarding to this subject.

Robert Paiste says that two cymbals with the exact same shape, modelled with differently shaped hammers, will not sound identical. This difference in sound would be caused by the dissimilar hammers.

Sabian, more or less on the contrary, claims that the fact that their hammerers all use differently shaped hammers, and that they all have their own style of hammering, does not influence the final result. It is, within the context of their type of manufacturing, just the profile that counts. Even if there would be a difference, they say, then it would be of minor importance when compared to the variations that originate in the rest of the manufacturing process.

This side of the story is again contradicted by the concept of the Zildjian Z series. The different shapes of the hammers that are used for these cymbals, such as the Five Point Star and the Closed Hex, are said to have a considerable effect on the sound of the cymbal.

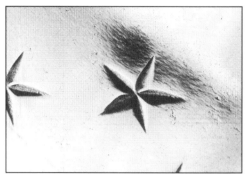

Zildjian Z series: the Five Point Star
Courtesy of Zildjian

Yes, No, Maybe

The statements above cannot lead to well-founded conclusions. They mainly indicate the complexity of this matter. This may be illustrated by the answer of a president of Research & Development, when asked: "If you have two identically shaped cymbals, the only difference being the number of hammer marks on each cymbal, will the one with the highest number of marks have less overtones?" His reply was classic: "Yes, no, or maybe."

Zildjian Z series: the Closed Hex
Courtesy of Zildjian

5.3.3. LATHING

The characteristic tonal grooves on the surface of most cymbals are created by the sharp cutting tools of the lathe operators. The cymbal, which is attached to a rotating lathe and worked with cutting tools, gets thinner and starts shining during this procedure. The sound changes considerably.

In some processes the stiffness of the cymbal—and thus the sound—is also influenced by the lathing procedure. Different results can be obtained by varying the method of lathing, or by using different lathing tools. The depth, the width and the shape of the tonal grooves all have their effect on the final sound. For instance, the lathe bands of the contemporary K Zildjians are much smaller than those of the old Istanbul K's, resulting in a more open, cleaner, brighter and "up-to-date" character.

Even

The more even the pattern of the grooves, the more even the sound will be. Uneven, meandering tonal grooves will result in a less even character. This phenomenon is partially responsible for the different sounds of the Paiste Formula 602 versus the Paiste 3000 series, having respectively even and uneven tonal grooves. The same differences can be spotted when closely observing the different types of the Paiste Line series, some of them having an even lathing pattern, others a more uneven one.

The specific sound of Paiste's brilliant Sound Reflection and Reflector cymbals, having more highs, is caused by applying special lathing techniques that shape the tonal grooves in a certain manner.

Lathed versus Unlathed

So far, the details that have been discussed may result in sleepless nights for Research & Development employees from time to time. To drummers they are of less importance.

Talking about the influence of lathing on the sound of a cymbal, the main subject for drummers is the difference between lathed and unlathed cymbals. The latter type will, in comparison to lathed specimens, sound more aggressive, more compact, tighter and less bright. The stick definition of unlathed cymbals is very clear. The greater mass gives them higher pitch and more volume potential.

Different lathing tools at UFIP
Photo by the author

Less Metallic

When lathing a cymbal, the outer layers that were hardened by hammering are removed. This makes the cymbal softer, as it were. A less metallic sound is the result. Lathing opens the cymbal up and makes it sound more musical. The grooves that are created by lathing help spread the sound around the body of the cymbal. They enable the sound to dissipate much easier.

Lathing also results in a distinctive irregularity of the surface of the cymbal (picturing the tonal ridges and grooves as peaks and valleys), which will slightly decrease the amount of overtones. This is largely compensated for by the lesser weight of a lathed cymbal. Such a cymbal is richer in harmonics and overtones than it was before this application.

Theoretical

This comparison, it should be added, is rather theoretical. Most unlathed cymbal series are not just cymbals that have not been given the lathing treatment. The 16" Rude version of the former Paiste 1000 series, for instance, weighed 12% less than its lathed brother. This is the opposite of what might be expected.

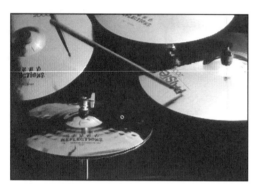

...applying special lathing techniques...
Courtesy of Paiste

Again, varying any of the other parameters in cymbal making can compensate, more or less, for the characteristic sound of unlathed cymbals. Shape, thickness and other factors play an important role here.

In 1992 Istanbul added some variations to the theme of lathing with their Ottoman, Vezir and Sultan cymbals, being lathed on one side, in circles, or in combinations of these options. UFIP's Natural Sound cymbals are lathed on the bottom only.

5.3.4. BUFFING

Buffing, or polishing the cymbals with high-speed cotton discs became popular around 1985. Before that time these shiny "Brilliant" cymbals mainly caused frowning eyebrows.[4] This was not only because of the specific visual appearance of the Brilliant cymbal. Buffing was thought of as a process that mainly took the tone out. To a certain extent that is correct, yet at the same time buffing adds a certain character that appeals to a lot of drummers.

Buffing a cymbal causes the sound to change in three ways:
–The friction-induced heat tempers the cymbal a little and makes it a bit harder;
–The ridges of the tonal grooves are somewhat flattened;
–A small amount of bronze is removed from the cymbal.

In terms of sound, buffing takes the edges off of the sound. It smooths and cleans the sound, it reduces the spread and makes the sound a little warmer and more mellow. The same terms are often being used to describe the characteristics of aged cymbals (see 5.3.6.).

Disagreement

There are, on the other hand, people who claim that a brilliant cymbal sounds brighter, having more high-end than a regular one. This disagreement may be partially caused by the specific cymbals that people have been listening to. Buffing had a different sound effect on UFIP's Solid Rides than it has on K's or HH's. Different results can also be spotted when comparing the various series and types of one brand. Additionally, such disagreements may be caused by plain subjectivity of the ears—and of the eyes.

As a side effect of buffing, brilliant cymbals sound different because the surface is evened out a little. Therefore more of the tip of the stick is hitting the cymbal, instead of being broken up on the ridges.

Compensate

When polishing, a number of parameters will compensate for each other. The increased hardness theoretically makes the pitch a little higher, while the decreased weight lowers the pitch again. Because of such factors, it is very possible to find a buffed and a regular cymbal of the same type and size that sound very much alike.

Something similar may happen with Zildjian's Platinum series, versus the regular A's. The Platinums are first polished, after which a microscopically thin layer of metal is added, giving the cymbal a silverish shine. This application also has its effect on the sound, yet there are regular and Platinum cymbals that have an identical sound. The exact effect is hard to describe.

The indication Brilliant, by the way, is only used for the polished B20 cymbals of Sabian and Zildjian. Some B8 series of cymbals are also polished, but they are not indicated as Brilliants. Such cymbals generally sound brighter than similar non-polished cymbals.

5.3.5. THE FINISH

A number of series of cymbals are finished with an extremely thin layer of transparent lacquer or wax, aiming to preserve the brightness and shine for some time. The influence on the sound of such a finish is said to be close to non-existent. As there have been some "anti-lacquer" drummers playing finished cymbals—without knowing or noticing it—this subject will not be discussed here.

Black and Red

Colored cymbals, having largely vanished some years after their introduction in 1984, definitely were influenced by the lacquer that was used. It was mainly the weight of the pigment in those lacquers that muffled the sound. These cymbals, when compared to regular ones, sounded much more compact, having a strong definition because of the absence of harmonics. They also had a very short sustain and a limited projection. Some drummers state that they have clearly perceived differences between otherwise identical black and red cymbals. Were they right? Yes, no, or maybe. The difference between various pigments may have contributed to this, but it could also be claimed that minor differences in the cymbals themselves will have been of more importance. Besides the fact that different dyes may have different weight, a black cymbal is almost bound to sound darker than a bright red one....

5.3.6. AGING

Within the general lack of uniformity, there is one subject that ranks highest: the

...buffing adds a certain character...
Courtesy of Sabian

The Platinum crashes are a little more contained because there's something on the cymbal that constricts them a bit; it makes them *mellower.*
—Simon Phillips

A number of drummers claim that the (Platinum) electro-plating results in cymbals with a noticeably more *piercing* sound.
—Kenny Aronoff

...differences between black and red cymbals...
Courtesy of Paiste

influence of age on the sound of a cymbal. In the case of aging it is not the manufacturer, but time and wear that organize the vibrations.[5] This process starts at a very early stage.

The sound of a cymbal changes from the moment that the ink of the logo is still wet up till a few days or weeks afterwards. Because of the intensive processing of the metal, the molecules are stirred considerably and it takes them some time to get in position again.

Some experts say that the molecules expand in that period, others say that the structure is getting closer. One thing is certain, however: in that period—its length depending on the alloy and other parameters—the sound of any cymbal improves audibly. "The internal molecular structure has the tendency to float within the metal of the cymbal. After some time the molecules actually begin to bind together as the metal settles," according to Billy Zildjian.[6] Because of this, manufacturers always try to keep a certain stock, giving the bronze a chance to come to rest before it is shipped. But what happens afterwards?

...exposed to dust, dirt, sweat, drinks, food, cleaners, heat, rain...
Leidseplein, Amsterdam
Photo by Tineke van Brederode

Closet

If a cymbal is left in its bag and put in a closet, it is very unlikely to change at all. At a certain moment, at the most after half a year, the metal has reached a final structure. After that it will stay the same. "Cymbals are made from bronze, not cheese," Roy Burns once graphically remarked.[7]

Most cymbals will not spend their lives in such circumstances. They are being played, so they will be exposed to dust, dirt, sweat, drinks, food, cleaners, heat, rain and, ultimately, to a constant stream of strokes. The fact that cymbals tend to "mellow down" after a couple of years is not so much due to structural changes in the metal caused by the vibrations. Everything that falls on it and sticks to it is of much more importance. Dust is an excellent muffler of vibrations. As such it will unquestionably reduce some of the higher overtones. Coca-Cola, beer and fast-food work even better. This muffling results in what many people refer to as "the disappearance of the harsh edges."

Coarse types of cymbal cleaners may have a similar effect. By smoothing down the ridges the sound will be "sweetened," similar to the buffing process. On top of that, certain cleaners will leave residues on the surface of the cymbal when they are not rinsed carefully after the cleaning. These residues have the same effect as dust, soundwise.

Eventually you can wear a cymbal down, sure. So yes, you can have changes soundwise. But you'd better have some audiometric testing from twenty years ago up to now, because I think your ears will change quite a bit in that period of time.
—Dan Barker

Something Has to Give

Many drummers have observed that their favorite cymbal has become better and better sounding in the course of the years. That might be explained by the above-mentioned factors. On the other hand, it might also be their ears, which have grown accustomed to the sound of that specific cymbal. It is a plain fact that this sensitive part of the anatomy is more likely to change than a piece of metal ever will.

On the other hand, it is hardly conceivable that twenty years of intensive use will leave a cymbal unaffected. Whether an instrument is being played on extremely hard for a short while, or somewhat easier for a decade or two, something always has to give. That is pure physics. Of course, the sticks are always the first victims. The bronze, however, will structurally respond in one way or another also. What might happen?

First, there should be a minimal wearing down process of the metal because of the repeating stick contact. This is of negligible importance. Second, and more crucial, there might be changes going on in the molecular structure of the metal. On this point experts disagree.

Harder

Billy Zildjian, who at times used to arm himself with all kinds of advanced electronic equipment on his journeys into the depths of cymbal-making, claimed: "...there are two kinds of crystals in the metal: hard crystals and soft crystals. The hard crystals are relatively unstable, and over the years they will gradually break down and form medium-hard crystals, medium crystals and medium-soft crystals, so as the cymbal gets older it actually becomes softer, though it sounds harder and more brittle."[6]

This statement might contradict the general perception of the mellowed-down sound of aged cymbals. An R&D employee of one of the major companies distinguishes two different phenomenons in this context: aging-in and aging-out. "The pitch of a good cymbal will, after some time, raise just a little because of the fact that the metal gets a little harder; the cymbal is aging-in. If the pitch drops slightly, I'd call that aging-out. Aging-in can be compared with what happens when you buff a cymbal. In that process the metal is hardened just a little, making it a little better."

Softer

The process of the metal getting harder is contradicted by other experts, who are convinced that older cymbals get softer: "If you give a cymbal to a heavy metal drummer, you will see a wearing down process in most alloys. The grains are beaten all the time, so it will loosen up. At least, it feels like it is loosened up, in terms of playing." Whether the same would happen if a cymbal were played by a more relaxed type of drummer for years cannot be proved, but it is assumable to say the least.

According to metallurgists, metal that is repeatedly being exposed to intense vibrations gets harder, and thus more susceptible to breakage (metal fatigue). "The harder a cymbal is, the better it sounds," claims a cymbal making expert. "I have a theory of my own that some of the best sounding cymbals that are made are the ones that are just a little harder. Sad to say, they are therefore more susceptible to breakage as well."

There are also authorities who emphasize the loss of tension in a cymbal as a second factor, next to possible changes in the molecular structure. "The tension that is hammered into the cymbal decreases gradually over the years. The cymbal gets a little softer, so to speak."

Ears

The result of a test, initiated by the Zildjian R&D team, probably says more than all theories combined. A number of professional drummers and testers were invited to listen—blindfolded—to a mix of old and new cymbals, in series of ten cymbals each time. In one series, an old cymbal came out first. In another series, a brand-new one. Their conclusion? "Yes, something definitely changes, but we haven't yet been able to find what it is exactly."

The most important factors in the changing of the sound of a cymbal, again, are dust and dirt. The fact that our ears are not consistent in what they hear over the years, as well as the subjectivity of human perception, should be seen as major second on the list. Changes in the cymbal itself are hardly perceivable by the human ear. The ultimate test? Have a drummer in a dust-proof area play a set of cymbals for five years daily. Record him digitally in the beginning and in the end. Then listen to the results. Any volunteers?

Non-professional Cymbals

The above goes especially for professional series. Some low-budget series will clearly show a decreasing sound quality in a couple of years. Spinformed cymbals that have been hammered little or not at all are claimed to be most susceptible to this phenomenon. The metal is worked less intensely. The process of making the cymbal is aimed more towards the shape of the cymbal and less at the tension in the metal. If, just by playing it a lot, the tension decreases, the sound will become dull.

5.4. AND FINALLY

No matter how extensive this subject is dealt with, the story will never be complete. Just take the people who still always torture themselves wondering about "the" secret of the old K Zildjians. Could it have been the inconsistency and impure mixture of the alloy? Could it have been the charcoal that was used to heat the ovens? What role may have been played by the smaller diameter of the hole? Could it have been the crooked cups on some of these cymbals?

In most contemporary factories much less is left to coincidence. Alloys are being calculated exactly, thermostats regulate the temperatures of the ovens and computers have made their entrance. Yet the R&D employees continue their experiments.

What will be the result if you temper a cymbal in oil or in sand, instead of using water? What happens to the sound of a cymbal if you freeze it for a couple of days? What about cymbals with the cup purposely located off center, or cymbals of which the thickness changes in steps, instead of the common even taper? These and many more questions have been the subjects of real experiments.

Some of the things that I was told during my visits to the major Western factories were quite amazing—and off the record. Nobody can tell whether these or any other experiments will ever launch a revolution in the world of cymbals. The sheer fact that even the experts do not know it all is, to say the least, a cheering and stimulating thought.

Notes:
1 "Vibrations of Plates, Gongs and Cymbals," by Thomas Rossing and Richard Peterson, *Percussive Notes*, vol. 19, no. 3, PAS, Urbana, Illinois, USA, 1982, pp. 31-41. For more information on this subject, please refer to the appendix Source Material, Physical Studies of Cymbals.
2 Idiophones: Rigid instruments struck, plucked, blown, or shaken to produce musical effects caused by the vibration of their primary elements. Definition according to the *New Grove Dictionary of Musical Instruments*, vol. 1, s.v. cymbals, drum set; vol. 2, s.v. idiophone, as referred to in the article "Manufacturing Secrecy: The Dueling Cymbal makers of North America," by David H. Shayt, IA, *Journal of the Society for Industrial Archeology,* Volume 15, Number 1, Washington D.C., 1989.
3 Also refered to as Paiste Signature or Paiste *Paiste* series.
4 Zildjian applied buffing before World War II. The old Chinese cymbals (Bo), pictured in Chapter 1, were also buffed.
5 Exceptions to this statement may be Zildjian's Pre-Aged cymbals and UFIP's Natural Sound series. The latter, according to the company, have been subjected to a special tempering process that pre-ages the cymbals.
  Metal bars of mallet instruments are, in some cases, also pre-aged, preserving them from going out of tune over the years.
6 "Inside Sabian," by Chip Stern, *Modern Drummer*, vol. 7, no.11, Modern Drummer Publications, Inc., New Jersey, USA, 1983. Billy Zildjian is a former Vice-President of Sabian.
7 "Cymbals; Tips and Myths," by Roy Burns, *Modern Drummer*, vol. 5, no. 11, Modern Drummer Publications, Inc., New Jersey, USA, 1981.

There was a drummer who opened a drumshop years ago. He used to take all his deliveries and bury them in the back yard for two weeks. He felt this really aged in his cymbals.
—Dan Barker

K Zildjian Pre-Aged Dry Light Ride.
Courtesy of Zildjian

6. INFLUENCING THE SOUND

Contrary to common belief, the sound of a cymbal can be influenced in many ways. The possibilities are somewhat less obvious than would be for drums, but a little experimenting can lead to interesting results. This chapter is deliberately not called "changing" the sound of a cymbal. That would have indicated more than is possible. You simply can't make a brilliant crash out of a badly manufactured heavy ride cymbal, and exchanging cups is, sad to say, also impossible. What you *can* do is bend a cymbal to your will, to a degree. One of the major ways to achieve this is by learning how to play it.

...you can bend it to your will, to a degree...
Les DeMerle
Photo by Tom Copi

6.1. THE ART OF CYMBAL PLAYING

Why are people like Tony Williams, Jack DeJohnette, Mel Lewis, Elvin Jones, Danny Gottlieb and many others so famous for their characteristic cymbal sounds? Surely it is not because they play the finest cymbals ever made. Even on an instrument far below the dignity of many drummers they would still know how to make Music. Charlie Parker once played a plastic saxophone, and nobody could really tell the difference.[1]

The major reason these people sound good is not the instrument they happen to be playing, but the way they are playing it. It is their "touch."

First, of course, there are numerous ways to hold a stick. When holding a stick firmly with the full hand, the cymbal will sound a lot drier than when the stick pivots between the thumb and the index finger. There are a wide variety of subtle differentiations possible between these extremes.

Elvin Jones has the ability to make an 18" machine-hammered ride cymbal sound like a 22" hand-hammered sizzle, just by the way he plays it.
—Terry Clarke

Variables

In this context the three major variables are the exact place were the stick is held, the amount of pressure that is applied, and the amount of meat that is put at the stick. The way you hit the cymbal also influences the final result. A light, smooth action of the wrist produces a different effect than a movement that makes people think you recently broke your arm.

There is no valid reason to try to bash right through a cymbal. Maximum volume can be attained with a relatively modest stroke, and there is no way to get any louder than that. Of course, a certain sound effect can be realized by striking the cymbal with extreme force. It goes without saying that this effect will not enhance the quality of the sound or the life expectancy of the cymbal.

Kenny Clarke had one cymbal; it wasn't very big. We used to call it the magic cymbal because when somebody would sit in on drums and use his set, it would sound like a garbage can, but when he was playing it, it was like fine crystal.
—Dick Katz

Deadsticking and Glancing

If the stick remains on the cymbal for a short time after the stroke, the sound will be slightly muffled. As long as this technique (pushing the stick into the cymbal, or "deadsticking") is used intentionally, it will enhance the number of sound options. Deadsticking can be used with ride cymbals as well as—with a little more practice—crash cymbals.

Crash cymbals sound warmer when they are hit with a sweeping, horizontal movement. This technique, glancing, will make mainly the low frequencies respond. If, at the same time, the stick is being pushed into the cymbal a little, the high frequencies will be somewhat suppressed.

Contrary to this, a short fast stroke, practically at a 90-degree angle with the cymbal, results in a much sharper and more aggressive sound that contains a larger amount of high frequencies. This technique can be dangerous when you don't pull your stick back fast enough, but Billy Cobham, Simon Phillips and many others have sufficiently proven

The interaction between your arm, the stick release and the cymbal is irreplaceable.
—John Robinson

If you really can pull the sound out of a cymbal, you get tone plus sustain. It's like "snapping" it.
—Billy Cobham

that it *is* possible to apply it without breaking three—or less—crashes a night.

Different Places

There are numerous sound variations possible by playing the cymbal in different places. The edge (crash), the bow (ride) and the cup (bell sounds) are the most well-known examples. Here, too, it is the subtle differentiations that make all the difference.

Some drummers characteristically play their ride cymbals quite close to the edge. Others go a bit more towards the bell, making the sound higher and clearer, and adding more definition to it. The search for the "sweet spot," the place where the cymbal's sound is at its optimum, is inextricably bound up with learning to play a newly acquired cymbal. Last but not least, the angle at which the stick hits the ride cymbal also determines the definition and the character of the sound (see 6.4.). To get a tight and even sound it is important to play the cymbal in the same place, time after time. On the other hand, when intentionally varying the spot where the cymbal is hit, an extra dimension will be added to the sound.

Shoulder or Tip

Apart from the place where the cymbal is played, there is another factor that influences the sound: the part of the stick it is played with. A Latin rhythm sounds a lot more powerful when the shoulder of the stick is used to hit the cup, rather than the tip. When hitting a crash cymbal with the butt-end, the sound that will be produced differs significantly from the sound that is generated with the part just behind the tip.

All these variations and ideas seem straightforward enough. Still, these are often the things that separate the pros from the amateurs.

Different Paths

Although "embouchure" is a term reserved for players of wind instruments, this word could be applied to drummers as well. When a hundred drummers play the same cymbal with the same stick, a hundred different sounds will be heard. The possibilities are unlimited. Reading a book, by the way, is not the best way to explore this field. Playing and listening a lot works much better, and so will a good teacher.

A final remark about this subject: having played on quite diverse cymbal series frequently (for review purposes), it has become increasingly clear that not only do drummers influence the sound of a cymbal with their manner of playing. The reverse occurs as well. A set of Paiste 3000 Rude cymbals inspires different ideas than a set of old K Zildjians. Sabian Sound Controls may lead one down different paths than UFIP Rough Sounds.

6.2. ALTERNATIVE PLAYING TECHNIQUES

Apart from hitting them with the all too well-known pair of sticks there are many other, less obvious ways to create cymbal sounds. Pitch-bend effects can be realized by hugging a cymbal in horizontal position to your belly, one hand holding the edge. The other hand holds the sticks. By putting pressure on the cymbal, it can be bent a little, thus varying the tension on the metal and therefore the pitch. This might not be an ideal style of playing to use in an intricate fill, but it works nice for an effect. Les DeMerle is known for similar pitch-bend techniques.

Cymbals can be scraped with coins or with the butt-end of a stick. The stick must be at right angles with the cymbal, being moved near the cup. Quite some pressure should

...without breaking three—or less—crashes a night...
Billy Cobham
Photo by the author

be applied. When performing the latter in the right way, weird, howling overtones are generated, the existence of which may be pleasantly surprising.

Similar effects can also be produced by using a double-bass, cello or violin bow on the edge of the cymbal.

A very soft and subtle tremolo effect can be realized by moving your hand, with fully extended fingers, up and down rapidly just above the cup, right after a stroke. Cymbals that produce relatively high frequencies are best suited for this technique, which can be combined nicely with the scrape and bow techniques mentioned above.

6.3. DIFFERENT STICKS FOR DIFFERENT TRICKS

Not everybody subscribes to the viewpoint that "a drumstick is as critical to a drummer as a violin bow is to a concert master."[2] On the other hand, no one can deny the striking difference in sound between a 2B, a pencil-thin model and a 7A on the same cymbal.

A wide variety of sticks enhances one's creative possibilities and available sound options to a great extent. Sections 6.3.1. to 6.3.5. apply to ride cymbals in particular. The sound of crashes and (pseudo-) chinas are not so much influenced by the choice of sticks, mainly because this kind of cymbal is usually not played with the tip of the stick.

Different sticks for different tricks
Photo by Bas Westerweel

6.3.1. CONSISTENCY

When talking about sticks, the sound of a cymbal is determined by various aspects. The material, the weight and the model of the entire stick and the bead are the most important parameters. Because wood is a natural material, differences in sound among sticks of the same brand and type are common.

Using sticks with nylon tips, the differences between "identical" sticks are considerably smaller. Variations in the stick itself may be partially disguised by the inherent consistency of the tips. Synthetic sticks and other non-wood sticks are the most consistent as far as sound is concerned. Not only the tip, but the entire stick always has the same density and weight. The fact that such sticks never gained vast popularity shows that consistency and solidity are not the major considerations. The sound and the feeling of wood are apparently more valuable.

6.3.2. THE MATERIAL OF THE STICK

The hardness and density of the stick primarily influence the clearness of the sound. Some types of (rarely used) wood seem to filter out all the high frequencies. Other types can be used to achieve a reverse effect. Because of their smaller mass, lighter and less dense types of wood will generate less harmonics than heavier species.

Asian oak, American hickory and maple are, in order of hardness, the three types of wood that are most widely used. The harder the wood, the clearer the ping and the broader the sound spectrum that is being triggered; this seems to be a logical assumption. Nonetheless, there is the usual amount of differences of opinion over this point. The most widely accepted explanation is simply that each type of wood produces its own sound. For that matter, in most cases the model of the stick determines the sound to at least the same degree as the material.

6.3.3. THE MATERIAL OF THE BEAD

Compared to wooden-tipped specimen, sticks using nylon beads or tips of other

Back during the war you just couldn't get no sticks. We played with chair-arms, and it sure did swing, man.
—Art Blakey

I don't think you should dig such a hole for yourself that you say, "I use 5A sticks and nothing but 5A," because obviously, you're going to use different sizes for different types of things.
—Alan Dawson

Of course wooden sticks never sound the same. That's because Mother Nature has the final say, and there's nothing you can do about it.
—Herb Brochstein

synthetic fiber produce a more transparent and clear high-pitched sound. The "ping" is more evident and so the projection is better. The harder the tip, the better certain partials and overtones will become audible. The fact that there may be less agreeable overtones in this spectrum suggests that nylon tips are a little more critical when it comes to the quality of the cymbal.

Wooden tips are always softer than nylon ones and produce relatively less high frequencies. They make cymbals sound warmer, fuller and lower. The softer the type of wood, the more audible this effect is. Splintered wooden tips do not sound like much at all.

Although wooden tips are commonly believed to produce the most "natural" sound, nylon tips have many loyal supporters. The greater durability and clarity of the definition play a decisive role in this matter. In a Dutch survey over 60% of the respondents said they mainly use wooden tips.[3] Less than 10% used both types, depending on where and what they play.

Nail Polish

Not only manufacturers, but musicians as well have always been on the lookout for new developments. Legend has it that Harvey Mason used to break off the beads of his sticks. He then sanded the ends lightly. This gave him a cymbal sound containing relatively many overtones that blended extremely well with the rest of the music.

Nylon tips produce a slightly softer sound when you treat them with crude sandpaper, producing numerous small, "muffling" irregularities in the surface. The same effect can inadvertently be produced by a burr on the tip, caused by bad workmanship.

The clarity and durability of wooden tips can be enhanced by treating them with a hard impregnating type of resin. Nail polish has been used here, though this doesn't last too long.

6.3.4. THE SHAPE AND SIZE OF THE STICK

The larger the mass of the stick, the more audible the lower frequencies become. The volume increases and the sound loses definition while becoming more powerful. A thinner stick makes a cymbal sound higher and "thinner."

Because there are less audible harmonics, the chances of producing unwanted frequencies are also lessened. This means that lighter sticks are less critical than heavier ones. They tend to accentuate the more pleasant overtones of the cymbal. The model of the stick itself, the main factor being the tapering, is of less influence.

However it can be safely said that a relatively thick throat will produce more overtones than an equally heavy stick with a thin throat, having the weight more towards the back. The first stick will trigger more frequencies of the cymbal's spectrum, the second one will make for a more delicate sound.

A stick with a longer taper and a thin throat tends to rebound from the cymbal faster, allowing every bit of impact to spread around the material and to vibrate. With sufficient technique this can also be achieved with heavier sticks.

Heavy Sticks

In principle, heavier sticks are used for larger, thicker cymbals—by heavier drummers. The loss of definition, caused by the mass of the stick and the size of the tip, is compensated for by the relatively limited amount of harmonics of a heavy cymbal. A light stick basically does not have enough mass to move a relatively great amount of metal.

A thinner cymbal is usually done better justice by using lighter sticks. A relatively

I used to use two different sticks. My thought behind it was that I like a real heavy snare, so I had a 2B for a snare stick, and I would shift between a 5B or a Rock stick for the ride because some of the songs are so fast.
—Lars Ulrich

I use certain sticks with certain weights to really get the best sound. If you use a smaller stick you get the higher frequencies. If you want a full-bodied sound, then use a big bead; that gives it a real punch.
—Paul Wertico

heavy stick like a 2B will produce many overtones—and thus a more washy sound—on a medium ride cymbal. Such cymbals will produce better definition with lighter sticks. Thin cymbals, especially crashes and splashes, are easily damaged by heavy sticks, and they can be easily overplayed. The same goes for butt-end playing.

6.3.5. SHAPE AND SIZE OF THE BEAD

The influence of the shape of the bead on the sound is mainly related to the amount of wood touching the cymbal. A smaller tangent plane will produce a better defined sound, because certain overtones will not be activated. A larger tangent plane will trigger more frequencies of the cymbal and thus create a fuller sound. This can be heard clearly when an acorn-shaped tip is used.

Varying the angle at which the cymbal is played will have a direct influence—because of the shape of the tip—on the size of the tangent plane, and therefore on the sound. In the case of a round tip such a difference is virtually non-existent.

Round tips result in a better definition of the sound. Elongated acorn tips usually have the opposite effect: more overtones, less ping and a better blend.

Heavy and large tips produce a full-bodied sound. The volume increases, the cymbal builds up more rapidly and the entire frequency spectrum of the cymbal will be triggered.

The higher frequencies will be clearer when using a stick with a small tip, while the lower frequencies will have less volume. A relatively large stick with a small bead will, on the contrary, cause a considerable amount of lows due to the mass of the wood.

For butt-end players it might pay to have a look at the way this part of the stick is formed. Some are close to spherical, others are cut off almost straight.

As with cymbals, the parameters of sticks are all interrelated. A rather thin oak stick with an acorn-shaped bead will have a somewhat nylonish sound, while a very small round nylon tip on a stick with a short taper will produce a sound with a relative woodish character. Joe Calato is said to be able to make any nylon-tip stick sound as a wooden one, and vice-versa, just by changing the angle between stick and cymbal and by using certain playing techniques.[4]

6.3.6. KNITTING NEEDLES AND SAWS

Apart from using sticks, cymbals can be played by hands, timpani sticks, mallets, knitting needles (beautiful), brushes, Blasticks, Splitstix, Hot Rods, Rutes, Rakes and other items. Twentieth-century composers make percussionists use coins, triangle beaters, triangles, combs, bows, and even files, rasps and saws.

The observations of Gardner Read in his book *Thesaurus of Orchestral Devices* are most notable: "For cymbals, more often than for any other percussion instrument, composers explicitly indicate which model and type of stick should be used."[5]

6.4. CYMBAL MOUNTING

Many drummers know the problem of a ride cymbal that builds up too much, losing its definition in an abundance of overtones. This problem can be suppressed in different ways.

First, the cymbal can be mounted at a very steep angle. The angle at which the stick hits the cymbal will then get bigger, resulting in a lighter and better defined ping with less overtones. The sound becomes a little drier. A horizontally mounted cymbal will

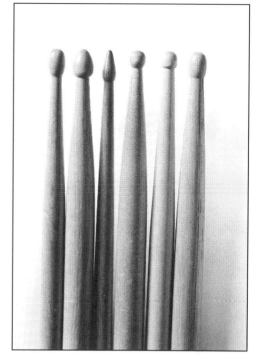

...the amount of wood touching the cymbal...
Photo by Bas Westerweel

I also hit the cymbals with the side of my hand, which is tightly closed into a fist. By the way, if your cymbals aren't real heavy, this can bend or warp them, so be careful about that.
—Tommy Aldridge

"If you want a cymbal to sound the way that it really sounds, it should be horizontal and not clamped down. At one time, I thought that having the cymbals at an angle gave me a certain stick-to-cymbal attitude. I thought it was a good setup for me. It wasn't. It gave me some real problems with my playing. I just wasn't making good contact with the instrument."
—Peter Erskine
Photo by the author

produce more volume, a broader sound and more spread.

A cymbal that is mounted at a very steep angle also will be a little muffled, because the power of gravity will do its utmost to get it back into a horizontal position, applying extra pressure to the cup. To keep the cymbal at such an angle, the wingnut needs to be tightened, enhancing the muffling effect even more.

The audience will hear the sound of a vertically mounted cymbal differently, because the underside—instead of the edge—of the cymbal points in their direction. In short, an obliquely mounted cymbal, firmly tightened, will have a drier, darker, more "bare" and more defined sound than a loosely mounted one.

A cymbal will sound most natural when mounted parallel to the floor, not being hindered by felts or tight wingnuts. The optimal way of freely mounting a cymbal appears to be suspending it. When experimenting, be careful not to interfere with your playing comfort.

Wingnuts and Washers
Tightening the wingnut exerts extra pressure on the cymbal. This has a dampening effect on the building up of harmonics. It also enhances the chance of breaking cymbals, especially thinner ones. The use of more and bigger felt washers will result in a less lively sound. This technique may be applied to rides and crashes, but also to Chinese cymbals. Stuffing the entire cup of such a cymbal results in a less "trashy" sound.

Stronger muffling effects can be achieved by mounting the cymbal on an extremely large felt washer (2"-5"). Such a washer should then be supported, for example by a small thick cymbal. Regular metal washers would be too small to keep the felt in touch with the cymbal. A very simple way to try out this effect soundwise is to slide a sponge over the tilter and then place the cymbal on top of it.

Hi-hats
The sound of the hi-hat is partly determined by the type of felt washers under the bottom cymbal and on both sides of the top cymbal. Large, soft washers have a muffling effect, diminishing the harshness of the chick as well as the overall volume somewhat. Small hard washers on each side of the top cymbal result in a more open sound and more volume. Replacing felt washers with rubber or fiber ones will result in a chick with more definition.

If the clutch is not tightened sufficiently, the chick sound will get sloppy. A very tight clutch will deaden the sound of the hi-hat. The volume will be limited and crashes on the hi-hat cymbal will sound thin. When playing in low-volume situations, you may of course purposely go for that effect. The amount of volume can be influenced by setting the gap between the cymbals. Hi-hats can also be made to sound different by simply reversing top and bottom.

Chinas and related types will sound different when you mount them upside down, simply because the cymbal will be hit in other places and at a different angle. More details on mounting cymbals can be found in Chapter 7.

6.5. THE CYMBAL STAND
Even a cymbal stand influences the sound that is being produced, to some extent. Especially when playing on a hollow wooden stage, the difference between a light stand and a heavy boom stand can be easily detected.

If you mount a ride cymbal on a fully extended boom-arm and give it a good blow, you will be able to feel the vibrations in the stand. This will, in some cases, be audible as "rumble." On a straight stand, in contrast to a boom-model, most cymbals will sound slightly more tight.

There are drummers who, for no other reason than the sound produced, swear by stands with a massive upper part. Others tend to stick by heavy stands or, conversely, extremely light ones. Listen for the differences and decide for yourself. It goes without saying that there are plenty of other reasons for choosing a certain type of stand.

6.6. TAPE, VARNISH AND DUST

There are many ways of limiting the freedom of a cymbal that is too brilliant. The well-known roll of gaffer's tape is very convenient for this purpose. Don't use masking tape, because after some time the glue will stick on the cymbal when trying to get the tape off. Usually, tape is put on the underside. Putting it on top makes it easier to change its size and position in on-stage situations. It might look better for the audience as well.

A cymbal that produces too many high frequencies can be fixed with one or two pieces of tape on the inside of the cup. An overabundance of low frequencies can be somewhat suppressed by taping the edge in one or more spots. Always listen to the result from a distance.

Due to different modes of vibration within the cymbal you might get different results depending on the exact location of the tape. Varying this location within imaginative lines or circles will produce various effects. Trial and error is a tedious method, but works best here. If you need to use more than a few inches of tape, you'd probably be better off with another cymbal. This advice does not include experiments like Fred Van Vloten's. He completely taped up the bell of an 18" jazz ride. This created an exotic, cowbell-like "wet" cup sound, while the crash sound became dry as dust.

...a "wet" cup sound, and an extremely dry crash...
Fred van Vloten
Photo by the author

Varnish and Dust

A less well-known method of dampening a cymbal is using transparent varnish. Spraying an extremely thin layer on the cymbal may produce satisfying results. Use a type of varnish that can easily be removed. This method is not to be compared with the tarnish retarding and other protective techniques that are applied by a number of companies.

The most effortless way to muffle a cymbal is to refrain from cleaning it. Dust and dirt have, in the long run, exactly the same effect as varnish (see 7.2.).

In the end, purchasing a cymbal with the desired character of sound will always be a more musical solution than applying tape, felt, lacquer or any other muffling devices.

6.7. RIVETS

The first use of rivets dates back to the golden age of Dixieland. They had hardly been used for many years when Art Blakey and other drummers started to work with sizzle cymbals again, around 1950.

Mounting a number of rivets does not so much influence the sound of the cymbal itself. It merely adds another dimension to that sound: the sizzle. The spread increases, especially in the high frequencies, and the resonance is prolonged. The definition of the ping will be lessened as it is blurred by the sound of the rivets. Partly for this reason, sizzle cymbals are used mainly by jazz drummers, particularly when playing brushes.

With brushes, the response of a cymbal is normally quite low. Especially the higher frequencies are hardly heard. When rivets are mounted, a gentle touching of the edge suffices to achieve a bright, sustaining sizzle effect. Rock drummers such as Cozy Powell, who uses riveted 18" and 20" Paiste 3000 crash cymbals, apply rivets to other effects.

As a conventional cymbal maker, I don't like rivets.
—Robert Paiste

Sizzle Cymbals

Not every cymbal will make for a "regular" sizzle cymbal. It has to have at least a moderate sustain, yet it shouldn't be too heavy either. Heavy cymbals have a slower response. This results in the rivets vibrating at higher volumes only, usually not producing the desired result. It may, however, be what you are looking for. The sound-effect will be more separate from the cymbal's sound, leaving more room for the definition to the ping.[6] A minimal "edge" will be added to the sound if two or three rivets are used in such a cymbal.

A prospective sizzle cymbal shouldn't be too thin either. The weight of the rivets would tend to muffle the sound too much. If played harder, the motion and the effect of the rivets would be difficult to control because of the fierce vibrations of the cymbal.

The "standard" sizzle cymbal, as it was sold by Zildjian, used to be a 20" medium-thin ride with six rivets, evenly divided in a circle, about 1" to 1 1/2" (2.5 to 3.8 cm.) from the edge. Sabian recommends their Light Ride as a standard. Except for Istanbul no factory listed riveted ride cymbals in the early 1990s. Some factories offer the possibility of making sizzle cymbals to order. The type and size of cymbal, the location and the number of rivets desired can then be indicated.

...a 14" K with fifty holes and four rivets...
Steve Gadd
Photo by Lissa Wales

Home-riveting

Cymbals may also be home-riveted. There are many different types of rivets on the market for this purpose. The hardness of the material, the size of the head and the length and diameter of the shaft all play a part in determining the effect. For more information on the influence of the number and location of rivets, and how to mount them properly, refer to 7.7.

Rivets have always been very popular to use in Chinas and related cymbals, which sometimes contain up to forty of them. Occasionally rivets are also mounted in hi-hat cymbals, top or bottom. The rivets, enhancing the brightness of the sound, produce their effect especially when the cymbals are played in half open position, or in open/close patterns.

Of course, rivets can be mounted in any other type of cymbal, and any other configuration is possible. Colin Schofield mentions Charlie Drayton's 12" splash with twelve rivets, a 14" K with fifty holes and four rivets as used by Steve Gadd, and riveted flat rides.[6]

I have one Paiste and one Zildjian rivet in my sizzle cymbal, and it really makes a difference. The Paiste one is a little heavier and gives the initial sizzle. The other one is a little lighter, giving extra length and adding just a little bit more high. Two Zildjians would be too light, two Paistes would weigh the cymbal down too much for my taste.
—Paul Wertico

Sizzling without Rivets

To achieve occasional sizzle effects, there are various sizzlers or "rattlers" that can be mounted on a cymbal without any modifications. Usually they consist of one or more pieces of small beaded chain. The chain is attached to a device that is mounted on the tilter. Such sizzlers can be home-made.

Affix a piece of the same sort of chain to a piece of thin nylon thread. The thread is then tied to a rubber ring, which is simply put over the thread of the tilter. The shorter and the lighter the chain, the smaller its dampening effect, and the lighter and higher the sizzle will be. A length of plastic-bead necklaces may also be used, though this will have a less brilliant effect than metal beads. Try out various locations of the chain by varying the length of the thread.

The edge is the part of a cymbal that vibrates the most, so the chain will have to touch the cymbal in or near that area. A disadvantage of working with such sizzlers is that you can easily hit the chain instead of the cymbal itself. Gravity will cause the chain to rest on the lowest section of an angled cymbal, which usually is the part that is being played on.

Coin

Another method is even more simple. Take a piece of adhesive tape and use it to fix a small coin about $1^{1}/2$ inches from the edge of the cymbal. Obviously such a construction will not last long, but it will do for just one song, or even one (quiet) night. A sporadic sizzle effect can be achieved by playing the cymbal while resting a thin stick or knitting needle on it. A bunch of keys, held to the side of the cymbal, will do the trick as well.

6.8. METAL ON METAL

Generally, drummers try to avoid the clatter of metal on metal. There are others who aim for just these effects. Double deckers are combinations of two (or more) cymbals, one of which is mounted inside, or directly on top of the other.

The Zildjian Piggy Back
Courtesy of Zildjian

Some of the setups in Chapter 4 offer examples of this technique. Splash cymbals, mounted in a China-type or on a crash cymbal, are very convenient for this purpose. Such combinations produce very short, almost electronic sounding noises, with a metallic bite. The sustain can be adjusted by the degree with which the cymbals are clamped together.

Zildjian developed the Piggy Back cymbal, a thin 12" China-like cymbal, that is especially intended for mounting in or on other cymbals. Other small Chinas work well, too. There is no need to limit the possibilities to combinations of small and larger cymbals. A 20" China on top of a 20" ride cymbal offers intriguing effects also.

Spoxe

Similar effects can be created by mounting a cymbal in the frame of a Roto-tom. This was originated by Terry Bozzio, in cooperation with Remo Inc. The frames are separately available under the name of Spoxe since the latter part of 1986.

Michael Blair mounted two small Spoxes on his hi-hat pedal, instead of conventional cymbals. Later he started using an 8" bell cymbal combined with a Spoxe on a remote hi-hat, and a 20" Spoxe with a 14" cymbal inserted.

Terry Bozzio, with Spoxes (left) and
double deckers
Photo by Lissa Wales

Chris Parker used to have toy cymbals sitting on top of his regular cymbals. Not in order to obtain an additional rattling effect, but the opposite: "It has a great dampening effect. I get a nice clean ride, and the overtones don't build up as much."[7]

6.9. CHANGING THE CYMBAL ITSELF

This is a sensitive subject. To what degree can you change the sound of a cymbal by re-working it with buffing wheels, lathes, hammers and other tools? Some drummers have home-hammered their cymbals, or have slimmed down a cymbal that was—to them— too thick. Whether they were right doing so is not an issue in this book. As long as the result is satisfying, there should be nothing against such operations. Except for one.

There is a good chance that irreparable harm will be the result when surgery of this kind is performed. On top of that, no warranty will ever cover the remnants of what once used to be a cymbal.

One quite drastic treatment sometimes may be just unavoidable: making a smaller cymbal out of a larger one. This is frequently done when the cymbal in question is cracked at the edge in one or more places. In that case, surgery becomes imperative; the torn cymbal would otherwise be unusable. To do something like this just because you want a smaller cymbal is mainly stupid (see 7.5.).

Polishing

The polishing of cymbals causes changes in the sound, though it is usually performed for the sake of outward appearances. Depending on the intensity of the polishing treatment the sound becomes a little mellower as the sharp ridges of the tonal grooves are flattened down. Buffing the cymbal with an electric device may generate so much heat that the cymbal is actually retempered, resulting in brittle spots. It is safer to go out and buy a Brilliant or any other shining type of cymbal.

Re-hammering a cymbal yourself may very well result in cracks, either in the act of hammering, or later on, as a result of tensions that are caused by working the bronze.

Cracks can also be the consequence of exposing the cymbal to excessively high temperatures in the course of grinding—or lathing—treatments that are performed without due experience.

Second hole

Another, rather exceptional form of influencing the sound is the drilling of a second hole in the cymbal. Armand Zildjian once did this to a flat ride: "I still think that we should carry this idea further, but it appears that I'm the only one who thinks so...."[8] In this cymbal, the extra hole is located about 1" from the original hole. When using the second hole, the cymbal produces a lower pitch and considerably less harmonics. This effective way of dampening a cymbal is strictly a one-way street. There is no way to get rid of the hole.

Inside Out

A bit simpler effect, but of a similar radical nature, is turning a cymbal inside out. This *can* only be done to thinner cymbals, and it *should* only be done to cheap ones—they might even benefit from it. The sound takes on an Oriental character. When applying this trick once too often on the same cymbal, it will crack on the "kink."

...drilling holes in the bottom cymbal...
Factory-drilled, UFIP Rough Sound Series
Photo by Bas Westerweel

The Bottom

The most widely used way of home-processing cymbals is drilling holes in the bottom cymbal of the hi-hat, in order to avoid an underpressure occurring between the cymbals during the closing (air-lock). This is safer than turning a regular pair of hi-hats into Sound Edge imitations. For further technical details on modifications to cymbals, see 7.5. Air-lock is dealt with in 2.3.

Finally, a tip for purists. Colored varnish has, as mentioned before, a muffling effect on the sound of a cymbal. The same thing goes for the ink used to furnish cymbals with type, brand and series indications. Removing these marks will therefore, theoretically, enhance the clarity of the sound. Nail polish remover works best for this goal.

Notes:

1   The famous Massey Hall concert, May 1953, released by Prestige Records PR 24024, *Jazz At Massey Hall, The Greatest Jazz Concert Ever*, 1973.

2   Quote by Herb Brochstein, president of Pro-Mark drumsticks, USA.

3   Stokken-Enquete (Survey on Sticks), by the author, *Slagwerkkrant* nrs. 31 and 32, Amsterdam, Holland, 1989.

4   Joe Calato, president of J.D. Calato Manufacturing Co. Inc, USA, producer of Regal-Tip sticks.
     5 *Thesaurus of Orchestral Devices*, by Gardner Read, 1953.

6   "Cymbal Rivets," by Colin Schofield, *Modern Drummer*, vol. 13, no. 9., Modern Drummer Publications, Inc., New Jersey, USA 1989.

7   "Chris Parker," by Robert Santelli, *Modern Drummer*, vol. 9, no. 10, Modern Drummer Publications, Inc., New Jersey, USA, 1985.

8   Armand Zildjian, interviewed by the author, December 1986.

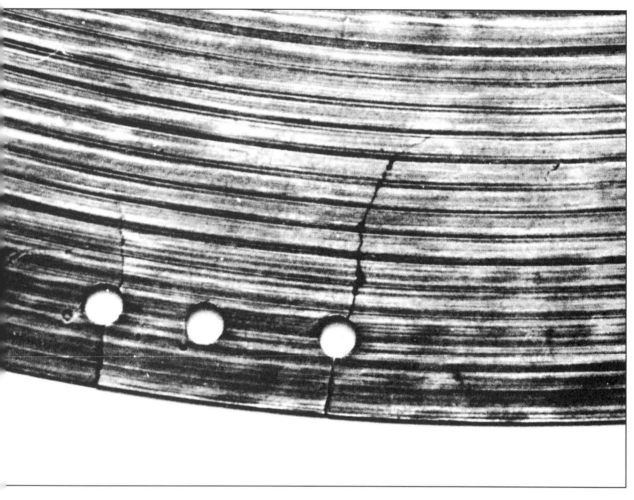

CYMBAL CARE
...drilling holes, mounting rivets
and other jobs...

7. CYMBAL CARE

As basic an instrument as a cymbal seems to be, there is quite a lot to say about how to take care of one. The first section of this chapter deals with the dos and don'ts of mounting cymbals. Cleaning, something every drummer seems to have his or her own ideas about, is the main subject of the second section. In the third section some suggestions are given for those who carry their precious bronze around in an old blanket—being just one way to diminish their prospects of a lengthy career.

The fourth section of this chapter is dedicated to some more thoughts and theories about breaking cymbals. Tips on repairing cymbals that did not live through previous sections, and advice on drilling holes, mounting rivets and other jobs can be found in the last sections.

7.1. MOUNTING CYMBALS

Getting the most out of a cymbal, while limiting the risk of breaking it, requires that it be mounted on a stand correctly. This definitely sounds silly, yet lots of sins against the following rules have been registered. Er, rules? No. Tips.

7.1.1. SLEEVES, WASHERS, WING NUTS AND STANDS

The nylon sleeves, that cymbal stands come equipped with, wear down after a while, and in many cases they are lost before they even had that chance. Spare sleeves are as imperative as spare sticks. Using a ragged sleeve or no sleeve at all will make the cymbal rub against the threaded stem of the cymbal tilter. This causes a lot of noise and, ultimately, a worn-out hole in the cymbal. Such "keyholes" reduce the cymbal's value as well as its life-expectancy.

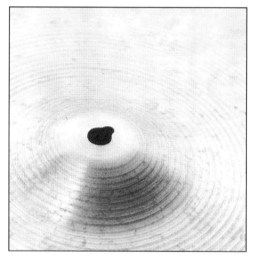

...using a ragged sleeve or no sleeve at all...
Collection Piet Klaassen Drum Service
Photo by Bas Westerweel

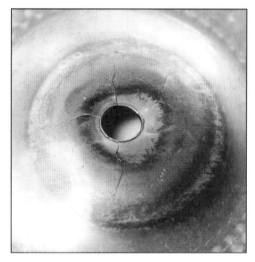

The wingnut:...exaggerate its purpose...
Collection Piet Klaassen Drum Service
Photo by Bas Westerweel

Groove

Because nylon is softer than metal, cymbals will eventually wear out a groove in the sleeve. Such a groove might catch the cymbal and cause damage as a result of the extra stress around the hole. Frequent inspection of these sleeves is prerequisite. Be aware that sleeves wear out on the side you're not looking at.

Instead of standard nylon sleeves, you can use fuel hose or plastic water hose (as used in aquariums). Being softer than nylon, these materials are better at preventing unwanted sounds, especially when playing cymbals with mallets. Of course, plastic and rubber wear down faster.

The percussion industry has also come up with alternatives.

Beato's Cymbal Shock Absorbers are soft sleeves that expand under the pressure of the wing-nut. Filling the hole entirely, the sleeve prevents the cymbal from swaying too much, without restricting its vibrations. Pearl, Yamaha and others have made one-piece combinations of nylon base-discs and sleeves.

Washers

The metal washers that are supplied with cymbal stands have one disadvantage: they're made out of metal. Adding leather washers on one or both sides, or using them instead of the metal washers (only with small, lightweight cymbals) helps prevent metal-clatter. Gaffer's tape may also help to reduce such sounds.

The size, hardness and thickness of felt washers affect the sound of the cymbal, as is extensively discussed in Chapter 6. Some washers are too thick in relation to the length of the thread, leaving no room for the cymbal to move after the wing nut has been mounted. Simply slice them in half, or replace them by thinner ones. Using small felt washers, like the ones used for hi-hats, on top of the cymbal will leave more room for your sticks.

Wing Nuts and Alternatives

The traditional wing nut has a few drawbacks. For one, it seems to invite people to exaggerate its purpose, with due risks of damaging their cymbals. Secondly, it tends to loosen up while playing, which may result in the above. Thirdly, every time a drumset is set up, at least one nut is bound to fall.

The easiest and fastest way to mount cymbals is by using T-Tops (e.g. Camber) or Cymbal Snaps (Zildjian). The cymbal is simply slid over the T-shaped nut and will then be mounted as freely as possible. If the threaded stem on the tilter is long enough, it is even possible to use an ordinary nut to keep the sleeve and washers in place.

Tama's Cymbal Mate and Meinl's Cymbal Clip are clever combinations of a wing nut and a sleeve. Others, like the Sonor Cymbal Clamp, are just easy-operation alternatives for wing nuts.

Spring-mounting

The Aquarian Cymbal Spring holds the cymbal between two rubber washers that are mounted on a double or triple coiled spring. The spring assembly absorbs a great deal of the impact, reducing the risk of breaking cymbals. The Flex Tilt Cymbal Shock Mount (Silver Fox Percussion) is comparable to the aforementioned item.

Chinas and related cymbals will especially benefit from spring-mounting. Being mounted at a steep angle and upside-down as the usually are, huge strain is exerted on the inside of the hole and therefore on the cup. Spring-mounting allows for tightening the cymbal in order to keep it steadily in position, reducing the chance of breakage at the same time.

Drummers are subject to physical laws of nature. One of them states that if you drop a wing nut, it will roll under the bass drum.
—Roy Burns

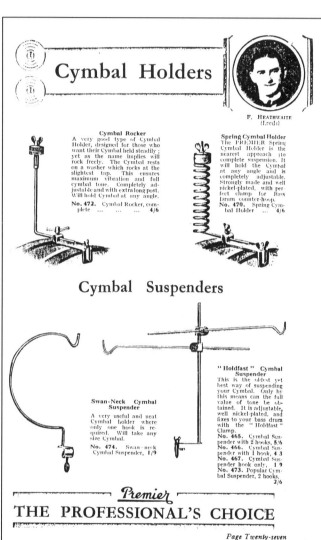

...the nearest approach to complete suspension...
Spring Cymbal Holder (top right), early 1930s Premier catalog
Courtesy of Premier

The idea of mounting cymbals on springs is, by the way, quite old. Premier listed a Spring Cymbal Holder as early as 1930.

Cymbal Stands

Cymbal stands, apart from having a certain effect on the sound of the cymbal (see 6.5.), are not to be dealt with in depth here. One remark should, however, be made. When using a stand with considerable maximum height in a low position, rattling might be caused by the inner tube vibrating against the outer tube. A piece of tape around the bottom of the inner tube will do in most cases. This is less radical then cutting off a piece of the tube, which in itself is a very effective solution.

Pulling out both tubes the same distance (instead of pulling out just one) can also prevent such sounds.

7.1.2. MOUNTING HI-HATS

The top hi-hat cymbal needs some freedom of movement in order to sound its best and to limit the risk of breakage. Tops that are too tight or have too hard washers may crack around the edge of the cup. Basically, the clutch has to be set so that the cymbal can keep turning for a while after you give it a spin. The vertical play (at the edge) shouldn't be too much either. If it is too loose the chick sound will get sloppy or even lost—loose nuts loosen up automatically.

The relatively limited amount of play a top cymbal has may cause it to wear out around the hole, especially if the cymbal is used as an additional crash. Note that there is no shock-absorbing nylon or rubber around the hole, as with the other cymbals.

Most clutches have some kind of braking system in the bottom nut. Preset the tension by tightening the two nuts above the cymbal against each other in the preferred position, after the bottom nut has been tightened as far as it will go.

Washers

The top cymbal has to be mounted between two felt washers. A felt washer as well as a metal one under the bottom cymbal will prevent rattling and cracking. Instead of felt washers, rubber or fiber ones may be used. Being harder they will enhance the definition of the chick sound.[1] Never put the bottom cymbal directly on the metal washer or the tilter. Felt washers may condense with age and should then be replaced.

In order to be able to splash the hi-hat cymbals softly with the foot, the washer under the bottom cymbal should provide sufficient stability. A too-soft washer will make the bottom cymbal give too much under the pressure of the top cymbal.

Angle

The angle of the bottom cymbal is usually adjustable by a tilting mechanism. This angle prevents the creation of a dull sound as a result of air-lock (see 2.3. and 3.4.2.). Different rooms and different cymbals may require different settings.

The distance between the two cymbals, again, largely depends on personal preferences. A gap that's too small will limit the maximum volume. A large gap results in less control and more volume. Another point of departure may be the most comfortable angle of the footboard, regardless of the width of the gap between the cymbals.

7.1.3. CYMBAL LOCATION

The only general advice on the location of your cymbals is to arrange them to fit yourself—not yourself to fit the cymbals. Try to find a position for each cymbal where it can be played in any conceivable way, without causing undue strain. Keeping them relatively low will save you extra energy in keeping your upper arm in mid-air all the time.

Put your cymbals as close to you and to each other as possible, keeping enough space to move your arms. No matter how fast you are, it takes time to travel. The location of your crashes and splashes depends on the way you play. If you do a lot of hi-hat timekeeping, for instance, you might want to put a splash in that vicinity.

Adapt

The location of certain cymbals may also be varied with the volume that is required. Playing hard usually implies larger distances between the crashes, creating more room to move. Softer music may lead to locating them closer by. The speed, originating from the larger distance to move your arm, could otherwise result in too-loud accents.

Humans are quite able to adapt to varying distances. Even if you have a new car, you don't have to get out to see whether you can pass between the ones of your neighbors.

In a nutshell, playing comfort is the most important consideration. Yet drummers put their cymbals way up in the air for show, or in order to be able to see their fellow band members, or to prevent the sound from leaking into the drum mic's. Have it either way.

7.2. CLEANING CYMBALS

Some drummers spend an excessive amount of time trying and testing all possible and impossible ways to get their cymbals clean and shiny. Others never do; they just go for the mellow character that dirty cymbals achieve over the years.

Even among the group first mentioned there is a lot of disagreement. One author advises Brasso "...rubbing it gently on with a clean cloth in the direction of the lathe cuts...",[2] while a fellow writer positively warns against the same product because "It will actually eat away your investment".[3] Brand-name cleaners (almost every cymbal manufacturer has one) and household articles such as Zud, Comet and Ajax have led to similar heated discussions.

7.2.1. CAUSES AND PREVENTION

A great deal of confusion can be solved by distinguishing three cleaning problems on cymbals, as Rick Van Horn does:[4]

1. Dirt and dust
2. Tarnish
3. Dullness

1. Dirt and dust affect both sound and looks. Dust is easy to remove with a dry piece of cloth, as long as your cymbals aren't so dirty that the dust sticks to them. Everything that has sticking qualities should therefore be avoided. This is not always as simple as it may seem. There is even grease in the air (nicotine, for one). Covering your set when it is not in use helps.

    Grease that is transferred to the cymbals by the tips of your sticks and your hands can be avoided by frequently cleaning all four of them. Handling your cymbals only with gloves is not a popular solution, yet a very effective one.

    Spilled drinks and fast food are two examples of dirt that can easily be removed, if you do it quickly.

Another thing I try to do [in recording] is to position the cymbals as high as possible. I know I'll get many an argument here, but the idea is to keep the cymbals from bleeding into the drum mic's, ensuring a more discrete cymbal mix. But don't try anything too radical. After all, you've got to be able to reach the things without upsetting time, or getting a hernia, both of which I've managed more than once!
—T. Bruce Wittet

As cymbals get dirty, they take on a personality of their own.
—Steve Gadd

I have never really touched my cymbals since I bought them, 24 years ago. For years now, I've been playing them in every kind of weather, indoor and outdoor. The only thing I do every couple of years is take a wire brush and run it through the grooves to clean off some of the dirt that accumulates.
—Hal Blaine

Much to some people's amazement I use the shower attachment in the bath and clean them in warm water, giving them a rub with a lintfree cloth.
—Mark Brzezicki

2. Tarnishing is a chemical process. The metal is affected by oxygen, which again is a basic ingredient of air. Also acids, as secreted by human skin, cause dullness of the cymbal's surface. Tarnishing affects only the appearance of the cymbal; the sound will not suffer in any noticeable degree.

   There is nothing you can do to avoid this process. The protective films that many cymbals are provided with helps to some extent and for a certain period of time. These finishes have been carefully developed in order not to affect the sound. Spraying cymbals yourself is therefore not recommended, unless it is being done to muffle unwanted harmonics (see 6.6.).

3. As the influences mentioned in 1 and 2 will continue forever, the shine of your cymbals will always be under attack. Hence continuously shining cymbals require continuous cleaning. A shine that lasts forever can otherwise only be produced by applying wax or lacquer of a quality that no doubt will kill the sound.

7.2.2. VARIOUS PRODUCTS

Some products are well suited for producing a nice shine, but are not effective when it comes to removing dirt. Others detach dirt, but won't give any shine. The right product depends on the extent to which the cymbal is dirty and/or dull, and on what you want to achieve.

Water and soap are cheap and effective in cleaning. Do not expect any shine. Rinse the cymbal carefully to remove any residues of the soap, which otherwise might produce stains. It has to be dried extensively afterwards, as water contains oxygen—and oxygen causes corrosion.

Adding the juice of a fresh lemon to the water will bring out some shine, as the juice's acid has an abrasive quality. If the cymbal hasn't been cleaned for a long time, it might help to leave it in a tub with water and soap overnight.

A nail brush or toothbrush can be used to get the dirt out of the tonal grooves. Always rub with the lathe cuts—no matter what product you are using—to minimize the risk of damaging the ridges and to improve the result.

Cymbal Cleaners

Various cymbal cleaners are listed in percussion catalogs. Most of them are liquid, others are so-called "dry cleaners": a kind of powder that has to be used with water. These cleaners, with a single exception, have a chemical as well as a mechanical effect. Chemically they help remove tarnish; mechanically they remove dirt, but also small particles of bronze (and the ink of your valued logo). The stronger the abrasive effect, which partially depends on the size of the chalk particles in the cleaner, the faster it works. On the other hand, the stronger the abrasive effect, the more you will affect the sound of your instrument.

Danger

The chemical ingredients of these—and many other cleaners—are usually not without danger. If the cleaner stays on the cymbal too long, it might actually cause some form of tarnish, usually visible as a blackish shine. This tarnish is hard to remove. Always work the cymbal in small segments to avoid this effect. Again, rinse and dry them extensively afterwards.

The transparent protective films mentioned above are not resistant to such cleaners. New cymbals—when being finished this way—therefore should only be cleaned with a

I never clean my cymbals at all, unless somebody spills a Coke and a dish full of Lasagna over them. If they really are sticky, then I just put them with the dishes.
—Fred van Vloten

...no cymbal manufacturer will sell a product that ruins his own cymbals... Courtesy of Zildjian

dry or damp soft cloth. Liquid glass cleaners may help also, though some of them may leave a dull film. Similar cleaners are available from percussion companies.

Different Answers
Professional cymbal cleaners cost considerably more than comparable household products. On the other hand, you have the confidence of knowing that no cymbal manufacturer will sell a product that ruins his own cymbals. Since such cleaners are not meant to be used weekly, they will also last a long time.

To find the right cleaner is basically a matter of trying several brands on your least popular cymbal. It is even cheaper to ask around for experiences other drummers had; you'll get a lot of different answers.

7.2.3. AUTO POLISHING COMPOUND, KETCHUP AND BRILLO
Van Horn mentions a number of products that he worked with, and regarded as rejects:[4]

— **Ketchup.** It leaves a residue and doesn't cut dirt. The acid in the ketchup works in removing tarnish.
— **Baking Soda paste**, which is non-abrasive, requiring strong arms to cut old dirt. It won't remove tarnish or leave a shine.
— **Spray Cleaners.** They may leave a dull film and only work on relatively fresh dirt.
— **Comet cleanser,** because it is very abrasive and may cause scratches. It is hard to rinse off and leaves no shine. When applying such cleaners, always use them with plenty of water.
— **Silver polish.** It leaves a nice shine but doesn't work on very dirty cymbals.
— **Brasso.** May be dangerous because it can break down the metal alloys due to the ammonia it contains.

Van Horn favors the use of White Auto Polishing Compound. According to his experience, this buffing compound, meant for auto body work, removes tarnish and is effective at removing dirt. Besides, he says: "...it smooths out scratches in the surface of the metal as you clean. Not enough to affect the grooves, but only the tiny scratches made by previous cleaning with abrasives, or wear and tear from carrying....It does take a lot of rubbing....the attractive look of the cymbal lasts for two or three months."

Lemon
In a survey conducted by the author, methylated spirits (alcohol) and benzine were mentioned besides most of the products mentioned above.[5] Benzine leaves a greasy film. Alcohol can be used for removing light dirt and dust. Rubbing the cymbal with a sliced lemon enhances the shine for reasons mentioned above. Turpentine affects bronze the same way as Brasso. The same has been said about oven-cleaning compounds.

Strongly abrasive and scratching powders and liquids are very effective in removing dirt, but also in removing bronze. If you don't want to turn your heavy ride into a paper-thin cymbal or just into a bad one, do not use coarse household cleansing powders, steel wool or sandpaper. Such products erode your cymbals, damaging the ridges and producing severe (and dirt-holding) scratches.

7.2.4. BIZARRE SOLUTIONS
The aforementioned survey also led to the discovery of a few unconventional, or rather bizarre ways to clean cymbals.

A drummer recalled his experiment of boiling the cymbal in water for a couple of hours. Possibly due to the excellent heat-conducting properties of the material, the cymbal gathered so much heat that something went wrong with the temper. The cymbal cracked the first time it was played after this bath.

Extremely dirty and tarnished cymbals have been cleaned with hydrochloric acid. This acid is used by artisans when working with bronze. The cymbal should be put in a tub with highly diluted hydrochloric acid (maximum 10%), stirring it gently and continuously. Immediately after the tarnish is gone the cymbal should be put in a second tub, filled with ammonia. The ammonia will neutralize the effect of the hydrochloric acid, which in itself has a corroding effect. Afterwards the cymbal should be rinsed very extensively.

Another procedure, which was successfully applied at least once, is to dip a stick with its tip wound in cloth in the hydrochloric solution and rub the cymbal with it. Work in small sections at a time, neutralize with ammonia and rinse, rinse, rinse.

WARNING: Improper or careless use of hydrochloric acid and/or ammonia can result in serious injury and/or damage to equipment. When using such liquids always use proper safety precautions, follow instructions given on the product, and keep out of reach of children.

7.2.5. MISCELLANEOUS TIPS

— **Cleaning cymbals** is a time-consuming affair that takes a lot of elbow grease. Yet never be tempted to use electrically driven polishing discs as they may generate enough heat to destroy the temper of a cymbal, which may result in cracks

— **Colored cymbals** should not be cleaned with cleaners that have even the least abrasive qualities. Paiste advises to use only a dry or damp soft cloth on such cymbals.

— **The acid** that is secreted by the skin of your fingers may work strongly on the colored coating. The corroding effect of this acid depends on its chemistry, which differs per person.

— **Dirt** doesn't adhere as well on Brilliant cymbals as it does on other cymbals. The buffing procedure smooths the surface, giving less hold to dirt and dust. The more often you clean your cymbals, the less work it will be. Hence the temptation to use strongly abrasive cleaners or electric tools will be less, too.

— **The ink** of the factory's logo will not resist many cleaners. If you want to get rid of the logos even faster, use nail polish remover.

— Be aware of **residues** that may be left by various cleaners. These residues may affect the sound of the cymbal more than dirt and dust ever will.

— **The ideal cleaner** doesn't exist. Again, too much depends on what you want to achieve and on how dirty your cymbals are. Experiment.

7.3. TRANSPORTATION

The sound of a couple of cymbals hitting the ground is impressive, but often fatal. A survey of drummers, conducted by Meinl in 1987, showed that many drummers carry their extremely expensive bronze in extremely cheap blankets. Others prefer towels and sleeping bags. A good cymbal bag, however, doesn't cost more than a low-budget 16" crash. It should have a thick impact-resistant padding, an oversized zipper and solid handles that do not cut your fingers. Some kind of fortification at the bottom is also highly desirable. That is it usually hits the ground, and that's where the cymbals' edges are.

Cases

Good cases, usually made from the same vulcanized material as drum cases, are sturdy and can handle quite a few blows. Some of them have a central bolt, over which you slide your cymbals. This way, a shock will be absorbed by the less-vulnerable cups of the cymbals inside, instead of by the edges. If dropped from a sufficient height, the cups will crack anyhow.

The bolt should penetrate the lid of the case, as the considerable weight of the cymbals would otherwise tear it out of the base. A round case should be at least two inches larger than the largest cymbal you have, so you don't have to turn it upside down to get the contents out.

Next, there are the some luxurious cases, such as the Zildjian Cymbal Safe, developed by ex-Clapton drummer Jamie Oldaker. Meinl, Paiste and Sabian have developed their own cases also, made of ABS, fortified glass fibre or such materials. All of them feature a central bolt, some kind of padding, and lots of protection. These cases weigh considerably less than the traditional wooden flight cases. The latter offer best protection.

Crowd

A blanket can act as additional protection, and is a good alternative for the central bolt. If you like to keep your cymbals bright and shining you may even consider putting a layer of cloth or foam plastic between every two cymbals. This is especially important for colored cymbals, which scratch easily. Cymbal Sox give extra and more professional protection against scratches.

Be advised to leave your cymbals in their bag or case up till the moment you're actually going to mount them. People who crowd the stage have probably damaged as many cymbals with their feet as drummers have with their sticks.

7.4. HOW (NOT) TO BREAK A CYMBAL

Although every manufacturer claims that *they* have never had problems with *their* cymbals breaking, many drummers have the experience that cymbals actually can crack. Even cymbals that were taken perfect care of, cymbals that were not being continuously overplayed and that never were dropped in their lives, have been known to give up. It is, however, not as bad as some people think. Following are some hints that may well enhance the life-expectancy of your instruments, most of which are likely to be able to last at least a full-time career.

Too Tight

As mentioned before, cymbals should have enough freedom of movement—especially crashes and splash cymbals. If a cymbal is struck and it can't move, then all the energy of the blow will have to be absorbed by the cymbal itself. A punch in the stomach, after all, hurts considerably less if you move with it.

Cymbals that have been mounted too tightly may, strange as it seems, crack at the opposite side. This can be easily explained. Every time you hit the cymbal, you allow the area that you're hitting to vibrate. When you come down again at that same spot, you're muffling it. You stop the motion caused by the first stroke at that point.

The vibrations, however, travel through the body of the instrument like a wave form. This wave form builds up at the other end of the cymbal, where the vibrations are not limited by each subsequent stroke. The cymbal is not allowed to release that stress factor, so it splits where the peaks of the vibration are highest and the valleys deepest: at the edge.

I have this 24" HH medium heavy that I used on *Think Of One,* which is a *bad* cymbal. It has a great big bell, and it's powerful, but I couldn't get a case for it, so I don't take it out much anymore.
—Jeff Watts

Sticks, heads and cymbals are disposable items...
—*Music Trades*, April 1992

I did once have a beautiful 18" medium-thin Paiste crash, but in the first week it split. So it's usually Zildjian, 16" and 18" crashes, on the lighter side. But I break those, too, because I don't like them to sway around, and so I tighten them up perhaps a little too much.
—Dan "Woody" Woodgate

Horizontal

If you mount your crash cymbals horizontally and at considerable height, you're likely to hit them at an angle of 90 degrees—at their most vulnerable part in the least desirable manner.

The best way to strike a crash cymbal is usually described as the "glancing motion." Mounting cymbals horizontally may be done without danger if sufficient technique is at hand: this implies pulling the stick back immediately after the blow ("popping").

It has been said that thin cymbals do not break that easily, because they give. The more flexible something is, the harder it will be to crack it. Though this might be true to some extent, a thinner cymbal will crack before a thicker one will, under the same circumstances. There simply is less metal to be fractured.

Extracting the Sound

Be aware that pretty much any cymbal can crack, especially if you do not follow the rules mentioned above. No matter how solid the instrument may look, it is not a sheet of stainless steel. It is very possible to get the maximum volume out of a cymbal without ever breaking it. As far as playing is concerned, this boils down to the difference between either extracting the sound from the cymbal or beating the sound out of it; between glancing the cymbal with a twist of your wrist or trying to cut through it in one straight blow.

Maximum Volume

Each cymbal has a certain maximum volume. Once that point has been reached, it is of no use trying to get more out of it. The volume will not increase. The result of beating it even harder will be a slight increase of the lows in the initial attack, an altering decay and, in the end, a new cymbal.

If you are frequently lacking power, buy a set of louder cymbals or invest in some kind of amplification. The latter solution has its advantages: louder cymbals will definitely sound different. Heavier sticks may produce more volume also, but may not be the best solution if you want to keep your cymbals from cracking.

Warranty

Some brands offer official warranties against cracking. Even after the warranty period it may happen that a broken cymbal is replaced, as soon as the crack or any other damage is found to be the result of a manufacturing flaw.

For an experienced eye it is not hard to find the cause of a crack. Clever stories are seen through immediately. In case of doubt, the manufacturer will be in touch with you and ask intimate questions about your relationship with the damaged cymbal.

There is, by the way, one manufacturer who does not supply any kind of warranty, because they "do not want to make their customers unnecessarily imprudent." Returning a cymbal for warranty should be done through your retailer or distributor: they know the formalities and the best way to package and mail it.

7.5. REPAIRING CYMBALS AND OTHER JOBS

Four things can be done with a cracked cymbal. Get rid of it, wait for the crack to grow larger (which it will by itself), attempt to prevent further damage, or create a rattler by binding all leftovers together. The latter has been done with the remnants of a few Chinas, and it worked. Do not bother to send broken cymbals to the manufacturer as "scrap—to be remelted." They have plenty of alloy as it is. Apart from cracks there are

If you want your cymbals to live longer, there's a certain angle of attack. Mine are towards me at an angle now. Over the years I've had to turn them a bit lower towards me. I don't crack as many cymbals as I used to, and I'm still hitting as hard as I was.
—Nicko McBrain

There's such a big difference between extracting the sound out of a cymbal or trying to beat it out. Some people seem to try to hit right through the cymbal. Sometimes that's part of the show, but in most cases it's more of a bad habit.
—Lennie DiMuzio

I carry different sets of cymbals with me on the road—A's, K's Platinums and Z's—so if one night I'm not hearing enough overheads, I can ask my drum tech to put on the Z's to get more of a cutting sound.
—Gregg Bissonette

A cymbal only can explode so loud, and then it's not gonna get any louder, so there's no need to try to beat the shit out of it.
—Lennie DiMuzio

various other situations that may lead to the use of tools.

7.5.1. CRACKS

Repairing cracked cymbals comes down to removing material from the cymbal. Small cracks have an irresistible tendency to grow. All you can do about it is cut the bronze that surrounds the crack. Yes, this will affect the sound of the cymbal—mostly depending on the quantity of material to be removed. And no, it isn't always as bad as it sounds.

Depending on the exact location of the crack, the thickness and the material of the cymbal and the quality of the repair, a cracked cymbal can last quite some time, varying from a few days up to several decades. Ride cymbals that have been repaired according to the following guidelines, have been known to survive for long periods of time.

There are several places for cracks to occur: somewhere within the cymbal, at the edge, or at the hole. Next to some similarities, there are different ways to treat different types of cracks.

Contemplate

Before getting started, spend a moment contemplating your skills as a metalworker. Besides good, sharp tools you need a considerable dose of courage, tact and dexterity, a steady hand and a feel for the material. Should you have any doubts, have somebody else perform the following tips. Some drum shops offer such services.

7.5.2. DRILLING BRONZE

The safest way to drill a hole in a cymbal is to use a drill press or a brace in which a hand-drill can be attached. This will prevent the drill bit from slipping and being jiggled, and it lets you concentrate on the main work.

Using a center punch to provide the bit with a starting point has been done, yet never without the risk of starting another crack. Instead of a center punch, pieces of gaffer's tape can be applied. Cross-glue them over the exact location. The only problem may be to locate that position when it's covered by tape. Sticking the bit through the tape when positioning will help. The use of a drill press or a brace should make the use of tape unnecessary.

Use sharp HSS bits, with a diameter of about 2/16" (3.5 mm.). Dull bits generate too much heat. Speeds of 1100 and 1350 rpm respectively are advised. Drilling at too high a speed could—because of the high temperatures generated—result in loss of temper.

Do not exert any pressure on the drill; let the bit do the work.

Applying cutting oil will prevent the cymbal and the bit from gathering too much heat. Drilling a little at a time or rinsing the drill with water will prevent this, too.

Prevent the drill from suddenly punching through by positioning the cymbal upside down on a wooden board. Some assistance is very helpful in this phase.

7.5.3. CRACKS PARALLEL WITH THE TONAL GROOVES

Performing surgery on a crack or split parallel with the tonal grooves always starts with drilling a hole at each end of the crack. This, ideally, should stop the crack from continuing any further. It is a matter of interrupting the fault-line.

Generally, the crack will be retarded rather than stopped. A major problem is locating the exact end of the crack. Cracks often do not stop where they seem to stop. Beyond what's visible, they continue as invisible hairline cracks. Use a magnifier and good lights, and look at the crack from every angle in order to find the places to drill. If you

... if you don't gamble, you will lose anyhow...
Collection Piet Klaassen Drum Service
Photo by Bas Westerweel

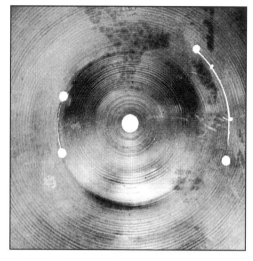

...harder, if not to impossible, to stop...
Collection Piet Klaassen Drum Service
Photo by the Author

don't gamble, you will lose anyhow. Mark the locations with a felt-tipped pen, and drill a hole at each marking. Then widen the crack with a small rat-tail file, so the edges of the crack don't touch each other any more. The colliding edges will otherwise cause further cracking, and they would be audible when playing. The less material you take away, the better the original sound of the cymbal will be preserved.

Parallel cracks in the cup or the cup-area are harder, if not impossible, to stop. First, the bronze is thicker and will therefore easily hide internal hairline cracks. Second, the frequency of the vibrations in that area is extremely high.

7.5.4. CRACKS FROM THE HOLE

Cracks that originate from the hole, mostly due to extreme tightening, may be treated the same way as in 7.5.3. Small cracks, up to 1/8" (3 mm), can be removed by simply enlarging the entire hole. Use a rattail file. Should the hole grow slightly too big as a result of such an operation, a metal grommet can be inserted. Such grommets are used to protect the leather straps of marching cymbals, but may also be applied to protect cymbals. A cymbal with a keyhole can be helped with a grommet as well; the keyhole will stop growing, and its edges will not cause any more damage to the nylon sleeve.

7.5.5. CRACKS AT THE EDGE

Cracks that start at the edge can be dealt with in different ways. The first way is the most radical one. By making the entire cymbal a couple of inches smaller, the crack will simply disappear. The sound of the cymbal will change considerably at the same time. Removing an inch (25.4 mm) or more from the outer edge alters the ratio of the profile of the cymbal and its diameter. This affects mainly the pitch.

That cracked bottom cymbal, that's been that way a long time now. About seventeen years. It cracked and the crack was just like a half moon, and I let it go. It turned round to the edge again and one night it just fell on the floor.
—Idris Muhammad

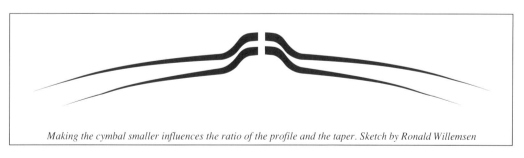

Making the cymbal smaller influences the ratio of the profile and the taper. Sketch by Ronald Willemsen

Taper

Something similar happens to the taper, as the outer edge becomes too thick in relation to the diameter of the cymbal. This changes the characteristic of a former crash cymbal towards that of a far less explosive band cymbal. The only way to solve these problems is to have the cymbal hammered and lathed again.

Removing too many inches from the cymbal (i.e. turning a 16" into a 11") may result in a reversed profile and a sound that can best be compared to that of a lesser quality dinner-gong.

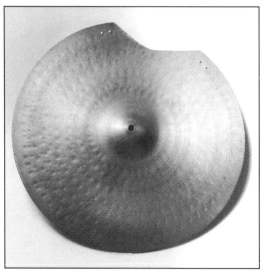

...survive for long periods of time... Tosco ride, 20"; rivets on either side of the notch. Author's collection Photo by Bas Westerweel

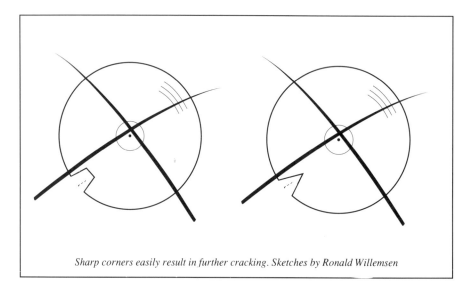

Sharp corners easily result in further cracking. Sketches by Ronald Willemsen

V-shaped Notch

The second method to remove cracks at the edge is much easier. The bronze around the crack can be removed with a metal saw or a grinding machine. On very thin cymbals a pair of sheet-metal shears can be used instead. Very small cracks at the edge can sometimes be removed with a round file.

The result of such an operation should have somewhat of a flat triangular shape, the longest side of which is formed by the (no longer existing) edge of the cymbal. The corners of this triangle should be curved, not sharp. Sharp corners easily result in further cracking.

Start by drilling a hole at the end of the crack. This will prevent it from increasing as a result of the jiggling effect of the sawing motion. The use of cutting oil facilitates the sawing.

The edges and the corners of the V-shaped notch have to be finished off with a smooth file, followed by a final polish with smooth waterproof sandpaper.

Hairline Cracks

Because of the possible existence of invisible hairline cracks, a sufficient amount of bronze has to be cut off. The more bronze removed, the less risk of further cracking. On the other hand, the more bronze you remove, the more the sound of the cymbal will change. By cutting a piece out of the cymbal some of the original vibrational patterns (see 5.1.) will definitely be distorted. Apart from that, cymbals with a large cut-out triangle might audibly start to "wobble."

Nevertheless, the notch has to be at least half an inch deeper than the visible end of the crack. If not, the whole operation becomes meaningless. This leads to one simple conclusion: Put the cymbal aside as soon as you notice a crack, as small as it may be, and do not play on it until it has been repaired.

The fact that creating a notch will make a number of tonal grooves end at the newly formed edge can do no harm in itself. Proof of this can be found in the existence of octangular shaped cymbals, such as Sabian's Rocktagon, and of various bottom hi-hat cymbals that have factory-made notches.[6] You could even consider making a whatever-odd-tagon out of a cymbal that has cracks at various places around the edge.

Remaining hairline cracks may be discovered by gently playing the cymbal with a soft timpani mallet. Hold the edge of the cymbal close to your ear, spinning it slowly, and closely listen around the entire edge. Remaining cracks will be audible as a high-pitched sizzling sound.

When inserting rivets in a ride cymbal that has been repaired this way, it is suggested to mount them near or on either side of the notch. This will prevent playing on the heads of the rivets, as the excavated area will automatically move upwards on a tilted stand.

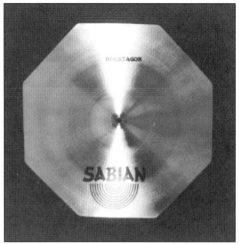

...tonal grooves that end at the edge...
Sabian Rocktagon
Courtesy of Sabian

And Furthermore
Do not bother repairing authentic Chinese cymbals in any of the ways given above. They will continue cracking anyhow. Repairing splashes and thin crashes is also likely to turn into an ever-repeating affair. Some cymbals just do not live forever.

Because of all the warnings stated above you might hesitate to repair a cymbal. That's completely justified. Of course, if you don't do anything, the cymbal will be ruined anyhow. It might be better to ruin it yourself.

Do not try to solder a crack. Apart from the fact that the solder will detach from the cymbal because of the vibrations, soldering will generate considerable heat, resulting in loss of temper around the crack. Soldered cymbals usually are as brittle as cookies around that spot. And welding? No.

7.6. DRILLING HOLES IN HI-HAT CYMBALS
Another reason to go for the electric drill is the wish to provide the bottom hi-hat cymbal with holes, to prevent air-lock effects (see 2.3. and 3.4.2.). Do not try, in an attempt to imitate Paiste's Sound Edge hi-hats, to create waves around the edge of the cymbal. Before drilling, refer to 7.5.2. Holes that are meant to prevent air-lock are larger than indicated in that section.

Instead of drilling a large hole in one step, start with a small hole, increasing its diameter in two or three steps (e.g. 3 mm, 6 mm or 2/16", 1/4", etc.).

If such an operation is not performed perfectly, the cymbal will start cracking as a result of the holes. This seems to contradict the advices above. Repairing, however, is a necessary evil.

Before you start drilling, please realize that the effect might not be what you had in mind. Besides, the value of your hi-hats on the second-hand market might considerably decrease. Buying a pair of factory-drilled hi-hats instead of creating them yourself is not a bad idea, really.

7.7. INSTALLING RIVETS
Installing rivets also requires drilling. Refer to 7.5.2. for technical information. The effect of rivets on the sound of a cymbal is dealt with in 6.7.

7.7.1. NUMBER OF RIVETS

The number of rivets usually varies from two to eight. Using more rivets will muffle the sound because of the weight of the rivets. The extra rivets do not give that much more of a sizzle, either. Factory-riveted cymbals generally hold (or rather: held) six rivets. Depending on the type of cymbal and on your taste, any other number may be chosen.

A popular combination is mounting two rivets about one inch from the edge and one inch apart from each other. The "trio" (three rivets in a row, or in a triangle) has its fans also. The effect of such combinations is quite subtle, and the chances of hitting rivets with your stick decrease.

Heavier cymbals require more or heavier rivets to make the sizzle sound become audible in relationship to the stronger definition of such cymbals.

7.7.2. DIFFERENT RIVETS

The number of rivets to be used is not solely determined by the type of cymbal and your taste, but also by the material and the size of the rivets that you intend to use. The harder the material of the rivets, the stronger and the more brilliant the effect will be, and the less rivets are needed to obtain a certain effect.

Copper and brass rivets produce a relatively low sounding sizzle. Steel, nickel-silver and nickel-silver-plated ones sound higher. Hardnesses may vary per material, also.

Next, there are considerable variations in the size of the head of different rivets. A larger head will produce a louder sizzle when mounted in a heavy cymbal, but it will take the highs out of lighter cymbals. Heavier rivets respond slower than lighter ones and their sizzle will be lower in pitch.

There are also differences in the length and the diameter of the shaft. For thinner cymbals it is best to use rivets with a relatively small head and a short, narrow shaft. Such rivets will result in a more easily controllable sound.

Some cymbal manufacturers have their own brand-name rivets. Rivets are also for sale at hardware stores and the occasional saddle makers that are still around. Metal split pins, available from any office-supply store, feature easy (un)foldable wings. This makes them easy to use as temporary rivets.

7.7.3. IN ADVANCE

It is not so hard to find out how a cymbal will sound once it is riveted. Attach a small coin or a small piece of chain to the cymbal, using a tiny bit of adhesive tape or a nylon chord (see 6.7.)

This will not produce exactly the same effect as a few inserted rivets, but it will be sufficient to base further decisions on. Whether to put a pair, a trio, or more rivets in the cymbal can be found out mainly by listening to comparable cymbals that have been riveted. Ask around before you start, and consider the possibility of ordering a custom-riveted cymbal instead. Most companies offer that service.

7.7.4. WHERE AND HOW

Rivets, as a general rule, are to be put at about one to one-and-a-half inches from the edge of the cymbal. To prevent the cymbal from future cracking, it is advised to slightly vary this distance per rivet, e.g. 15/16" (24 mm) to 17/16" (27 mm). This will help prevent the creation of a fault line. The same theory has been applied to rivets that are mounted in one line across the center of the cymbal.

Drilling holes less than an inch from the edge is like begging for trouble. Enlarging the stated distances from the edge will decrease the effect of the rivet—or increase the quality of sound you are looking for. Trilok Gurtu has been using a 22" ride cymbal with four rivets at about 4" from the edge, for instance. Rivets in the cup of a cymbal are not very effective.

Avoid drilling in or directly around the imprinted trademark. When putting rivets on a 20" cymbal at more than an inch from the edge, these rivets are going to scratch your 18" cymbal when carrying them around in a case with a center-bolt.

Spinning

Mark the places to be drilled with a marking pen. If more than two or three rivets are to be put in, they are usually spread evenly around the circumference of the cymbal, as the figures on a clock.

In order to find the best location for a pair or a trio of rivets, see if the cymbal has a heavier side by spinning it around on a tilted stand. If it stops in the same position time after time, then put the rivets at the highest side to prevent playing on their heads.

Rivets in Chinas

The ideas about the best location of rivets in a China cymbal differ—again. Colin Schofield advises to put them roughly at the same spot as in other cymbals; not exactly in the bottom of the turned-up edge, however, but slightly towards the edge.[7]

Others contend that the bottom of the flange *is* the best location, preventing the rivets from causing a muffling effect due to their oblique position when put somewhere in the turned-up edge. The risk involved is that the flange itself may be a weaker point in the cymbal. Before mounting the rivets, decide whether the cymbal is going to be used upside-down. Rivets do sound silly with their heads down.

Riveting hi-hat cymbals

Both hi-hat tops and bottom have been riveted, in numerous variations. Usually eight rivets in four groups of two are put in the bottom cymbal. Again, study some factory-riveted hi-hats before starting yourself.

The most common location of the rivets in hi-hat cymbals is halfway between the edge of the cup and the edge of the cymbal. Positioning them more towards the edge will decrease the effect ("swoosh," as Schofield calls it in the aforementioned article). After all, the edge is dampened completely when closing the hi-hats.

7.7.5. SIZE OF THE HOLE & FLARING THE RIVETS

The hole should be 1/16" (1 to 1.5 mm) larger than the diameter of the shaft of the rivet. Zildjian rivets, for instance, are 2/16" (3 mm), and the company advises using a 3/16" (5 mm) drill. If the hole is too big the rivets may come out after a while. A too narrow hole will give them too little room to move.

For the actual drilling, please refer to 7.5.2.

Rivets with a cylinder-shaped shaft can be flared with the use of a tapered punch. The punch should be wide enough to prevent it from getting stuck in the rivet. Have an assistant hold the cymbal upside down, resting the head of the rivet on an anvil.

Lacking such a device, the side of a hammerhead or any other flat and heavy piece of steel can be used. Because the shafts are quite thin there is no need to apply excessive force.

Various possibilities: 8 rivets (standard), trio and Trilok Gurtu's solution
Sketch by Ronald Willemsen

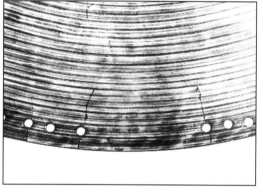

...drilling the holes too close to the edge is like begging for trouble...
Collection Piet Klaassen Drum Service
Photo by the author

Split-pin rivets can be bent open with a screwdriver. Hold the head of the rivet with a pair of pliers, so there will be no force applied to the cymbal.

Doubling for a Sieve

The sound and life expectancy of a cymbal will not be noticeably influenced by a couple of proficiently drilled small holes. The number of rivets, therefore, can be reduced afterwards–even to zero. Exceeding eight holes may affect the sound as well as the durability of the cymbal. Besides, again, a cymbal will decrease in second-hand value even if just one hole is found in its surface. A cymbal that is capable of doubling for a sieve won't be worth anything at all. And of course, riveting a bad cymbal will make a bad sizzle cymbal. Rivets add to the sound, they do not improve it.

7.8. FINISHING OFF THE HOLE

Though most manufacturers have replaced the old press drill by a punching device, there still are cymbals on which the center hole is not as smooth as it should be. As the rough edges of such a hole will wear out the sleeve in no time—which, in turn, will damage your cymbal—it is wise to finish off such a flaw.

If there is actually a point of metal sticking out into the hole, use a smooth file to remove it. Be careful not to file the hole out of round, thus starting a keyhole effect yourself. Minor flaws can be removed using waterproof sandpaper, twisted around a screwdriver. Existing keyholes can be disguised and prevented from growing by inserting a metal grommet (see 7.5.4.).

7.9. ENGRAVING

Serial numbers in cymbals may prove to be very helpful if you need to identify your cymbals after they've been stolen—presuming you have jotted the numbers down and remembered where you put them. Most manufacturers do not imprint such numbers. This omission can be made up for by engraving your name and zip code in the cups of your cymbals. The material at that point is usually thick enough to withstand such a treatment, assuming it is being done with proper tools and care.

7.10. BUFFING, LATHING AND HAMMERING?

This chapter is mainly meant as a guide to performing *necessary* acts of surgery and care on cymbals. Repeating what has been stated in Chapter 6, it is advisable to buy a cymbal that pleases you, rather than trying to buff, lathe or hammer a dissatisfactory cymbal yourself. Basically, this goes also for some of the other tips given in this book.

WARNING: Improper or careless use of (electric) tools can result in serious injury and/or damage to equipment.

Notes:

1   "The Care & Feeding of Cymbals," by Frank Kofsky, *Modern Drummer*, vol. 5, no. 6, Modern Drummer Publications, Inc., New Jersey, USA, 1981.

2   "Cymbal Acoustics, Selection and Care," by Larry C. Jones, *The Instrumentalist*, USA, March 1979.

3   "Tips on Cleaning Cymbals," by Chris King, *Modern Drummer*, vol. 7, no.1, Modern Drummer Publications, Inc., New Jersey, USA, 1983.

4   "Cleaning Your Set," by Rick Van Horn, *Modern Drummer,* vol. 4, no. 5, Modern Drummer Publications, Inc., New Jersey, USA, 1980.

5   Survey by the author, 1988.

6   Zildjian's discontinued Amir and Impulse bottom hi-hat cymbals had such notches, as well as Sabian's first EQ-Hats (see Chapter 9)

7   "Cymbal Rivets," by Colin Schofield, *Modern Drummer,* vol. 13, no. 9, Modern Drummer Publications, Inc., New Jersey, USA, 1989.

8. THE MANUFACTURING PROCESSES

No matter how advanced a synthesizer may be, a cymbal will always be a harder instrument to make and to select.
—Giovanni Spadacini

The strangest stories are told about the way cymbals are made. An inquisitive visitor once asked a cymbal maker how he was "capable of rolling this copper wire so tight that it actually stays together?" There are many less bizarre, but equally wrong stories around. In an authoritative book, rumor has it that various kinds of mystic oils and herbs are applied to temper the cymbals.

As the six Western cymbal factories have cooperated to great extent in supplying the necessary information, such tales can be avoided on the following pages. For dessert, this chapter offers a short trip to the way cymbals were made in ancient times.

8.1. WOODEN LOGS AND COMPUTERS

The methods being applied by modern factories are, at some points, as different as day and night. Where one manufacturer has adapted every technological development, another factory uses methods that date back to the beginning of this century, and before. In other words, in one factory the process is largely left to computer-controlled machines; in the other, workers still heat the cymbals in a woodburning stone oven.

Sometimes these differences can be accounted for by the available resources, sometimes by more-or-less idealistic convictions, often by tradition, sometimes by a lack thereof.

And for every way of doing something a reasonable explanation can be found. If—because you can't afford a machine—you persist in doing things by hand, you will stress the artisan character of your product. If you use a computer—because you never learned to do it by hand—you will accent the consistency of the sound of your cymbals.

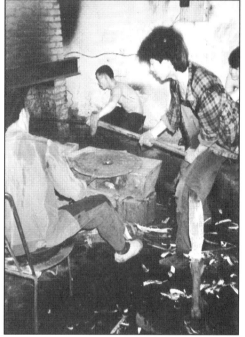

Plate hammering at the Wuhan factory, China, late 1980s Photo by Paul Real, Paul Real Sales/PR Percussion

Turkey Dinner

When visiting a number of cymbal factories, a confrontation with undisclosed traditions is unavoidable. Sometimes these traditions have quite logical explanations. There is a story about a family gathering for the yearly turkey dinner.[1] The turkey, according to a mysterious family tradition, is served in parts instead of in one piece. Why, somebody wants to find out. Eventually grandma reveals the secret: her granny's oven was so small that the turkey simply *had* to be cut up.

The Final Result

No matter how modern or how old-fashioned the process is, every manufacturer is convinced of being right, and they are all right in doing so. All of them have a very thorough knowledge of what they are doing and why they are doing it that way. That is something that drummers benefit from every day.

Every company also has its secrets, and this book never had the goal of revealing any of those secrets. It was amusing, however, to see how one manufacturer proudly showed every detail of the machine that was fearfully kept covered by his competitor.

The fact that one process takes more words to explain than another has nothing to do with the quality of the resulting product. It's not the way a cymbal is produced, but the final result that counts. At the same time, you might be able to conceive the sound of a cymbal just by taking a close look at the factory, which, at least to some extent, reveals some of the underlying philosophy. The fact that you can

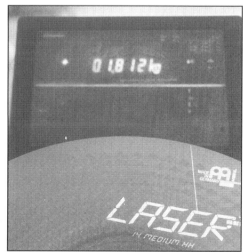

Digital technology at Meinl, late 1980s Courtesy of Meinl

pretty often hear that philosophy in the cymbals is happily considered a positive thing.

Turkish, Swiss/German, Italian and Chinese
The various production processes are classified by the countries of their origins, and subsequently by the various ways of hammering. This classification does as little or as much to contrast and equate various production processes as any other classification would. The choice was arbitrary. The goal of this section is to provide insight in the way cymbals are being made, but not to qualitatively compare or judge those various methods. Regarding the many ways each style can be—and is—applied would make such a comparison impossible anyhow.

Figures
In this chapter, figures such as temperatures, weights of castings, expansion-measurements and such may vary from one company to another. The printed figures sometimes are identical to what was told by one of the companies; in other cases they are averages of figures that were given in different (but comparable) companies. Not every possible exception on general processes has been mentioned. Most of the information was gathered between 1986 and 1988. Updates were made in 1992. All photos, except for those in 8.7., represent the actual situation in the late 1980s.

8.2. IN ADVANCE
There are a number of important treatments that are basically applied to every cymbal. This basic knowledge will enhance the understanding of the sections that follow, and at the same time shed some light on the terminology.

The Disc
There are three basic ways to obtain the flat discs that will be transformed to cymbals. In the Turkish tradition they are rolled out of small, thick, individual castings. The Swiss and German factories, by tradition, have their discs made by external manufacturers. The Italians pour the liquid bronze into—rotating—molds that have somewhat of the profile of the future cymbal in them.

Semantics
These three methods are difficult to give exclusive names to. A short trip to the area of semantics, therefore. When distinguishing between Turkish and Italian versus Swiss/German-style cymbals, the terms "cast" and "non-cast" are often used. As the metal of the latter type of cymbals has been cast also, these terms are not accurate. The only difference is that the bronze for these cymbals is cast in larger quantities and outside of the actual cymbal factory. As a matter of fact, Italian-style cymbals are the only ones that are really cast: as soon as the mold is opened, the shape of the cymbal is already recognizable.

The Swiss-German cymbals are sometimes referred to as "sheet-metal" cymbals. A non-specified number of discs are cut or stamped out of large sheets of metal, as opposed to the Turkish style, where each cymbal has its own casting. This casting, when milled down, becomes a sheet, be it a small one. The only difference, in this stage of the process and in this semantic context, is again the quantity of the materials. These quantities are co-determined by specific characteristics of the various alloys.

For Swiss/German type cymbals the terms "Euro-style" or "European" are used as well. A minimum amount of geographical knowledge, however, suffices to make one

...really cast...
Courtesy of UFIP

realize that both Italy and Turkey—at least the part Istanbul is in—belong to Europe as much as Switzerland and Germany do.

Accepted Terms

Setting the semantic hairsplitting aside, it is generally accepted that "cast" cymbals, contrary to "non-cast" species, start out as *individual* castings. The term "sheet-metal cymbals" has also become accepted. None of these terms, ultimately, are widely used among drummers; they belong more to the vocabulary of the marketing managers who created them.

Shaping

In ancient times cymbals were hammered into shape by hand. As technology advanced, manufacturers have been searching for ways to achieve the same results in a less labor-intensive way. At first, heavy machine hammers were used just to pre-shape the flat discs. Later on, faster and more controllable machine hammers allowed for complete machine-hammering. Automatic and computer-controlled hammering machines, the latest additions, just have to be set.

In 1992 these methods were all being applied.

Hammering

As in daily life, this book distinguishes hand-hammered cymbals from the ones that are hammered by machines. However, some of the "hand-hammered" series are—partially—hammered by the same kind of machine that is used for cymbals that do not fit that category.

The similarity is that the machine moves the hammer, and the man behind it guides the cymbal. The difference is the style of hammering. Hand-hammered cymbals basically have an irregular hammering pattern, while the other types have a regular pattern. In both cases the worker can directly influence the result. The consistency and the character, in terms of sound, depend largely on the goal that is set by the designer of the cymbal.

The difference between automatic hammering and computer-controlled hammering is marginal for drummers.

It is possible to shorten the amount of time needed for hammering by pressing the cymbals into a preliminary shape. In most cases this treatment is only part of the entire process. Cymbals that are only pressed are very rare and usually very cheap.

Spinforming

In spinforming, a machine presses the rotating cymbal in shape, after which some hammering might be done. This technique is mainly applied for low-budget series.

The cups are usually pressed in, in some cases after applying heat to that area or to the entire cymbal. Exceptions are the Italian-style cymbals of which the cups are shaped by the molds, and the spinformed cymbals. The spinforming machines shape both cup and profile. Spinforming should not be confused with the Italian technique of rotocasting.

...mounted on a high-speed lathe...
Courtesy of Paiste

Lathing

The last major step in the process is the lathing. The cymbal is mounted on a high-speed lathe and worked with sharp cutting tools. At this point the tonal grooves are created, the sound opens up and the cymbal starts shining. In most factories this is by hand.

Tempering

Tempering is an important procedure in many processes: At a certain point the cymbals are heated and cooled down quickly. This treatment causes changes in the molecular structure, enhancing the workability of the metal as well as the sound and the life expectancy of the cymbal.

...each cymbal starts out from its own block of metal...
Zildjian castings
Courtesy of Zildjian

8.3. THE TURKISH STYLE

The process that stems from the patriarch of modern-day cymbal making, Avedis Zildjian, forms the basis of the professional cymbals of Zildjian, Sabian and Istanbul. It was because of the activities of Avedis and his descendants that "regular" rides, crashes and hi-hats are collectively indicated as Turkish cymbals. It also led to a large number of brand names that refer to his family name, to the city or the country where it all started, or to the Armenian heritage.[2]

History and Introduction

The Turkish style of cymbal making dates from the first half of the 17th century. The oldest factory in this particular field, Zildjian, applies this method in the most modern way. A relatively large part of the process has been mechanized, or automated. At Sabian, in 1988, more treatments were still executed by hand or by more basic machinery. Istanbul, the smallest of these three companies, makes their cymbals almost entirely by hand.

These differences do not affect the results in sound, per se. It takes a very good set of ears to perceive whether a cymbal has been heated by a 21st-century oven, or by a wood-fire. On the other hand, the differences between "identical" cymbals will be bigger as more is done by hand.

In short, the Turkish method means that the manufacturer composes and melts his own alloy. The bronze is poured in small, round molds, one for each cymbal. These castings are rolled down to flat discs. After the cup has been pressed, the discs are made red hot and cooled down in water, at which point they are no longer brittle. Shaping and lathing transforms them into cymbals.

Control

Because of the many, mostly small-scaled, treatments in this method, the differences between "identical" cymbals traditionally have been relatively large. A 16" thin crash that turned out rather heavy was—and is, sometimes—allowed to weigh exactly the same as a 16" medium-thin crash that turned out quite light. These differences can be explained by the nature of the alloy and by the fact that each cymbal starts out from its own block of metal.

On the other hand it has to be stated that, wherever companies have chosen to go for that route, these differences are much smaller then they used to be. The tolerances in the various parts of the process have been notably reduced.

The assertion that "the type of cymbal is defined at the end of the line; in advance they do not know what they're going to make" is therefore outdated—with the exception of Istanbul, to some extent. New machinery and a never-ending growth in controlling specific parts of the process does not only lead to greater consistency of the cymbals. It also enhances the control of the parameters; it increases the number of options to organize the vibrations.

In the early '90s, this has lead to the development of types of cymbals that could not—not in such quantities, in any case—have been made before that time.

8.3.1 THE ALLOY

The alloy that Zildjian, Sabian and Istanbul use is based on a way of mixing tin and copper that was pioneered by Avedis Zildjian in 1623, and kept—almost—secret ever since. The striking thing about this bronze alloy is the large amount of tin, which basically makes it very brittle. It was Avedis's merit that he saw a chance to turn this good sounding, but inflexible, alloy into a very malleable material.

The industrial name is B20. Chemists are more accurate: SnBz 20 is a bronze (Bz) alloy with 20% tin (Sn, Stannum) and 80% copper. Besides these two metals a minimal amount of silver is needed, acting as a catalyst—a bond between the copper and the tin. This silver is either added, or traces of silver are present within the copper.

The fact that the ingredients are known doesn't alter the secrecy of the formula. The formula is not about what the alloy consists of, but the way it is prepared: which temperatures are applied, in which order are which metals added, etc. The slightest variation in these parameters may cause dramatic changes in sound, appearance and durability of the cymbal. As Armand Zildjian put it: "Our secret is not in the composition. It's not a written-down thing or a recipe. It's a technique you have to watch and learn over time—like the cake that Grandma made."[3]

Bullet-proof

According to one of the companies, the fact that the alloy is prepared in smaller quantities is not responsible for the tolerances in the sound of the finished cymbals. Modern techniques provide superfluous ways to control these processes. In earlier days this was not the case, which is one of the reasons behind sound variations in "old" K's.

Besides the well-known sound properties of B20, it conducts heat very adequately. "That characteristic would make it the ideal material for car radiators," Sabian's Nort Hargrove said, not planning to sell any for that purpose. Hargrove also established by experiment that the castings are bullet-proof: "Some pieces came out; but when I took a piece of steel as thick as that casting, I shot right trough it."

8.3.2. THE MELTING ROOM

Very few people are allowed to enter the melting room; journalists do not belong to this elite. Yet, there are a few things that can be told. Istanbul uses old-fashioned logs to heat the melting pot. The other factories apply more up-to-date and controllable techniques. Metallurgical-grade charcoal is, in some cases, used as a flux to take the oxides out of the metal, resulting in a purer alloy and thus a better casting.

The bronze is heated up to 2200°F (1200°C), and poured into molds of various sizes, for various sizes and types. The smallest casting weighs about one pound, the heaviest up to 20 pounds. Further narrowing the weight ranges per type has two advantages, as Zildjian's Colin Schofield explains: "If the range of a casting for a 10" splash is between 3 and 3.5 pounds, half a pound of bronze may be wasted; the splashes that started off from a heavier casting will sound different as well."

Before being transported to the rolling mill, the castings may rest a couple of days, giving the molecules a chance to settle.

8.3.3. ROLLING

Rolling the thick castings into flat discs is one of the most time-consuming parts of the Turkish-style process. It takes about 45 minutes to heat the castings up to the point where

Oven and rolling mill at Istanbul, 1988. Third from left: president Mehmet Tamdeger
Photo by the author

they almost start melting again (around 1500°F / 800°C). The traditional type of oven bears clear resemblance to the ones found in Italian restaurants, and is therefore affectionately referred to as a "pizza oven."

When the castings have reached the desired temperature, they are taken out with long shovels and, one by one, fed between the steel cylinders of a respectably sized rolling-mill.

Depending on the size and type of cymbal, this process is repeated between about seven (for a heavy ride) and fifteen (a splash) times. For every pass through the mill the cymbals have to be reheated. By reducing the gap between the rolls every time the casting passes through, the original thickness of the casting is reduced about 50%. The diameter, depending on the size, has then increased by 4" to 8". The outside of the disc, which can be severely cracked because of the nature of the process and the material at this stage, is cut off and melted down for future use.

Interlocking Crystals

The castings are cross-rolled: with each pass the casting is rolled in a different direction. This results in a even thickness and an optimal molecular structure, referred to as "a basket-weave of interlocking crystals" or an "interweaving grain." Swords used to be forged in a comparable manner: the metal was beaten flat, folded double, beaten flat again, etc. This way of treating the metal prevents weak spots and warpage. It also helps transmit the soundwaves more quickly around the body of the instrument, which is nice for cymbals and less important for swords.

Flames

Zildjian and Sabian make one type and size of cymbal "per oven." An "oven" can contain, for instance, eighty future 20" cymbals or two-hundred 8" splashes. At Istanbul various types and sizes of cymbals are heated and rolled in one load. The wooden logs that heat the stone oven do not allow for contemporary thermostatic controls. Because remainders of the glowing charcoal sometimes stay affixed to the cymbal when it passes through the rolling mills, spectacular flames may be seen. This casts an impressive artisan effect over the scene, yet may leave small spots on the discs.

Variables

Heating and rolling are two sources for future differences in sound between "identical" cymbals. The cymbals that are put in first come out last and will thus be heated longer. The cymbals in the middle are generally subject to higher temperatures than the ones on the sides. Next, there is the heat-induced uncontrollable expansion of the steel cylinders of the rolling mill.

These minimal variables definitely have their effects, which may or may not be compensated for in the run of the process to follow. In the late eighties Zildjian introduced a new type of oven. This so-called "rotary hearth" makes sure that every cymbal in the oven is heated for exactly the same period of time and at the same temperature.

The *rotary* hearth and the *rotary* hammer (see below) should not be confused with the Italian system of *rotocasting*, as they have nothing in common.

8.3.4. CUPPING

Chalk marks are drawn on the flat discs to indicate the position of the cup, which is then pressed in with hydraulic presses. The cymbals are prepared for this treatment by being heated entirely. In this phase the discs have a dull, grayish tint and an undefinable, dull, muted clang for a sound. Besides, they are very brittle. If thrown to the floor they'll shatter into many pieces.

8.3.5. TEMPERING

It is hard to imagine that a disc, at one time so brittle, can be subjected to heavy and intense hammering a short while later. It would be impossible indeed, if it wasn't for tempering. B20 is a so-called three-phase metal; while heating the cymbal, three different phases can be discerned. By heating the cymbal and cooling it immediately afterwards, the metal will be frozen (quenched) in one of those phases.

In most metallurgical processes this technique is used to make the material harder (i.e. steel). Where cymbals are concerned the idea is to bring the metal into a phase where it is malleable.

During their last visit to the oven the discs are heated until they are glowing red. The workers use long shovels to flatten out the ones that warp under the intense heat. When the discs reach the proper temperature they are taken out and dumped in a basin of water, one by one. The difference in temperatures between water and cymbals causes a muted-gunshot-like sound, that begs to be sampled. If the cymbals or the water do not have the right temperature, the entire oven of cymbals may be wasted. Even the angle at which the cymbal hits the water is said to be important.

After rolling, the discs are cooled before being subjected to tempering. Courtesy of Sabian

Sea Air

From times immemorial cymbals were washed with a saline solution before tempering: in combination with the heat of the oven, the salt eats away the tin-oxide that's responsible for the grey/blackish look of the cymbals in that phase.

At Zildjian the salt has been replaced by another solution that works the same. Sabian noticed in time that the salt didn't eat away only the tin-oxide, but also tended to devour the oven and the supporting beams of the roof. As the tin-oxide is taken away during lathing anyway, they discarded the use of salt. Only the unlathed Sabian Leopards still are treated with salt. At Istanbul such problems never occurred. Salt, after all, doesn't like stone as much as steel.

Legend has it that Aram Zildjian and his nephew Avedis III chose to establish the first Zildjian factory near the sea, because they thought that the salt sea air would benefit the quality of the secret alloy. Truth is always less romantic: they just needed salt water.

8.3.6. CIRCLE SHEARING

After tempering, the holes are drilled or punched in and cymbals are cut into the shape of circles. At Istanbul a circle is scratched on the cymbal with a steel compass. It takes two men and a lot of time to cut the cymbal. One very slowly turns a large handle while the other feeds the cymbal cautiously between two cutting wheels. This procedure demonstrates why 16" wasn't (or isn't, in some cases) always 16".

Washing the cymbals with salt water. Istanbul Photo by the author

Circle shearing of an Istanbul cymbal: Arman Tomurcuk, son of one of the presidents, on the left.
Photo by the author

8.3.7. SHAPING HAND-HAMMERED CYMBALS

At this point in the process the discs are quite flat, but they're round, they have a cup and a more-or-less finished edge. Like a cymbal, almost. The next step in organizing the vibrations is the shaping. This section describes the making of "hand-hammered" cymbals. Next sections deal with automatic and computer-controlled hammering processes (8.3.8. / 8.3.9.).

Hand-Hammering

In Istanbul the hammerers are seated on kitchen chairs, an anvil between the knees, working the cymbals completely by hand. In theory, the cymbals are hammered on the bottom side first, turning the cymbal inside-out. By working the topside afterwards the cymbal takes on its convex shape. Then the bottom side is taken care of once more. In reality, the cymbals are turned around and about all the time, in a way that seems to be completely random. They do know, however. It takes about an hour and a half to finish a 20" cymbal, says Istanbul.

...each hammerer has his own style...
Sabian
Photo by the author

...just the shape that is being controlled from time to time...
Sabian
Photo by the author

At Sabian the HH cymbals are pre-shaped by a large mechanical hammer, the so-called bumper or Quincy drop-hammer. When pre-shaping, piles of about three cymbals (depending on the size) are put on a guiding pin and turned around slowly, while letting the bumper do the work. This treatment saves the men with the hammers a lot of time. An experienced hammerer will work on a 16" crash for about fifteen minutes.

The K Zildjian cymbals are mainly hammered with the help of a smaller type of mechanical hammer, which attacks the cymbal with a few hundred beats per minute. The man at the machine guides the cymbal without any pins or anvils, just by hand and apparently at random. The resulting pattern, however, can better be described as irregular. Hammering completely "at random" would hardly result in a sellable cymbal. The cymbals are then finished with the ancient hand-held hammer. Zildjian also uses a bumper in some cases.

One company has also been using a press in the process of shaping such cymbals, guaranteeing an optimal consistency of the low profile. Other companies do not use such a press for these cymbals—because of the low profile.

Style of Hammering

Drummers will immediately notice that each hammerer has his own style of hammering, varying from a tight grip to the loose relaxed way of "playing" that drummers are supposed to be capable of. The shape of the the head of the ballpeen hammer, which is ground daily, is adapted to the hammerer.

These personal differences have no measurable influence on the final result, according to Sabian. Zildjian basically says the same: "You don't control the hammer marks. You control the shape, because that's what makes the sound."

The image of the man who hits the cymbal a few times, then changes his hammer for a stick to control the sound, is wrong. It is just the shape that is being controlled from time to time. The Zildjian and Sabian hammerers use templates for this purpose. At Istanbul they trust the naked eye.

Backbending
Courtesy of Sabian

8.3.8. SHAPING AUTOMATIC-HAMMERED CYMBALS

Shaping an A Zildjian or an AA Sabian is done in three basic steps: backbending, pressing and hammering. For backbending, small stacks of cymbals are put behind a solid rail that is attached to a workbench. Subsequently, the stack is bent backwards to an angle of about 90 degrees a couple of times, in different positions and directions.

This sort of loosens the metal. It takes the elastic deformation out, bringing it from an elastic state to a plastic state, helping the future cymbal take on the shape of the die. It would otherwise jump back to its original shape, like a spring.

Pressing is done by huge hydraulic machines, with a pressure of eighty tons per square inch. The cymbals are washed first: the smallest piece of dirt would cause disastrous effects under these circumstances. The profile that is pressed in is preliminary, except for Sabian's Jack DeJohnette series and the Zildjian Earth Ride: for these cymbals, pressing is the last major step.

Pressing the preliminary shape of a Sabian AA: eighty tons per square inch.
Courtesy of Sabian

Hammering

The automatic hammering machines push up the bow and put more tension in the metal. The A's and AA's are hammered in circles. For each type of cymbal the distance between the circles (varying from the cup to the outer edge), the distance between the hammer marks and the force of the hammer (somewhere between 1,000 and 1,500 pounds) can be adjusted.

This setting is not entirely standard per type and size. Because of small variations in the cymbals per "oven," the machines have to be set for every load, which takes a few test-cymbals each time. The same goes, by the way, for hand-hammered cymbals: the first cymbals of an oven always take more time. The hammerers have to get acquainted with the feel of the newly born discs. As the control over the preceding processes grows, such adaptations become less necessary.

The regular hammering pattern gives the A and AA cymbals not only a cleaner, faster and brighter sound. It also causes a harder playback; hand-hammered cymbals are

Automatic hammering of an
A Zildjian
Courtesy of Zildjian

If they don't press the right hardness in the right way, or if they make too many passes, the temper goes right out of the cymbal and it sounds like a piece of wet leather.
—Billy Zildjian

"softer to the touch."

In the mid-eighties Zildjian designed and built a rotary hammer, which is being used for the A and K Custom series, the latter being hand-hammered as well. This device was yet to be revealed to the public's gaze when this book was printed.

Sabian built new hammering devices too, as used for the AAX series. The importance of technical details of such machines is largely surpassed by the sheer fact that they allow for more control over the process, and thus for new types of sounds and improved consistency.

8.3.9. COMPUTER-HAMMERING

As stated before, the oldest factory in this field is using the newest equipment, wherever the character of the instrument allows it. The Z Zildjian cymbals are the only Turkish-style cymbals that are hammered by a computer-controlled machine. The advantage of such a machine is that the hammers, the patterns, the power and all other variables can be set, changed and retrieved very easily. For understandable reasons Zildjian was not prepared to go too deeply into this subject. The various shapes of the Z hammers, contrary to what has been stated before, *do* influence the final sound to some extent.

8.3.10. LATHING

Lathing looks deceivingly simple. In reality, it's easy to ruin a cymbal in this process. The friction of the spinning cymbal and the cutting tool generates so much heat that the temper of the cymbal can be lost completely.

First the bottom is lathed, moving the cutting tool in one easy motion from the cup to the edge. The oxidated outer layer disappears and the cymbal starts shining. Thinner cymbals have the tendency to warp during this process, sometimes to quite amazing degrees. Taking away material on this one side disturbs the balance in the cymbal.

Lathing the topside is done in two phases. At the first one, called roughing, the top layer of the cymbal is removed.

This procedure also puts the structure and the balance back in the cymbal. Because of the high speed and the inherent temperatures the cymbal is stiffened up to its shape. The backer of the lathing machine has the shape of the final cymbal. During the second phase the tonal grooves and the taper are created.

The stiffness and—therefore—the sound of a cymbal are largely dependant on the method of shaving. The width of the latheband, the pressure, the shape of the tool and the lathing pattern are just some of the variables.

Lathing
Courtesy of Zildjian

Shell

Slight variations in thickness of the castings can not completely be equalled out by lathing, as Sabian explains: "Cymbals that are made according to the Turkish tradition have a softer layer of material inside a harder 'shell.' Trying to compensate for thickness by lathing a cymbal a little extra would result in cutting right through, or removing, the harder outer layer. This would ruin the sound."

While shaving the outer layers off of the cymbals, possible pit dents or pit marks (small black spots, caused by dirt and/or oxidation) are effectively removed. It is also common habit to correct small spots by hammering the cymbal just a tad.

In most cases lathing is the final step. Some exceptions are Sabian's Sound Control series and their Thin Chinese models. The Sound Controls get their flange by being hammered after the first lathing. Afterwards they're lathed once more in that area. The Thin Chinese is entirely hammered and lathed twice. At Istanbul a second hammering, after the lathing process, seems to be a routine with most cymbals. Unlathed cymbals, for those who have not been paying attention, are ready after hammering.

8.3.11. BUFFING

The same machines, be they in another size, that can be admired in every shoemaker's shop are used to buff the various Brilliant series. Jewelers rouge is applied for polishing the cymbals. The aging-in process of B20 cymbals, which usually takes a couple of weeks, is reduced significantly by this process. Buffing induces temperatures that can easily demolish the temper of a cymbal.

*...thinner cymbals have the tendency to warp during lathing... Istanbul
Photo by the author*

8.3.12. FINISHING TOUCHES

In the early 1980s Zildjian started experimenting with tarnish retarding films, which were later applied to all regular-finish A and K cymbals. The extremely thin polyurethane misting disappears in the course of time. "Finding the right substance and a means to apply it without interfering with the sonic properties has been a subject of intensive studies," says Zildjian. Blindfold tests, in which Zildjian personnel tried to distinguish between finished and unfinished cymbals, were part of these studies.

While sophisticated systems may be used in one company, others have been experimenting with very basic bent pieces of steel-wire: hang the cymbal on the wire, dip it partially in a lacquer-filled basin, give it a good spin and ready you are.

The Platinum series (Zildjian) undergo another treatment. By an electrolytic process they are provided with a very thin chrome-tinted covering. No, alas, the name of the series is indeed misleading.

Sabian doesn't put a coating on their B20 cymbals. "It doesn't matter what type of coating you use, as soon as you put something on a cymbal you automatically put restrictions onto it. There are some good coatings out there, but we don't know if we'd ever go that route."

8.3.13. TRADEMARK AND LOGO

The very last step is to furnish the cymbals with their identification marks. In order to prevent cracking the cymbals by hammering the trademark in, machines have been developed that perform this procedure in a "rolling" fashion. Istanbul, some years after their start, initiated the habit of including the year of production with the trademark.

The type and series indications are put on the cymbals with ordinary stamps, with sophisticated equipment, or with techniques in between. Here again, more research is being done than one would think. Finding the right lacquer includes factors such as durability, visibility and non-muffling properties. At this point, marketing managers, accenting the first two aspects, and R&D divisions, wanting to avoid anything that might possibly affect the sound of their creations, have been known to strongly differ.

8.3.14. TIME-OUT

The entire process—from casting the bronze up to trademarking—takes about three weeks at Zildjian and Sabian. A huge part of that period is time-out for the cymbals: they get a chance to rest for a couple of days between each treatment. Heating, or more generally speaking, putting energy into the cymbal, excites the molecules. It is more effective to subject the metal to a next treatment when the energy of the previous procedure has dissipated and the molecules have come to rest.

This is a logical explanation, which can be heard at most factories in any style. It is again Istanbul that sets itself apart. The hammerers hand the cymbal over to the lathemen, sitting right next to them, as soon as they're through with their part of the job. And vice-versa, if needed. They have done so for decades—"So why change it?"

Logistics

Maybe, and this is merely conjecture, the theory behind a lot of things in factories of any kind has a very simple basis. Just think of that turkey recipe, for one. When producing huge quantities, you will simply *have* to set the half-finished products apart for a while in-between the various processes. That's a matter of logistics. If, at Istanbul, with a production of about 10,000 cymbals a year, the aforementioned theory would be applied, the workers would have to take a few days off after rolling, another three after hammering....

The difference in size of the factories involved is, of course, very notable at more than one point. The big companies have specialized top and bottom lathe-men, hammerers, and so forth. In Istanbul every man is needed when rolling, and all of them can be found in the same room during lathing and hammering.

8.3.15. TESTING

Every factory tests every cymbal before it leaves the premises. The trained ears of the testers allow for incredible speed. The starting point when testing a cymbal is the preferred sound of the factory in question. It is hard for new testers, usually drummers themselves, to put aside their own sound-preferences.

Before being submitted to the final test, the cymbals have been resting for a couple of days—at *all* companies. This may be considered as the first stage of the aging-in of the instruments. A cymbal that is still "warm" because of all the excitement in its molecular structure has little sustain and a sound that clearly hasn't opened up yet.

Zildjian

The Zildjian testers have a Standard and a Tuner cymbal of each type at their disposal. Those cymbals can be used as reference points for doubtful cases. The Tuner is closest to the Zildjian preferred sound of that type of cymbal. The Standard represents the largest permitted aberration of that sound. It doesn't need to be explained that the customer may prefer a cymbal that's closer to the Standard, assuming he would be able to spot the diminutive difference between the two.

Everything that is beyond the Standard sound is rejected—even the weird ones that you might prefer. Those are not bad cymbals, per se; they are just beyond the range. These ranges are smaller for A Custom cymbals than they are for K's, to mention two extremes. In testing, performance should be distinguished from the characteristic of the voice of the cymbal. A cymbal, therefore, should always perform as what is considered the optimum for that cymbal, in terms of its decay, its attack, its degree of high and low-end. "The human ear, however, will always be able to detect a characteristic in the voice of the cymbal that distinguishes it, however subtle that might be, from another cymbal. The consistency is in terms of the performance," adds Colin Schofield.

Sabian

At Sabian, the cymbals are tested once more just before shipment. The men who get the cymbals off their shelves literally work with a stick in their hand; usually a 5A is used for this purpose. Nylon tips are preferred because of their more revealing characteristics. Besides, they don't produce stick marks. Nort Hargrove: "If we got a problem, we always use a 5A to narrow it down. We're tuned in on that stick."

In testing it's the frequencies that may be missed that are paid most attention to: "It's not what's there I'm looking for. It's what's not there," says one of the Sabian testers.

The rumor about special or extremely well-turned out cymbals that are reserved for the endorsees is, naturally, denied at all companies. Of course, endorsees are involved in research and development programs, and thus have access to cymbals, such as prototypes, that never would have made it to the shops anyhow. As endorsees are so influential to drummers, on the other hand, they will usually not play full custom sets of cymbals that are not regularly available.

...tested once more before shipment... Courtesy of Sabian

8.4. THE SWISS/GERMAN STYLE

It was Michael Paiste who, around 1917, originated the basics of the Swiss/German way of cymbal making. This happened in Estonia, to be completely honest.[4] The cymbal industry in Europe didn't fully develop until the end of the fifties, when the Paiste Formula 602 series were introduced. In that same era Roland Meinl started hammering his first cymbals. It took another twenty odd years before UFIP, and later Sabian and Zildjian, started making cymbals in this "new" way, in addition to their traditional series.

Main Variants

It must be noted that distinguishing the Swiss/German method as one method is quite a generalization. The differences in production between Paiste and Meinl, the two main representatives, are at some points considerably larger than the similarity—the simple fact that both companies buy their discs, rather than making them themselves.

The Swiss/German method can be divided in two main variants:

1. The discs, supplied by specialized metal factories, are heated in the middle, the cup is pressed in and then the cymbals are shaped by mechanical (8.4.5.), or automatic or computer-controlled (8.4.6.) hammering devices.

2. Similar discs are shaped by a spinforming machine, which takes care of both cup and profile. The disc is mounted on a rotating backer in the shape of the future cymbal and forged into shape against this backer. Afterwards the cymbal may or may not be hammered and lathed (8.4.7.).

Shaping cymbals by pressing them could be considered a third variant. In this style, this technique is used only as a pre-shaping procedure, except for rare, very low-budget cymbals of mainly nondescript Asian and East-European origins.

Illusion

The mutual differences in sound between "identical" cymbals that were made in the Swiss/German style are smaller than they have traditionally been with cymbals of Turkish and Italian origin. One reason is the fact that the entire Swiss/German process of casting and rolling is done at a much larger scale, resulting in extremely small differences in the discs. Other procedures play their roles as well. To be complete it has to be noted that a metal consistency of 100% will be an illusion, even when this method is concerned. There will always be minimal variations in the basic material. Can they be heard? No.

8.4.1. THE ALLOYS

Traditionally, the main alloy used in this method is SnBz 8 (B8, to be short), a mixture of 92% copper and 8% bronze. This alloy was first used on a larger scale by Paiste, when they introduced the Stambul '65 and the Giant Beat series (1965).

The reason Paiste selected B8, instead of, say, B15 or any other mixture, was quite straightforward. B8 is a standard industrial alloy that is used for numerous other applications, so it was easy to obtain and relatively easy to have it produced. Of course, this production takes place according to Paiste's own specifications.

As is the case with any other composite material, its ingredients do not tell the complete story of its quality and characteristics. When metallurgy is concerned, and more specifically the production of cymbal-bronze, the quality of the material depends on the temperatures during mixing and rolling, the pressures applied, the order of mixing the ingredients, and so on. These variables influence, among others, tensile- (bending) and yield- (pull) strengths, hardness, malleability and hence the sound of the product. Therefore B8 is not always equal to B8.

Every factory in this field has, as indicated, its own patented and exclusive recipes. These recipes may differ per series: Paiste used a different recipe for their low- and medium-budget series than they do for the 3000 line.

Paiste Sound Alloy

Paiste is the only factory in this category that employs two more alloys for their professional series. Their B20, used for the Formula 602 and Sound Creation cymbals, is quite different from the "Turkish" species, as can be clearly felt and heard. For the Paiste Line (1989), also but incorrectly referred to as the Paiste Signature or Paiste *Paiste* series, a third alloy is being used. This was the first alloy ever specifically developed for the making of cymbals, according to Paiste. It was given the name Paiste Sound Alloy.

The exact ingredients of the alloy were not revealed by the company, but its basic ingredients would be, again, copper and tin. Based on the sound and the physical characteristics of the Paiste Line cymbals the assumption seems justifiable that the tin content of the Paiste Sound Alloy is considerably higher than 8%. More than 20% tin is unlikely, because such bronze would be too brittle.

Also, the color of the cymbals seems to indicate a relatively high tin content. As the color of a composite metal can be influenced by very small additions of any material this is no reliable indication. With the introduction of the new alloy, B8 may be expected to become of less importance in professional ranges in the future. Paiste's Sound Formula cymbals are made from the Paiste alloy as well.

Brass, Nickel-Silver and Others

For the production of the least expensive Swiss/German-type cymbals, brass and nickel-silver are used. Brass is a very yellowish looking mixture, containing 60% to 70% copper and 40% to 30% zinc. The name nickel-silver sounds more expensive than most of these cymbals are; the "silver" simply refers to the silverish shine of the nickel in this composite material. Besides 6% to 8% nickel it contains copper and zinc in various amounts.

These three metals are also used for Packfong, which is used for the production of professional gongs. The name Packfong is derived from the Chinese *Pait'ung*, meaning white copper.

For their short-lived Reference Class series (1989-1991) Meinl used a "custom made alloy which we developed ourselves. This alloy has a very special hardness and

The exact ingredients of the new alloy? It's strange; I've been working on it for over eight years, and now I suddenly seem to have forgotten all these figures...
—Robert Paiste

mixture," according to the company. In 1992 UFIP was experimenting with B12 for their Kashian Pro line of cymbals. Presumably, in the course of time, companies have used or will start using other variations on the aforementioned alloys.

8.4.2. CASTING AND ROLLING

"Basically, the process of making a metal plate is always the same. The materials are melted, mixed and stirred—cooked like a soup, you could say—cast in ingots of the desired size, and rolled flat afterwards," says Toomas Paiste. This goes for steel, aluminum and, yes, for bronze. One of the cymbal manufacturers in this category has his B8 bronze cast in huge square bars with a length of 35 feet (10.5 m). These bars are rolled into flat sheets of about 20 times that size.

...heated in the center...
Courtesy of Paiste

One direction

Unlike the Turkish-style process, the rolling of B8 bronze is performed in only one direction. Toomas Paiste: "Because of the lower tin content of B8, rolling in different directions has no effect on the quality of the material. B8 can also be rolled in larger quantities, and it needs less intermediate heating than B20, because it's less brittle." The Paiste Sound Alloy is, just like B20, rolled in different directions.

Out of the flat sheet, discs are cut or punched, in which form they arrive at the cymbal plant. Most factories have discs for every size made in a number of thicknesses. Usually one thickness is used for two different types: one for thin crashes and crashes, one for medium and ride types, one for power and heavy cymbals. Contrary to the Turkish-style B20 cymbals, B8 can be lathed indefinitely. According to Robert Paiste it would be possible to reduce a "power-thickness" disc to a thin crash cymbal. There are, however, more useful ways to spend the day.

8.4.3. CUPPING

For the pressing of the cup the cymbals are only heated in the center, except for the Paiste Sound Alloy cymbals that are heated entirely. After cooling down the cups are pressed in. In a few low-budget cases the pressing is done without any heating. The hole is usually produced by a punching device, rather then a drill.

8.4.4. NO PRESSING

Not one type of factory is completely free of persistent rumors. As far as the Swiss/German manufacturers are concerned, there always has been the big misconception that these cymbals are pressed into shape. At Paiste the bows of the professional cymbals are exclusively formed by hammering, Meinl states the same, yet uses a computer-controlled hammering device. Presses are not used in any of these processes, apart from those that shape the cup. Therefore, the terms "pressed" or "stamped" cymbals are wrong. The relatively flat bow of most Swiss/German-style cymbals may be explained

Punching the center hole
Courtesy of Meinl

by the fact that it would be very time-consuming to make a high profile just by hammering. Both factories have been using spinforming to (pre) shape lower priced cymbals.

Some other manufacturers do utilize hydraulic presses to provide their low and medium priced B8 cymbals with a preliminary shape. Right after this treatment the cymbals already have a more-or-less musical sound, yet with a lot of unpleasant harmonics. Hammering helps organize these frequencies.

...an irregular regularity...
Courtesy of Paiste

8.4.5. HAMMERING: MECHANICALLY AND BY HAND

The hammering machines of Paiste and UFIP are quite similar to the ones that are used for the preliminary hammering of the K Zildjian cymbals. At Paiste a hydraulically driven hammer hits the underlying cymbal, which is guided by hand, with 200 to 500 beats per minute. The power of the hammer is controlled by a footpedal. Because of the variations made possible by the guiding of the cymbal and the controllable power of the hammer, it actually is a—somewhat facilitated way of—hand-hammering.

Most, but not all Paiste cymbals and the Swiss/German-style UFIP cymbals are hammered in circular, even patterns. Naturally there will be slight differences between each cymbal that is made this way. Though Paiste always has stressed the consistency of their cymbals, they also do accent these tolerances. Robert Paiste calls it "...an irregular regularity; it's the difference between walking in a natural forest and a promenade in an artificial one, where all the trees are exactly lined up. Hammering the cymbals this way we can adapt the hammering to each individual cymbal, because no one is the same, and therefore no cymbal should be hammered exactly the same way."[5]

Guiding Pin

The Paiste hammerers have a guiding-pin attached to their thigh. The cymbals, which are completely flat before hammering (except for the cup), are laid over that pin and slowly rotated under the hammer.

There are different hammering patterns required for different types and series of cymbals. Also the power of the hammer may vary per type, or even for one specific cymbal, that needs a different depth or power of hammering on different spots. The strongly varied sounds within the Paiste Line is, among others, a result of applying very diverging hammering patterns: the Mellow types are hammered completely different from the Dry or the Power types. These series also contain types that have quite irregular patterns, which puts them in the "hand-hammered" category.

In order to develop the right feel, junior hammerers start their career making cymbals in the old-fashioned way: a hammer in one hand, the cymbal in the other. When they have mastered that art, they're allowed to start working with the machine-guided hammers.

After hammering, the cymbals are once more inspected and, if necessary, slightly corrected by hand. Drumsticks are not used in this phase. It's the right shape that counts now, not the sound. The sound will be changed considerably by subsequent lathing anyhow.

Hammering at Paiste; the mirror prevents the hammerer from being startled by sudden visitors.
Courtesy of Paiste

The discontinued Japanese Pearl 900 series were made in almost the same way as the professional Paistes. Roberto Spizzichino (Spizz) is the only manufacturer who has produced B8 cymbals that were hand-hammered the old way. This line (Spizz Three Series) was listed for a few years, around 1990.

8.4.6. HAMMERING: AUTOMATIC AND COMPUTER-CONTROLLED

The automatic hammering devices used for Zildjian's Scimitar series are identical to the machines that hammer their A's, though later a rotary hammer may have been applied. Different patterns, hammer shapes and power-settings are used for different series.

Meinl was the first factory to use a completely computer-controlled hammering machine. This device, which was first used for the Meinl Profile series (1984), has always been hidden from inquisitive eyes. It is used for most of Meinl's series, except for the spinformed lines. Due to the nature of the computer, differences between identical cymbals as a result of the hammering process are close to non-existent. This is exactly what Meinl is after.

According to Meinl they could very well produce cymbals that are "hand-hammered" by computer. They simply would have to program the machine to hammer in uneven patterns, possibly even varying the pattern per cymbal: "...but why should we? There are plenty of hand-hammered cymbals around as it is," says Reinhold Meinl.

The B8 Spizz cymbals, made by Bespeco (Italy), are entirely made by automatic machines according to processes that were developed by Roberto Spizzichino.

8.4.7. SPINFORMING
Spinforming is a technique that has been used in various industries for decades. Roland Meinl was the first manufacturer who developed a specific spinforming machine for cymbals, in the mid-sixties. Before, this technique was performed by hand. In the first half of the twentieth century a variety of spinformed or "spun" cymbals were made in the USA, available under the names of Ludwig, Davitian and others. Premier has also made such cymbals.

In one treatment
For spinforming, the flat disc is attached to a die that has the shape of the future cymbal. By pressing an oval-shaped roll, with a diameter of a couple of inches, against the rotating disc and moving the roller from the center of the disc to the outside, both cup and profile are realized in one treatment. Spinformed cymbals can be identified by a rather large groove that is caused by the edge of the pressure roll. This groove is, by its shape and size, often quite clearly discernable from regular tonal grooves.

Only the least expensive series are more-or-less ready after spinforming. The other series are subjected to hammering procedures, mostly by automatic or computer-controlled machines, and lathing. Spinforming on its own, after all, does not provide the tension in the metal that hammering does. This tension is largely responsible for the sound. In some low-budget cases, the hammering is mainly a matter of cosmetics.

At Sabian, spinformed B8 cymbals have been worked with the AA machines, using a different hammer, a different force and a different pattern. The spinformed Paiste cymbals have always been hammered by the same mechanical hammering devices as used for the professional series. This procedure also changes the profile, and "It adds life to the cymbal," according to Robert Paiste.

8.4.8. LATHING
Lathing is, except at Meinl, mostly done by hand. Micrometers are used to perform intermediate checks in thickness and taper. Unlike the thin species of Turkish-style B20 cymbals, even the thinnest of Swiss/German-style B8 cymbals do not warp when the bottom is shaved. Another difference is that lathing B8's does not alter the profile of the cymbals, as may be the case with some Turkish-style species.

Lathing section at Paiste; a third check of the cymbals takes place at this stage.
Courtesy of Paiste

The brilliant, high-polished look of Paiste's Sound Reflection and Reflector cymbals is accomplished when lathing. By using a special cutting tool the metal is given distinct light-reflecting characteristics.

Many of Paiste's professional series are hammered and shaved twice. This explains the jagged lines (tonal grooves) that can be spotted on many of their cymbals, especially on those of the Paiste Line. The grooves, resulting from the first lathing, are severely deformed by the second hammering. As with the aforementioned processes, cymbals get a chance to come to rest between the various steps.

Sponge

Meinl's Reference Class cymbals had a similar surface, which affected both the appearance and sound. No details were disclosed. The unlathed Meinl Raker cymbals are treated with a sort of sponge that closely resembles a piece of soft stone. This provides

"Pearl's unique professional cymbal sound is created thru a high heat process in their exclusive special oven."
Pearl catalog 1983
Courtesy of Pearl

the cymbals with a fine, delicate pattern. The same technique is used for some of the less expensive lathed Meinl series, giving the coarsely lathed cymbals a more refined appearance. The only cymbals that are lathed twice at Meinl are the bottoms of the Sound Wave (a la Paiste Sound Edge) hi-hats. The waves are made by a press, and lathed afterwards.

8.4.9. TEMPERING

Like Turkish-style cymbals, most Swiss/German-style cymbals are tempered. A secretive attitude usually surrounds the exact proceedings. Meinl Profile were, and Meinl Raker series are, tempered twice. Cooling the cymbals is done slowly in some cases, by just letting them sit, or fast with the help of oil, water or chemical substances in other cases. At no time are temperatures as high as in the Turkish-style process applied.

The B20 cymbals of Paiste are tempered at the beginning of the process. The temperatures are considerably lower than at Zildjian or Sabian: when the hot cymbal hits the cold liquid all you hear is a modest hiss, instead of the frightening shriek at the other companies. The tint of the Paistes changes during this process from a dullish gray into a nondescript sand-like color.

8.4.10. FINISHING TOUCHES

B8 is more sensitive to oxidation than B20. Finishing the cymbals with a protective film was already a common habit for the Swiss/German manufacturers at a time when their colleagues didn't even think about it. The way the protective layer is applied is quite similar in most cases. The cymbal is set in a spinning motion, mostly by hand, and then it is sprayed.

At Meinl the spraying booth is identifiable by the stacked containers of milk that surround it. The unhealthy volatile ingredients of the lacquer explain this. The Meinl cymbals are prepared for lacquering in a chemical cleaning bath. This results in a surface that, as pursued by Meinl only, will hold the lacquer for years.

Lacquering of Meinl cymbals
Courtesy of Meinl

Dye

Paiste uses what they call "wax", instead of lacquer. According to Paiste this film does not influence the sound of the cymbals. What, on the contrary, does muffle the sound are the colored lacquers with which Paiste caused a small but significant revolution in 1984. In order to make colored cymbals not too dull-sounding, a special series was developed that had an extra high-end boost. The main cause of the muffling effect is not the lacquer itself, but the relatively heavy dye.

Colored cymbals soon became quite rare again, as Paiste had predicted at their introduction. Besides Paiste, also UFIP, Headliner, Avanti and Vader have listed colored cymbals.

8.4.11. TESTING

The Paiste testers use so-called Master cymbals as a point of reference. The sound of the cymbals to be tested may diverge from the sound of the Master within closely defined ranges. The pitch, for instance, may differ somewhat, but most variables have to be close to identical to the Master. "Any Paiste cymbal that doesn't come in within a certain sound range of the Master cymbal is scrapped, even if it's a perfectly good sounding cymbal. It wouldn't be typical. If it's not accurate to what it should be, it won't be what the drummer expects," says consultant Fredy Studer.[6]

Paiste testers use a Master cymbal as a point of reference. Courtesy of Paiste

Larger Differences

Because of the more controlled character of the process (mainly referring to the rolling), the differences between one type of cymbal and the other are larger than in most Italian and Turkish-style series. At Paiste and Meinl there are also notable gaps between the tolerated weight of each consecutive type. Due to the broader frequency range of the Paiste Sound Alloy, differences between identical Paiste Line and Sound Formula cymbals are larger than between identical B8 cymbals.

Though Paiste knows the effect that aging might have on a Master cymbal—and this goes for other companies as well—they do not replace it from time to time. Chances are that the differences between the old and the new Master are greater than you'd ever get by aging, according to Robert Paiste.

Meinl

At Meinl, contrary to Paiste, the goal is very clearly to make a 100% identical cymbal time after time, which is aided by a large deal of automation. As little as possible is left to coincidence or, for that matter, to the human hand: "The brains are more important than the hands," according to Reinhold Meinl.

It still is men who control and set the machines, but other than that, hand work is only done when a machine wouldn't be more efficient per se, or too fast in comparison to the rest of the production. Meinl is, because of this philosophy, the only cymbal factory where the testers work without drumsticks. The final test is simply performed by weighing the cymbal. If the weight is correct, within very close margins, the cymbal is okay.

Too Self-willed

Even in the most modern factory possible, a metal consistency of 100% is idealistic. Reinhold Meinl: "Differences can appear between summer and winter: the temperature in the big plants where the metal is rolled may vary from 23°F in the winter to 100°F in mid-summer (-10°C to 40°C). This can result in differences in pitch of about 5% to each side of the desired pitch, which, by the way, is close to inaudible." Apart from that, it might be suggested that any cymbal is possibly just a little too self-willed an instrument to sound identical to any other cymbal.

According to a 1983 catalog, Pearl seems to be the only company who used "an advanced electronic sound data processor to check each cymbal for sound."

8.5. THE ITALIAN STYLE

The small Italian city Pistoia is the native region of the Etruscan art of casting and working with bronze. The Pistoian artisans, leaning on this old tradition, gained worldwide fame and recognition with their bronze church bells around the turn of this century. The step towards cymbal making has been a small one ever since.

The same material (B20) could be used, and the casting process could be more or less identical as well. Around 1910 Mr. Tronci cast and hammered the first Italian cymbals. In the years that followed a number of small factories were founded, of which a number were united in UFIP. This company, under the presidency of the aforementioned Tronci's grandson Luigi, has been the most important representative of the Italian cymbal industry, possibly with the exception of the short hey-days of Tosco.

Molds

Italian-style cymbals are the only genuinely "cast" cymbals. The liquid bronze is poured into molds that already have the preliminary shape of the future cymbal. In 1977 the Zanchi Brothers, of the former Zanki cymbal factory, introduced the rotocasting system.[7] This patented system, which will be explained later, improved the quality of the Italian cymbal considerably.

The Italian method of cymbal making is very labor-intensive, giving the process a very artisan character. This may be illustrated by the fact that the workers are generalists, rather than specialists—with the exception of the hand-hammerers. Every employee masters the entire process from casting to finishing, and each of them is fully responsible for "his" load of cymbals. As Luigi Tronci points out: "We each have two main machines down here: our right hand and our left hand."

Rotocasting; the liquid metal is poured in the mold.
Courtesy of UFIP

8.5.1. THE ALLOY

The alloy that is used by the Italians is—as far as the ingredients are concerned—identical to the bronze of the Turkish-style factories. It also contains a minimal amount of silver. The Italian recipe is not surrounded by any secrecy, as opposed to the Turkish formula. This may be accounted for by historic reasons.

First, Zanki, Tosco and Spizz originated from UFIP one way or another, so everybody just knew. Second, nobody has ever chased the Italian recipe. Some already had their own, and others preferred to use B8. Apart from that: UFIP is the only factory where you can bring your camera and register everything there is to see.

8.5.2. (ROTO)CASTING

At UFIP, the Chilean copper and the tin from Malaysia or Vietnam are mixed in a quantity of about 800 lbs (400 kilos). When the alloy is ready it is poured in double, cake-shaped castings that each contain 30 lbs (16 kilos). Before rotocasting, these cakes are melted again by heating them up to a temperature of over 1,800—F (1,000—C).

The rotocasting machines, which have interchangeable molds for the various sizes, are belt-driven. When a mold is at top speed, at about 1,000 rpm, the liquid metal is poured in through a heat-resistant filling pipe in the middle of the horizontal lid. As soon as this pipe is full, the cymbal cast is ready. This takes about twenty seconds for a 20" ride. The lid is opened and the casting can be taken out.

Centrifugal Forces

In the traditional Italian system, when the liquid metal was cast in vertically positioned, stationary molds, the alloy filled the mold just by laws of gravity. The advantage of rotocasting is that the bronze gets a denser and more homogeneous molecular structure, resulting in a better sounding and more durable cymbal. Besides, the centrifugal force pushes any dirt and metal impurities to the outside of the casting, so they will be automatically removed during lathing.

The molecular structure of the castings is quite unlike the structure of the rolled (Turkish-style) B20 castings. This partially explains the differences in sound characteristics between Italian and "Turkish" cymbals.

Preliminary Shape

Because of the fact that the casting is very porous at the outside, it has to be quite thick (about 1/10" / 2.5 mm). A casting that is too thin would never result in a smooth cymbal surface. The rotocasting system permits the castings being made a little thinner, which saves a lot of lathing-time. The old castings used to be up to 1.5 times as thick.

When the castings leave the mold they already have a cup and somewhat of a bow. The profile is raised by hammering. The castings that Roberto Spizzichino used for his former Spizz B20 cymbals were completely flat, as he preferred to press the cup. The additional tension as a result of this pressing process, he said, produced extra highs. Besides, it gave him a greater freedom in varying cup sizes.

The inventors of the rotocasting system used to come over to the UFIP plant once in a while to make their castings. These castings were then worked into Zanki cymbals at their own small factory, mostly in the same fashion as applied by UFIP.

8.5.3. TEMPERING

Just like any other cymbal of this type of bronze, the metal has to be brought into malleable state before doing anything else. It seems logical to lathe the thick castings before tempering (that would save time heating them), but the condition of the metal in this phase does not allow that. It would simply break under the cutting tools.

Tempering in UFIP's "pizza" oven
Photo by the author

Tempering is, again, quite similar to the Turkish way, the main difference being the numbers of cymbals: the 1988 UFIP oven had a maximum capacity of two castings. Before putting the castings in the oven they are prepared. With a wet bundle of straw that has been dipped in a bucket of molding sand, the cymbal is rubbed in. This archaic looking method prevents the cymbal from warping during heating.

This same oven was used to produce the bizarre colored effects on the discontinued UFIP Tiger cymbals. After hammering, the Tigers were subjected to a treatment with a grindstone and sprayed with a special lacquer. The heat of the oven colored the lacquer, especially on the grounded spots.

Spizzichino

Roberto Spizzichino, who has his discs supplied by other companies, used a few more procedures in his process. Multiple tempering is one step he mentioned. Spizzichino's 1992 Antique, Bygone Sound cymbals (discontinued) were also treated with a chemical

...big jumbles of bronze-wire...
Courtesy of UFIP

process after hammering: "This makes the cymbals harder, and at the same time it softens the sound to some extent. I do not understand why, exactly, but it happens," he explained.

8.5.4. FIRST LATHING

Because of the thickness of the castings, they have to be lathed before hammering. The top side is shaved off by hand. For the bottom side UFIP uses an automatic machine; it simply removes overabundant metal. An 18" cymbal loses over two pounds during this procedure. The resulting big jumbles of multi-colored bronze-wire that lay around are remelted and used again.

8.5.5. HAMMERING

The UFIP cymbals are hammered with the same machines that are used elsewhere. The cymbals are first subjected to a slower machine (300 bpm) that provides the cymbal with quite deep, large and very irregular hammer marks.

The second treatment involves a faster hammering device (500 bpm) with a smaller size of hammer. This machine was also used for the discontinued Ritmo series, that had a regular (A or AA like) hammering pattern.

Listening in the Future

As of 1992, all professional UFIP cymbals fit the category hand-hammered. After the initial hammering they are hammered by hand, which takes about fifteen minutes for an

Preliminary mechanical hammering at UFIP
Courtesy of UFIP

Hand-hammering at UFIP
Photo by the author

18" cymbal. Unlike his counterparts at any other factory, the hammerer at UFIP controls the sound of the cymbal in between hammering, just by playing it with a stick. Luigi Tronci: "We have always done it this way. If you'd give a cymbal in this phase to a drummer, he'd probably throw it away. The sound is far from ready now. It has to be lathed once more, and afterwards it'll need about two months to age in. Our hammerers, however, know what to listen for in this phase. They can 'listen in the future,' so to speak."

There are no presses used for shaping the cymbal or for the cup, which was already formed during casting.

Roberto Spizzichino's cymbals are entirely hand-hammered.

8.5.6. SECOND LATHING

The second lathing is done by hand. Compared to the first lathing, considerably less bronze is removed: about one pound for an 18". Contrary to what sometimes happens with the Turkish style of lathing, Italian cymbals do not warp, and the lathing does not involve any changes in the profile of the cymbal. The lower speed of the lathing machines might be the explanation.

8.5.7. FINISHING TOUCHES AND TESTING

At UFIP the cymbals are allowed a day or two off before their final hammering. To get the excited molecules to find their final position in the finished cymbal, the Italians keep each instrument for at least six weeks before shipment.

Roberto Spizzichino at lathing
Photo by Piero Principi

Considering the casting process and all the other hand work, it is logical that "identical" Italian-style cymbals will always sound different.

Up to the early '90s their sound, rather than their weight, was used to decide whether a cymbal would be stamped Crash or Thin Crash. With the introduction of the Sound Classification System (SCS), UFIP discarded these terms. Instead, each cymbal is marked with its exact weight and an indication of its sonic characteristics: Low, Medium or High.

Spizzichino's B20 cymbals, which are very rare, are the most "individual" Italian cymbals, being produced not as much in series as per piece. His instruments are based on discs supplied by other manufacturers.

The Italian cymbals do not have any protective films.

8.6. CHINESE CYMBAL MAKING

According to various sources, Wuhan, one of the largest Chinese cymbal making companies, has been in production for over 1900 years. There are two Wuhan factories, one of which has been housed in the same building since the beginning of the 19th century. Wuhan is the most prominent, but not the only manufacturer; the total number of Chinese cymbal making companies is unknown. Few Western people have ever had the chance to penetrate into one of those places and experience the ancient process.[8]

8.6.1. THE PROCESS

The production process of the Chinese cymbal has been somewhat subjected to 20th century influences, but not much has really changed. Casting and hammering a 20" cymbal may well take over a day. The hammering alone takes about three hours.

Supposedly, bronze in the classical composition of 80% copper and 20% tin (B20 again) is used. The exact ingredients and the mixing procedures are carefully kept secret. The appearance, sound and feel of Chinese cymbals justifies the assumption that the alloy is not always as pure, nor as constant of composition as other manufacturers are used to. These rather loose specifications might add up to the preferred raucous character of these instruments.

As in any similar process, the metals are melted, mixed and cast in molds. When the

...first hammering, spreading out the metal...
Wuhan factory, 1989
Photo by Paul Real, Paul Real Sales/PR Percussion

The lathing department at the Wuhan factory, 1989
Photo by Paul Real, Paul Real Sales/PR Percussion

castings are ready the endless procedure of multiple heating and hammering starts, until the desired thickness and shape are achieved.

It's not unusual if a relatively large cymbal goes in and out of the oven up to twenty times. This constant reheating is necessary because the metal is still very brittle in this phase.

Contrary to any other manufacturer, the Chinese temper their cymbals after hammering. In the Wuhan factory a machine hammer was later being used for the first hammering, spreading out the metal. After the casting has been hammered flat and to the desired thickness, the tuning and the shaping of the profile, the cup and the flange is done by hand.

Crust

Besides the hammering machines, the Wuhan company uses very simple presses and lathes. Lathing in China is more like scraping off the crust, formed by the multiple heating. The tonal grooves of Chinese cymbals, if any, are considerably shallower than those of other types of cymbal. Presumably lathes are also used to finish the cups, which are more even in thickness than they used to be. This can be seen by looking at the edge of the hole.

The fact that the hole of a Chinese cymbal is not always exactly in the center of the cymbal, and that the edges are not as neatly finished as with Western cymbals has to be accepted as is. Appearance does not have a high priority in the Chinese philosophy of cymbal making. Of course, the quality of the products differs per company.

After tempering, the cymbals are given a final precision tuning. The ideas about the ideal sound are quite different from what Western ears used to, and so are the testing procedures. The Master Inspector, at the end of the line, rejects about 40% of the cymbals, a rate that would put any Western factory out of business within a month.

In addition to being sold under their own name, authentic Chinese cymbals are marketed by various Western companies under different names. Up to 1989 Meinl imported such cymbals under the Dragon and Cobra names, both Chinese and Turkish types. Slightly warped cymbals were corrected by hammering them.

If a cymbal would take more than, say, twenty beats to get it straight, it got a one-way ticket to the garbage can. Other processes have also been applied to these cymbals.

8.7. CYMBAL MAKING B.E. (Before Electricity)

When lining up the sparse information about production techniques in the old days, two things can be noted. First, it becomes clear that a considerable number of techniques are still being performed in more or less the same way. Especially casting and hammering are—basically—the same as they were thousands of years ago. The main difference is that things are much more controlled than they used to be.

Second, and more interesting, it shows that the possibility of adapting the technique in order to obtain a certain effect or sound is quite new. Up till a few decades ago cymbal makers were governed by all kinds of technical limitations. A low-profile cymbal was not made because they preferred that type of sound, but simply because they were not able to make a high profile in an acceptable amount of time. Evidently, things have changed significantly.

8.7.1. ANCIENT TIMES

Metallurgists have performed in-depth research to find out how people were able to make relatively high-grade alloys 3,500 years ago. It is a known fact that they mastered this art perfectly, which goes for the working of the metal also.

Exactly how they did it will probably never be revealed, but a few things are at least suspected. Thicker cymbals and such instruments were cast in sand-molds, in a fashion that is comparable to the way church bells and Icebells are still being made.

From various archaeological discoveries it can be deduced that early cymbalsmiths knew how to make thin cymbals as well. Lathes were also used quite early in history. On a pair of small bronze cymbals, originating from Greece and about 2,500 years of age, grooves were discovered.[9] Whether or not they had a tonal purpose as well is not known.

8.7.2. TURKEY

The way cymbals are made in Istanbul today is reminiscent of the methods that were applied in the old K Zildjian days; the wooden logs, the charcoal, the stone oven, the hammering. However, a few things must have changed. How, for instance, were the rolling mills and the lathes driven in times in which engines did not exist? As documentation is less than sparse, oral traditions have to be relied upon.

Kerope Zilcan (1914), who worked in the old K factory for some years and got involved with Sabian later on, knows these traditions. Lathes and mills, according to what Kerope has been told, were set in motion by a treadmill: basically a wheel with large spokes, which was rotated by walking around the axle, pushing the spokes. Up until about 1880 the required energy was furnished by men.

Kill

Apart from the not-so-inspiring character of this kind of work, the management of the ancient company was often confronted with yet another problem. The men in question also represented the local fire brigade. Whenever they were called upon this duty, the entire factory was paralyzed. Kerope Zilcan: "One day, when the workers got back after extinguishing a fire, they saw this donkey. As I am told, they got mad; they thought they lost their jobs. 'Kerope Effendi!' they shouted to my grandfather, 'You have taken away our jobs. We kill you!' Kerope Zildjian[10] then replied: 'No, I have given the work of the donkey to the donkey, and I will give the work of the men to the men.' Why they didn't think of using donkeys before? Well, I guess it just didn't cross their minds."[11]

Eventually, gasoline engines were introduced. It was not until 1915 that the first electrical engines were installed.

The cylinders of the rolling mills were originally made of stone. The steel cylinders, which followed later, were driven by 4" wide leather belts up till the late 1930s.

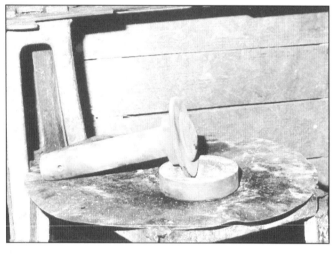

Dies to shape the cups in the pre-press era
Istanbul
Photo by the author

Cupping

A machine to press the cups in was an invention of later date also. Before that time a concave die, in the shape of the future cup, was used. A stack of cymbals was heated and laid on the die face down. The cup was then shaped with huge convex sledge hammers, or using a convex counterpart of the die.

Often this was done by three men: two hammerers, and one to rotate the stack of cymbals. It's no wonder the cups used to differ in size and shape considerably in those days; they could be shallow or deep, depending on their position in the stack. Periodically, this uncontrollable process resulted in crooked cups as well, and sometimes the hole seems to be drilled off-center, in an attempt to compensate.

Telephone-wire

Thermostats were, in those days, unheard of. The temperature in the wood-fire ovens couldn't be measured, let alone controlled. Another explanation for the limited consistency of sound of the old Turkish cymbals was the fact that there were no sophisticated ways to control the exact composition of the metal. Impure copper, tin or both were sometimes used.

In times of scarcity—the Turkish government had their share of problems and also caused a few now and then—the Zildjian cymbalsmiths had to settle with almost anything that was "acceptable." The purchase of a few hundred miles of telephone cable, made out of silver-bearing copper, is just one illustration.[12]

Progress

The basic method used to mix and melt the alloy has not changed since 1623, except for minimal refinements in the melting room, around 1935. Improved technology of the past decades now takes care of an absolutely constant quality of bronze, and that alone makes for a world of difference with the old K cymbals.

Another, seemingly minor, improvement was the upgrading of the quality of the cutting tools. Older cymbals have considerably shallower tonal grooves, not because people preferred them that way, but simply because the tools weren't able to cut any deeper. Again, this is an example of changes of sound due to technological progress, apart from any philosophy.

One thing is perfectly clear: "the" old K does not exist. In the old days, dimensions, material, treatments and other variables were subjected to many unreliable influences, and so, as a result, was the sound.

8.7.3. GERMANY and SWITZERLAND.

There are no exact records of the material Michael Paiste used for his first cymbals, early this century. Probably the alloy was close to B8. After World War II a mixture of copper, tin and 6% to 8% nickel was being used.

For lack of any machines or other devices, the entire cymbal used to be hammered by hand. To shape the cups a wooden die was used. The center of the cymbal was heated and worked with sledge hammers.

In the beginning, Paiste had to work without electricity as well. For driving the lathes a system was used that could best be compared to old-fashioned sewing machines: a flat board set in a rocking motion by the feet, driving the lathe via a number of connecting rods and a wheel. Around 1954 Paiste had their first mechanical hammering machine.

Spinforming

In the late forties Paiste made a series of spinformed cymbals, which were only sold in Germany. The flat disc was mounted on a rotating mold and forced into shape with lots of human power and a pole to which a small roller was attached. The worker wore a leather harness that was attached to a spot near the mold: leaning heavily into this harness produced more force at the other end. There may very well be a few small factories left in Eastern Europe where very low-budget cymbals are still being made that way.

Roland Meinl used this process from the first day he started making cymbals, in the early fifties. He ordered his metal sheets, collected them at the railway station by bike, and cut them in circles with an oversized pair of tin-snips. Some twenty years later he introduced the first computer-controlled hammering device in cymbal making. That was amazingly fast progress compared to the time it took Turkish cymbal makers to go from men- to mule-power.

8.7.4. ITALY

In Italy cymbals have always been cast, comparable to the way church bells were made. After the introduction of the mechanical-hammering device one more important development was to come: rotocasting (1977).

Lathing in the old days
Courtesy of UFIP

UFIP: tempering in the old days.
Note the wooden logs in the background
Courtesy of UFIP

Before rotocasting, the liquid bronze had to find its way into the vertically positioned molds by sheer gravity. This required very high temperatures, which were realized by wood and coal. The scorched walls of the casting room in Pistoia are the silent reminders of that period.

"It's impossible to make anyone understand how awful and tedious casting used to be in those days," Luigi Tronci of UFIP says. "During casting a working day lasted only four hours. Any longer would have been plain murder. The room temperature could easily rise to about 160°F (70°C)."

Covering the liquid bronze with a layer of charcoal was an attempt to prevent some of the air pollution, but this system wasn't perfect. "There was so much dust and smoke that you couldn't see your hands in front of your face," adds Tronci. Besides, the charcoal left unwanted residues in the bronze, resulting in a high reject rate.

An additional problem was the fact that the molds had to be opened at temperatures of about 750°F (400°C), by hand. Besides the rotocasting system, the introduction of gas-heated systems led to improved conditions for Italian cymbal makers.

Notes:
1   Story by Toomas Paiste.
2   The Armenian suffix "-ian", as Zinjian, Zenjian, Alejian, Kashian; Zildji- as in Zildjiaram and Zildji Vram;
    The city or the country, as in Stambul, Stanople, Super Constantinople, Istanbul and Krut (Turk, spelled backwards); various other names such as Zyn, Zymbor and Zilco.
    The Turkish legacy is also kept high in Amir, Scimitar (Turkish sword), Vezir, Ottoman, Sultan, and Turk (See Chapter 9).
3   "Manufacturing Secrecy: The Dueling Cymbal makers of North-America," by David H. Shayt, IA, *Journal of the Society for Industrial Archeology*, Volume 15: Number 1, Washington, D.C., 1989. Also published in *Percussive Notes*, October 1991. The quote that is referred to in this article is derived from "In Crashing World of Clang and Bang, Zildjian is the Cymbal of Excellence," by Peter Gorner, *Chicago Tribune*, May 18, 1983.
4   Estonia, south of the Finish Bay, alternately has been an independent country and part of the former Soviet Union. As of 1991 it is independent.
5   Interview by the author.
6   "A Visit to the Paiste Factory," by Simon Goodwin, *Modern Drummer*, vol. 9, no. 11, Modern Drummer Publications, Inc., New Jersey, USA, 1985. The same issue contains "Inside Paiste," by Robyn Flans.
7   Early 1992 the Zanki factory was closed. Two of the Zanchi brothers started working for UFIP (see Chapter 9).
8   The contents in this section was compiled from an article and stories of people who have visited the Wuhan company:
    - "Wuhan Gongs & Cymbals: Maintaining an Ancient Tradition," by Bruce Howard, *Modern Drummer*, vol. 6, no. 2, Modern Drummer Publications, Inc., New Jersey, USA, 1982;
    - information supplied by Paul Real of Paul Real Sales/PR Percussion, American distributor of Wuhan cymbals;
    - information supplied by Michael Ranta of Asian Sounds, Cologne, Germany.
9   *Percussion Instruments and Their History*, by James Blades, Faber and Faber Ltd., London, England, 1975. Revised and updated 4th edition: Bold Strummer Ltd., Westport, CT, USA, 1992.
10 Kerope Zildjian was president of the Zildjian Company from 1865 up to his death in c1909 (see Chapter 9).
11 Interview by the author.
12 "Inside Sabian," by Chip Stern, *Modern Drummer* vol. 7, no 11, Modern Drummer Publications, Inc., New Jersey, USA, 1983.

9. THE COMPANIES

The histories of the various cymbal making companies are quite diverse. Their philosophies may be as various, or as coinciding. At one point they are—with minor exceptions—all alike: every manufacturer accentuates the importance of making only cymbals that are "creating the possibility to express all your musical feelings," "cymbals that drummers want to use," and, last but not least, "cymbals that are meaningful." The end result of their efforts luckily shows a lot more variation.

Every manufacturer tries to make identifiable cymbals, cymbals that can be recognized as theirs. It may be considered a compliment to the individuality of drummers that there is not any other instrument being produced in such a variety of sizes, types, weights and sounds.

The histories and philosophies of the cymbal-making companies are the subjects of the first sections of this chapter. Each of these stories is completed with information on the products of the company, both from the present and the past, both under their own and other names. The second series of sections deals with the companies that have ceased to exist. In the last section some cymbal brands that were—or are—made by other companies are briefly depicted.

In most cases, dates and origins of series and brands have been mentioned, giving this chapter the additional value of an extensive guide or reference.

9.1. THE ZILDJIAN FAMILY

The history of the Zildjian family, having its specific character and length, is dealt with separately from the Avedis Zildjian Company (9.2.). The story has been published before in various magazines and books. These sources do not always coincide. In such cases both sides of the story have been mentioned, making the picture more complete than it has ever been before. As this is not a scientific historical book, no attempts have been made to prove which story is right; besides, they rather add than contradict.

Especially the resourceful publications of Chip Stern, *Inside Sabian*,[1] and Dr. Pars Tuğlacı, *Turkish Bands of Past and Present*,[2] should be mentioned; they were of great help.

All available information was brought together and combined with interviews with Armand Zildjian and two descendants of Kerope ("K") Zildjian. The quotes that are not accounted for in the footnotes are derived from interviews by the author. The extensions (I, II, etc.) refer back to the indispensable family tree that was made out of the sum total of—again, not always coinciding—information. Within this context the family tree is more a point of reference than a historically founded statement. In the past, a Zildjian Family Bible seems to have existed, but it has been lost. Years of birth and decease may, in some cases, differ.

9.1.1. THE EARLY DAYS

Almost every story about the Zildjian family starts off in 1623. In that year an Armenian alchemist named Avedis found a special way to mix eight parts of copper and two parts of tin into a bronze alloy for cymbal making. There's also a tale saying that Avedis was working on making artificial gold. The bronze, however, proved to be at least as profitable, and definitely more realistic. The way Avedis mixed and melted his alloy meant a large improvement. It sounded better and wasn't as brittle as bronze had been prior to that time. The same ingredients, after all, had been used for ages to make bells and other instruments. The thickness of such instruments and the way they were worked did allow for a brittle alloy, contrary to the requirements of a thinner cymbal.

Avedis won a lot of respect because of the quality of his cymbals. It gained him the

Armenian name *Zilciyan*, literally meaning Family or Son of Cymbalsmiths or -makers (*Zil* is "cymbal" or "bell", *ci* is "maker", *yan* is "family" or "son of"). The name, under Western influences, eventually altered to Zildjian.

A Small Proportion of Gold

According to Pars Tuğlacı, the family's cymbal-making history even starts one generation earlier: Avedis I's father, Kerope I, already made cymbals. He had migrated from the Black Sea Coast to Istanbul (then called Constantinople), where he worked as Chief Cauldron Maker for the Ottoman Palace. He started making cymbals later on. In the year 1623 he established the first Turkish Cymbal Factory, in the Constantinople quarter Samatya.

This quarter, in the European part of Istanbul, still bears that name. "In the garden of their workshop in Irekli Street there was a dungeon of 3 square meters, with iron doors and windows. Here, hidden from all eyes, the three sons who knew the secret formula would prepare the alloy...."[2]

Kerope, according to Tuğlacı, died at the age of 96. Avedis then took over "and developed his father's techniques even further. He discovered an alloy of tin, copper and a small proportion of gold." The gold, as is generally assumed, is merely mentioned to heighten the mystic aspects of the story. The names of Avedis' two brothers are not disclosed.

Avedis II

Little or nothing is known about Avedis' earliest descendants. Chip Stern's extensive research on the Zildjian genealogy picks up in the in the early 19th century, necessarily

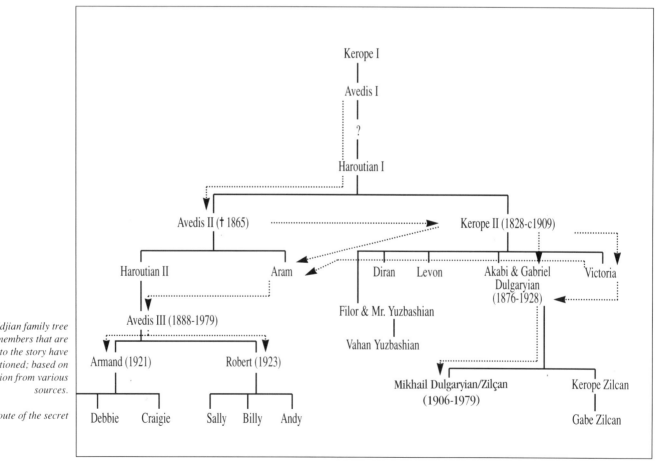

Chart 1. Zildjian family tree Only family-members that are relevant to the story have been mentioned; based on information from various sources.

············▶ *route of the secret*

skipping some generations.[1] At that time Haroutian I (in Armenian: *Hodja Artin*), is given the secret by his father. As tradition dictated, Haroutian passes it on to his oldest son, Avedis II, great-grandfather of Armand and Robert Zildjian.

According to Zildjian[3] and other sources, it was this Avedis who devoted a lot of energy to familiarizing the world with his "Turkish" cymbals. In 1851 he built his own schooner and sailed his cymbals to Industrial Exhibitions throughout Europe, gathering numerous decorations and awards at the London and Paris fairs that same year, and again in London in 1862.

From this time on the instruments of the company were refered to as Zildjian cymbals, instead of merely as "Turkish" cymbals.

Avedis II's children, Haroutian II and Aram, were not old enough to continue the family business at the time of his death (1865), so his younger brother Kerope II was next in line.

Avedis II
Courtesy of Zildjian

Kerope II

According to Pars Tuğlacı it was Kerope (1829-c1909) who made the rewarding journeys: He "was the most accomplished craftsman of this talented family. His cymbals surpassed any made in Europe in resonance, thinness and durability. In the second half of the nineteenth century Kerope Effendi made several journeys to Europe.... He participated in exhibitions in Europe's major centers of culture and trade, winning ten decorations and medals, and as many certificates of commendation."[2]

Tuğlacı mentions the same cities and years as Zildjian does, and adds Vienna (1873), Boston (1883), Bologna (1888, 1907 Grand Prize) and Chicago (1893). These cities are also featured in several Zildjian publications, and one of Zildjian's medals originates from the Worlds Columbian Exposition in 1893.

According to "The Avedis Zildjian Story," however, Kerope had "managed the business competently but without the imagination that his brother had shown. He continued to enter cymbals in appropriate exhibitions but did not make personal trips to stimulate business as his brother had done. He was more content to fill orders as they came in."[3]

Tuğlacı does not speak of Avedis II at all, contradictory to Chip Stern,[1] Zildjian, Armand Zildjian—his great-grandson!—and others. His book, though, contains some names that are not disclosed elsewhere. One of them is a third Haroutian.

Haroutian

Research in the Turkish Treasury Archives revealed to Tuğlacı that Kerope also had a brother by the name of Haroutian who was head of the family. At some point in history a number of fires had brought the family close to bankruptcy; they had debts to the Treasury and couldn't afford to buy copper and tin anymore.

A possibility to move the entire industry to Paris, France, was rejected, as the Zildjians preferred to stay in their native country. A settlement was then arranged to "pay their debts under specific terms," as the Sultan had "ordered that everything necessary be done to help the Zildjian family ."(1868)[2]

Karekin

Another story that should not remain unmentioned is the "often re-told, faintly alchemical saga" of Karekin Zildjian. "Outside the direct line of inheritance, this Zildjian stole away to

Mexico City in 1907 to set up his own cymbal foundry. His experiments ended abruptly in an explosion that tore his head off and 'encased his body in molten bronze.'"[4]

K. Zildjian & Cie.

Kerope was in charge of the company, then called K. Zildjian & Cie, from 1865 to his death in c1909. In the book *Music, Musician and Musical Instruments* (1869), it says: "Assisted by his brothers, the cymbal maker Kerope Effendi receives export orders from Europe for 1300-1500 pairs per year.... Recently experiments have been undertaken in Istanbul for the manufacture of other metal musical instruments.... Mastercraftsman Ali Baba has sent us some examples of these copper instruments, but although they are of encouragingly high quality, they are nevertheless incomparable to their equivalents in Europe. There is no doubt that the second best cymbal maker after the Turkish cymbal maker Kerope is M. Gautrot. Although M. Grapkin of Osker comes third, the sound produced by his cymbals is only average."[5]

It may be safely assumed, whether Kerope was or was not as inspired as his brother, that it was he who gave his initial to the original K Zildjian cymbals.

Kerope Zildjian II with his wife, their sons Diran and Levon, and daughters
Courtesy of Dr. Pars Tuğlacı, Istanbul

Kerope's Children

Gabe Zilcan (Sabian), great-grandson of Kerope, says that Kerope had twelve children; ten daughters and two sons. Victoria, the oldest daughter, was one of the few women ever in possession of the secret and in charge of the company.

"One of the other daughters, Akabi Zildjian, married Gabriel Dulgaryian, who also ran the company for some time. Their oldest son, my uncle Mikhail, took over in the 1920s. Filor Zildjian, a third daughter, was married to a Mr. Yusbashian. Their son Vahan cooperated in the company as well."

Presumably it was Victoria who passed the secret to the Dulgaryian family.

The contribution to the company of Kerope's sons, Diran and Levon, has allegedly not been of great importance.[2]

Not by Zildjians

As the American Zildjian company has regularly stated in older catalogs, from that moment on the Avedis Zildjian cymbals are "The only cymbals made anywhere in the world by Zildjians and their 300-year-old process." The K Zildjian cymbals of that time, after all, are made by people who also know and use the process, but who, being married into the family, do not bear the Zildjian name.

Two Places

It was the first time that the "formula" could be found on two places: Aram Zildjian, son of Avedis II, also got the secret. It was given to him either by Kerope or by his niece Victoria Zildjian, presumably around 1909. This eventually led to the situation where the descendants of Kerope II ran the old company in Istanbul, while the descendants of Avedis II, through Aram, started a new company in the USA. In the late seventies the descendants would be united again, be it for a very short time.

Aram Zildjian

Aram's older brother, Haroutian Zildjian, was offered the secret, too. Being a successful district attorney, he let it pass. "No wonder," says Armand Zildjian about his grandfather. "You couldn't expect anyone to make a living out of making cymbals in those days. If you got an order it was a dozen pairs. So you went out and bought the copper and the tin, you hired the same guys that helped you two months ago, and you opened the doors and made the cymbals. Aram, on the other hand, always wanted to make cymbals. He always felt that he was the real Zildjian, because of his last name."

Aram Zildjian, in the first decade of the century, was involved in severe conflicts between the Armenians and the Turkish, as an activist in the Armenian underground. After an attempted murder of the Sultan he had to run, or, as another story tells, he was exiled.

In Bucharest, Rumania, he started making cymbals, presumably under the name Zildjiaram. After some time he returned to Turkey and continued his work in the old factory. In the late 1920s Aram travelled to America to bring the secret to Avedis III, thus initiating the Avedis Zildjian Company (see 9.2.).

9.1.2. DULGARYIAN - ZILCAN

Mikhail Dulgaryian (1906-1978), son of Akabi Zildjian and Gabriel Dulgaryian, took over from his father in his early twenties. Gabe Zilcan, Mikhail's nephew: "He handled the business after Aram left Rumania to start the American factory."

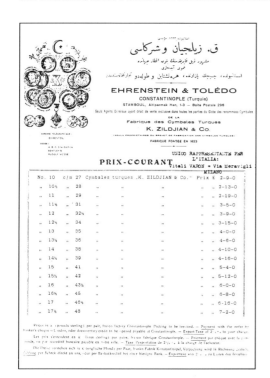

Price list of K. Zildjian & Co. Date unknown; presumably prior to the 1940's
Collection UFIP

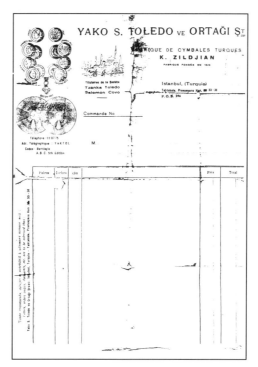

Order form of Fabrique de Cymbales Turques K. Zildian.
The caption says: Yako S. Toledo and Partners Company.
Collection Zilciler Kollektif Sirketi (Istanbul)

According to Robert Zildjian, Mikhail, at one time, followed Aram to Bucharest, where he stayed until "...he got bonkers, tore up the foundry, wrecked the machinery and returned to Istanbul, where the day-to-day management was being handled by Yako S. Toledo, a partner in an export firm."[1]

A receipt and a price list (dates unknown) show that Toledo played a main role in the company; his name is in the caption, in one case together with the name of one

The crew of the Turkish Zildjian factory in 1965. Mikhail Zilçan is seated on the far right. First from left is Mehmet Tamdeger, later manufacturer of Istanbul cymbals. Collection Zilciler Kollektif Sirketi (Istanbul)

Mr. Ehrenstein. Toledo's son in law, Salomon Covo, is listed on the receipt as a partner in the company.

Zilçan-Zilcan

Gabe Zilcan's family relationship to Mikhail Dulgaryian should normally have given him the same family name. Kerope Zilcan, father of Gabe and brother of Mikhail, sheds some light on this part of history.

In 1935 the Turkish government forbid any names with the Armenian extension "ian." Mikhail Dulgaryian cleverly used this event to change his name to *Zilçan,* meaning Bell *(çan)* of the Cymbal. In Turkish, this is pronounced nearly the same way as Zildjian (Zilch-ian). Because in the American alphabet the letter "ç" doesn't exist, it is later changed to Zilcan.

The End-the Beginning

In the 1940s the company was saved from bankruptcy by Salomon Covo. Covo then became the owner and general manager.[1] Some three decades later, having gained back all Zildjian trademarks, the Avedis Zildjian company closed down the Istanbul factory.

Gabe and Kerope Zilcan at Sabian, 1988
photo by the author

This happened around the time Mikhail Dulgaryian/Zilçan passed away, in 1978, according to Gabe Zilcan.

Kerope Zilcan cooperated in the Istanbul factory, yet only in the last ten years of its existence. "Our grandfather was of the opinion that there should be only one brother working in the factory at a time," Kerope Zilcan says. "I started working there in 1968, when I was 54 years of age. Before, I worked for a textile-paint company, right across the street. I never hammered cymbals, by the way, and I never had the secret. I worked with my eyes, not with my hands."

Kerope Zilcan went to Meductic in 1975, seven years after the Avedis Zildjian Company had established a second plant there (Azco Ltd., see 9.2.1.). His son Gabe followed him in 1977. A few years later Robert Zildjian established Sabian in that same plant. Kerope mainly worked for Sabian as a consultant (Sabian, see 9.3.).

Two former employees of the Turkish factory, Mehmet Tamdeger and Agop Tomurcuk, started their own company in 1981 (Istanbul, see 9.4.).

9.2. AVEDIS ZILDJIAN COMPANY: THE INCEPTION

In 1908 Avedis III, Aram's nephew, migrated to the USA, not having any intention to start making cymbals. Being Armenian, Turkey was not the quietest country to live in, and Avedis definitely didn't want to join the army.[1] Armand Zildjian: "When my father came to America he was something like 17 or 18. He first worked for a big candymaker, Segalian—whose nephew he had escorted—for a while. Later he started his own candy factory. The Armenians were big candymen in Boston at that time."

The Letter

In 1928 or 1929 Aram Zildjian, failing in health, wrote a letter to Avedis III. He notified him that he was to come back to Turkey and take over the Zildjian legacy. Avedis, doing well in candy making, was reluctant. Armand Zildjian: "At first he said: 'Jesus, that's a romantic story. You couldn't make a living of it.' It was my mother who inspired him to try it anyhow." After all, jazz was developing at their doorstep, and a large demand could be expected.

So Aram came to America and taught Avedis, who had once worked in the old factory at age 12, the art of cymbal making. "In 1929, right in the heart of the depression, they rented this garage, full of old taxi cabs. It was worse than the Istanbul factory when I saw it around 1957," laughs Armand Zildjian. This is when the Avedis Zildjian Co. is established.

9.2.1. THE FIRST CYMBALS

The first Avedis Zildjian cymbals were made in 1929, in a small plant at 39 Fayette Street, Norfolk Downs, Massachusetts. According to Aram's wishes, this plant was a close imitation of the one in Istanbul, also fashioned around a dirt floor. It was located near the sea, not necessarily because of the possibly beneficial influence of salt air, but simply because of the fact that salt water was needed for the production process.

"From the beginning, when Aram still was around and I was a kid, I remember the way they made cymbals back then. If they made half a dozen a day, it was a big number," Armand Zildjian (1921) recalls. Avedis had, in the meantime, hired three employees: a man who had worked in his candy factory and two recently immigrated metal craftsmen.[3]

The first American Zildjians, c1930. Aram is seated second from left, Avedis Zildjian III is seated third from left.
Courtesy of Zildjian

Name Drummers

Ten years later the original plant was destroyed by a fire. Avedis II built a new factory in North Quincy, Massachusetts. Not hindered by the conventional ideas of his uncle he created a more modern setup. The progress of the company was tremendously aided by the fact that jazz was developing fast.

Since its earliest days the Avedis Zildjian Co. was helped and advised by name drummers. Armand Zildjian remembers Gene Krupa coming by: "He said, 'We could

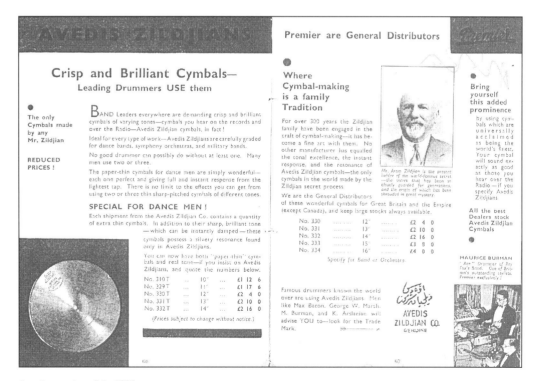

Premier catalog of the 1930s
Courtesy of Premier

use the cymbals you're making, but they're too heavy. Can't you make thinner ones?' So my father made thinner cymbals, and that originated the Paper Thin. And all the categories, the words Ride, Bounce, Swish—all those words came from terminology of Avedis Zildjian. Gene Krupa, Papa Jo Jones, Buddy Rich, Cliff Leeman... They were all wild about these thinner cymbals."

In earlier days drummers such as Chick Webb, Big Sid Catlett and many others also consulted the new factory. Avedis, being at the right place at the right time, easily overcame the initial mistrust against American-made cymbals.

Azco

In 1968 the company needed to expand. A site in Meductic, New Brunswick, Canada, was chosen, giving Zildjian a better access to the Commonwealth market. It was named Azco Ltd. Basically the idea was cast and roll in the Zildjian factory, and to finish the cymbals in Canada. "After closing the K factory in Istanbul, it was decided to bring the guys from Turkey to the Azco factory in Canada, and to produce the K's up there," Robert Zildjian recalls.[1] For some time in the 1970s a series of "Canadian K's" had been hammered and lathed at Azco.

After many decades, the descendants of Kerope II, now bearing the name Zilcan, were united again with Avedis II's offspring. Not for long, however. In 1979 Avedis III passed away, having given the secret both to Armand Zildjian and Robert Zildjian, his sons. As had happened before, the secret being in more than one pair of hands, trouble began.

After more than two years of negotiations, the brothers split up. Armand Zildjian gets all Zildjian trademarks and continues the Avedis Zildjian Company. In 1988 the company is officially recognized as America's oldest firm, being 365 years of age.

9.2.2. AVEDIS ZILDJIAN: THE COMPANY

In 1986 the Avedis Zildjian Company employed about 90 people worldwide, 45 working in the factory in Norwell, Massachusetts. This plant was established in 1972. Still respecting all traditions of the ancient way of making cymbals, it's the most modern factory of its (originally Turkish) kind. "Everybody remembers how Art Blakey, Mel Lewis, Elvin Jones and many others used to go down to Gretsch to select their old K cymbals: if they had one good one out of ten they were thrilled to death. Yes, the process of making them was the same, but it wasn't brought to modern technology standards," says Armand Zildjian, the only drummer amongst the cymbal presidents of the era.

Armand plays a main role in guarding the "Zildjian sound." Being closely involved in R&D activities and not being afraid of new experiments he will, more than once, use old Zildjian cymbals as point of reference—no matter how much the sound of a new series may deviate from what has been done before.

A Cleaner Operation

Apart from the Sound Lab, where new series and cymbals are being developed, there is constant activity in the area of developing new machinery. The basic idea is not to make a better cymbal—"We can only make different cymbals, not better ones." The intention is to improve consistency, to diminish the reject rate and to make the process less labor-intensive, while maintaining the quality and character of sound of each series and the individuality of each cymbal.

When Armand and Robert Zildjian parted ways, there were all kinds of predictions: Sabian would never have a chance against Zildjian; Zildjian would be severely crippled by Sabian; Sabian and Zildjian would split the Zildjian market to the point that neither company would be able to survive and Paiste would become the dominant force; Zildjian and Sabian together would blow Paiste off the map. Ten years later, all three companies had expanded. No one predicted what ultimately happened. Drummers simply bought more cymbals because there were more good cymbals to buy.
—Rick Mattingly

Armand Zildjian
Photo by the author

Compared to the old days of cymbal making a lot has changed at the Zildjian factory. Computers control the temperatures in the new rotary ovens, spec-sheets improve control over the process, automatic pad printers take care of the logos; modern equipment is being used throughout, and in the 1990s the ancient process has become a much cleaner operation. Yet, "We don't change the craftsmanship so much that it's no longer a handmade cymbal," says Charlie Yanizzi.

The two last names to be added to the huge list of Zildjians are the Armand Zildjian's daughters, Debbie and Craigie Zildjian. Both of them are directors of the company, involved in production and administration respectively. Armand's son, Rab, worked for the company during the early eighties, but eventually left to pursue other interests.

The Avedis Zildjian company in Norwell, Mass.
Courtesy of Zildjian

9.2.3. ZILDJIAN PRODUCTS

A lot has also changed when it comes to the cymbals. The A (for Avedis) Zildjian line gives a striking example of developments over the years past. In 1932 a Premier/Zildjian price list showed an 8" Sting, 10" to 14" Thin, 14" and 15" Heavy and 11" Special Hi-hat cymbals.

Fifty years later the A series encompasses 25 different models, each in one to eight sizes, available in regular, Brilliant or Platinum (1986) finishes. Next there are the hand-hammered K's, the computer-hammered Z series, the K and A Customs and two lines of B8 Scimitar cymbals.

8" Zildjian Sting, 1937 Premier catalog
Collection Classic Drum Museum, England

Bread and Butter

The A series, according to Armand Zildjian "the bread and butter of the cymbal game," are used in every style of music. Next to the huge increase of available types, existing models have also been adapted to changes in musical demands from time to time.

The all-American hand-hammered K's (1981), originally developed for jazz players, have also found their way into the realms of fusion and rock as a result of changing fashions, but also because of their updated character.

A specialty model within this series is the Pre-Aged Dry Light Ride, an extremely light cymbal that is processed to sound a lot older than it is (1991). In 1992 the name Avedis was added to the Zildjian logo on all A cymbals, and the words Brilliant and Platinum were added to the relevant versions.

Z series

The Z series (1986), the first Turkish-style cymbals to be hammered by a computer-controlled device, feature special hammer shapes and patterns that influence the sound of these unlathed cymbals. The concave hammermarks (Open Penta and Five Point Star) change the metal more dramatically than the convex marks (Closed Hex and Six Point Star); they make the cymbal thinner and denser at that spot, resulting in a faster response.

The Open Penta and the Five Point Star are used for rides and flanged cymbals (Power Smash, China Boy) respectively. Z's weigh about 50% more than comparable A's. The Z Mega Bell Ride is the first cymbal with a cup three times the size of a regular cup. Unlike the K and the A, the Z doesn't stand for anything on its own.

The first factory cross-matched hi-hats are a combination of the most traditional and the most contemporary Zildjian cymbals: a K on top and a Z on the bottom.

Avedis Zildjian series: 25 models, in 1 to 8 sizes, in regular, Brilliant and Platinum finishes (1992)
Courtesy of Zildjian

...new machinery and old style lathing patterns...
A Custom swishes
Courtesy of Zildjian

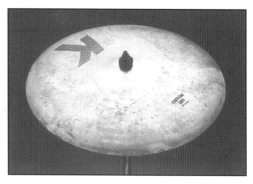

"Severely ultra-dry" K Custom Dry Ride
Courtesy of Zildjian

K Custom

In 1987 the K Custom cymbals were released in response to a demand for versatile cymbals, coming from people like Steve Gadd, Dave Weckl and Vinnie Colaiuta. They are also unlathed, but considerably less heavy than the Z's and featuring both hand- and a new type of automatic hammering. Two years later the "severely ultra-dry" K Custom Dry was added.

Scimitar Bronze (1990); the Noble & Cooley snare drum is made of Zildjian bronze.
Courtesy of Zildjian

A Custom

A new era of Turkish-style cymbal making was introduced with the A Custom series (1991). As Colin Schofield points out: "Five years ago we could have made five cymbals by hand that sounded like the A Customs, but we couldn't have made hundreds of them a day."

New machinery allow for increased consistency and smaller tolerances, which could not have been maintained with the regular machines. At the same time, ideas of the past have been applied: "We used an old-style lathing pattern, similar to the way the [A] cymbals of the forties and the fifties were lathed. That's why they do sound a little bit, to some extent, like those cymbals," according to Schofield.

Scimitar

In 1982 Zildjian introduced their first B8 alloy cymbals, the mid-price Amir[6] series, followed two years later by the unlathed (B8) Impulse series. The Impulse line was discontinued shortly after the introduction of the Z series. In 1990 the Amir's were replaced by an improved series, called Scimitar Bronze.

A heavier edition of these cymbals, Scimitar Bronze Rock, were introduced shortly afterwards. The name Scimitar (a Turkish sword) had been introduced earlier for a series of brass cymbals, released in the late 1980s. For Zildjian this was the first low-budget series. In 1992 they were replaced by the New Scimitars, now made of B8.

Other products

Next to the series mentioned above, Zildjian also lists a complete range of Drum Corps, Marching Band and Symphonic cymbals, as well as gongs (Turkish, Gamelan, Taiwan, China), crotales and Burma Bells.

In 1989 a snare drum, made of the Zildjian alloy was produced in cooperation with Noble & Cooley. It was discontinued in the early '90s. A special Cymbal Microphone

System, the ZMC-1, was launched in early 1987. In 1989 Zildjian acquired its own timber factory, and started producing drumsticks.

9.2.4. ZILDJIAN PRODUCTS FROM THE PAST

Though not having been made by the Avedis Zildjian Company, the old K Zildjians belong to its history. Less well-known products of the company are the Zilco, Zenjian and Alejian cymbals.

The Old K's

The old K, having been made in Turkey up till the late seventies, is and probably will always be one of the most sought after cymbals. There are collectors who'll buy any cymbal with the original logo, sometimes for as much as twice the price of a contemporary hand-hammered cymbal. Regarding quality of sound, this isn't always the best thing to do.

Being made entirely by hand, without any serious quality control throughout the process or afterwards, not always the most beautiful cymbals were produced. Consistency was hardly heard of in those days. It sometimes may even be the charm of things like an inclined cup or an out-of-center hole that appeal to K collectors. Such flaws do not mean the cymbals don't sound good. It's just one more indication that "the" old K doesn't exist.

Brighter Cups

There are considerable differences between each one, also depending on the time when they were made. As production techniques evolved, the cymbals changed. The shape of the bell, for instance, was at first not chosen because of sound reasons: the technique of consistently making large or high bells simply wasn't mastered completely. When the first "modern" dye-techniques were introduced, in the early sixties, higher, less clunky and brighter cups became an option for the first time.

Both heavy and, later on, thin cymbals were produced. The thinner ones became most famous, for their trashy sound, their spread, their warmth and their overtones. The cymbals, as they were played by Elvin Jones, Mel Lewis and others, represent what is generally indicated as "the old K sound." But there are also pingy K's around, be they not as often in the collections of jazz drummers.

Though old K's can be used in pretty much any style of music, many drummers choose not to use them live, especially in louder styles of music. Their irreplaceability, in many cases, is the main reason. There are not too many old K's around. In the fifties and sixties presumably no more then 40 to 45 cymbals were made per week.

Determining the Age

The age of old Zildjians can be sometimes determined from their trademark—the metal impregnation. As Constantinople was renamed Istanbul in 1930, cymbals bearing the first name can be safely assumed to be from before that time. This is with the exception of cymbals with the stamp *A Zildjian & Co. Genuine Constantinople Cymbals*, which was used on some models in the late seventies. The letter *A* in the stamp shows that these cymbals were not made in Turkey, where the *K* factory was located. For exact determination of the age of a cymbal the Zildjian company should be consulted; there are

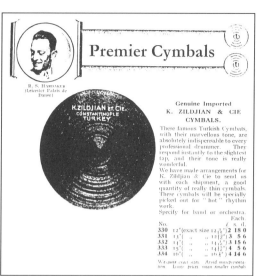

*...their tone is really wonderful...
section of a 1930s Premier catalog
Collection Classic Drum Museum,
England*

*Kerope Zildjian II who gave his
initial to the K Zildjian cymbals
(9.1.1.)
Courtesy of Zildjian*

too many variables (logos and trademarks, as well as cup sizes, lathing techniques, etc.) involved to give general written instructions.

Zilco

The Zilcos were about 25% lower in price. In 1939 Zilco also featured 11" and 13" Swish cymbals, "The new cymbal sensation; introduced by Gene Krupa and Dave Tough," according to a Premier catalog.

The tone that comes through... (Not guaranteed against breakage or warping).
Section of a 1937 Premier catalog
Collection Classic Drum Museum, England

The name Zilco was used again later on, for cymbals that were made in the Canadian Azco factory from 1968 to 1970 and from 1976 to 1979. There were two types. One was a second-line Zildjian, the other was a thinner cymbal that was not hammered.

The aforementioned Premier catalog also features Zinjian cymbals, which were, notwithstanding their misleading name, made by UFIP (see 9.7.1.)

Zenjian and Alejian

In the 1930s Zildjian made a second line of cymbals for Leedy, the famous drum manufacturer, under the name of Zenjian. Ludwig catalogs also listed these Zenjian cymbals, in various sizes and weights.

The 10" Deep Cup Version described as having a "penetrating 'squashy' ring that is plenty hot for modern cymbal socking."[7] In the 1940s Zildjian produced Alejian cymbals for Slingerland, in sizes from 8" up to 16" and in two to three different weights.

Individual Cymbals

The Avedis Zildjian Sting cymbal, giving an "individual 'sting' tone, in every keen drummer's kit" is listed in a Premier catalog of 1936/37. The 1948 Zildjian catalog contained the former Bop Flange Hi-hats (with flanged edges) and a Be-Bop cymbal, available in 18" to 26".

Also in recent years cymbals and series have been taken out of production, such as the Deep Ride, either because alternatives had been developed, or because the specific character of such cymbals was no longer in demand.

9.2.5. ZILDJIAN TRADEMARKS[1]

The route that was followed by the Zildjian trademarks was not as complicated as the one of the family's secret, yet some light should be shed on it. This also explains how the American company, at one time, could close down the Turkish factory, which had been in the hands of Kerope II's descendants since the early 1900s.

Agreements signed around 1926 by Aram Zildjian and—independently?—Yako Toledo with the Fred Gretsch Co. made the latter the exclusive distributor for Zildjian in America. Hereby Gretsch got the K Zildjian, A Zildjian and Zildjian trademarks.

Avedis III got the rights to the A Zildjian trademark back in 1951. Getting the K Zildjian trademark back into the family took a little longer. An attempt was made in 1955, but failed. Mikhail (Dulgaryian) Zilçan came over from the Turkish K company and testified for Gretsch that A Zildjian and K Zildjian were different instruments, and the case was decided in Gretsch's favor.

In 1968, K Zildjian Co. and all the European trademarks were bought back by Robert Zildjian on behalf of the Avedis Zildjian Co. Five years later Baldwin (who, at that time, owned Gretsch) was granted the exclusive distribution rights in the USA for ten years, in exchange for all other trademarks. Owning all Zildjian-related trademarks again, the Avedis Zildjian Co. was able to put an end to the Turkish factory.

9.3. SABIAN

Sabian has both a long and a short history. The products of the company are partially based on the centuries-old secret of the family of president Robert Zildjian, yet the actual history of the company starts in 1981.

...at the borders of St. John river...
Robert Zildjian (left)
Courtesy of Sabian

Two years after the death of his father, Robert Zildjian parted company with his brother Armand. He established Sabian—a composition of the names of his children, Sally, Billy and Andy—in the former Zildjian satellite-plant, Azco, in Meductic, Canada. Robert Zildjian had chosen this site, which he had frequently visited for fishing trips.

The original building, situated at the borders of St. John River, its corrugated iron walls then painted in Sabian burgundy-red, was never meant to house a complete company. Yet it wasn't until October 1989 that Sabian opened a separate office building, giving the company—60 employees in 1987—more room to breathe.

9.3.1. SABIAN: THE COMPANY

When Sabian first started, there were lots of other things to take care of besides making cymbals. "After the break-up it was decided that Sabian would not be allowed to enter the world market before January 1982. For the USA that date was set one year later," says Dave McAllister. As the former Azco plant had only been used for hammering and lathing, this delay was not too serious. There were no ovens and no rolling-mills, for example, so they couldn't start right away anyhow.

...Sabian burgundy-red...
Photo by the author

Sabian being an unknown name, the company decided to go for high-quality professional cymbals right from the beginning: "As the name doesn't sell the cymbals, the cymbals will have to sell the name," was the unofficial slogan. "Right after the break-up the product lines of both companies would have been seen as very close," McAllister says. "It's still the same family process. But since then, it seems that there's now two different directions: in product development, in the new sounds the companies have come up with. We have pursued a policy that's been dedicated to different sounds, to sound options. The first thing we did was to bring some off-the-wall products out of our vault, like the Rock Splash, the Leopard Ride and the Flange Ride, which later grew into the Sound Control series. One of the other things we have done is tried to create a new level of consistency, maintaining an individualized sound."

"...Let's redefine things...."
Kerope Zilcan (l) and James "Nort"
Hargrove (r)
Photo by the author

...the number of available HH
cymbals comes close to the figure of
the AA's...
Sabian HH Rock cymbals
Courtesy of Sabian

Sabian VSOP: Mini-Bell, Mini-Hats,
Dry Ride, Leopard Ride, Flange
Ride, Rocktagon and others
Courtesy of Sabian

Pointed Hats

Sabian has combined the direct knowledge of the ancient Turkish process—through former employees of the Turkish factory—with the ideas of people that were new in the field, such as James "Nort" Hargrove, who stated: "Let's redefine things. What we were told for years doesn't seem to be right always. They don't wear pointed hats in the melting room and they have no magic sticks." The Rocktagon cymbals and the unlathed Jack DeJohnette Crashes are clear examples of that part of the Sabian philosophy. The influence of the other side can still be found in the actual extensive hand-hammering process of the HH series.

9.3.2. SABIAN PRODUCTS

Within the span of a decade Sabian managed to introduce four series besides the more traditional AA and hand-hammered HH series. "The first developments of the HH line was with the symphonic, orchestral musicians in mind," according to McAllister. "The HH thing started because Robert Zildjian wanted to have a cymbal for symphonic percussion. That's his love, first and foremost. What we've tried to do is take the traditional Turkish hand-hammered type of cymbal, but give it a new musical dimension."

The HH series, being darker in sound than the AA series, are being used both in jazz and in rock and other contemporary styles. The AA series offered 105 different cymbals in 1992. The decrease compared to the 1988 catalog, listing 144 cymbals, is mainly caused by cutting down on sizes that lost popularity due to musical developments, such as 16" rides and 22" crashes.

Musical trends can also be traced from the number of available HH cymbals in 1992, which comes close to the figure of the AA's. Both series have been available in Brilliant finish since the first years of Sabian.

VSOP

In 1986 Sabian introduced the aforementioned Flange Ride, a design of Ed Thigpen. This light weight ride cymbal with its slightly flanged edge was the forerunner of the Sound Control Series (HH and AA, 1987), with which "the elimination of excessive overtones has been achieved." The Flange Ride was part of a number of specialty cymbals that were presented on a separate pamphlet, labelled VSOP. It contained the Mini-Hats, Sizzle and Rock Sizzle Hi-hats, the 18" Rocktagon, an exceptional heavy Rock Splash, and others.

Shortly before, the Leopard series, an unlathed and heavy variation of the hand-hammered HH, had been released. The Leopard hi-hat bottoms were later to be combined with either AA or HH top cymbals in the "cross-matched" Fusion hi-hats.

Signature Cymbals

In 1989 Sabian released a small series of unusual cymbals that were neither lathed nor hammered, including two very dark and dry crashes and a China: the Jack DeJohnette Signature series.

Later on DeJohnette and Sabian started working on additional cymbals of a different character.

With these series giving artists' names to cymbals was re-introduced (see 9.5.3.). Simultaneously Carmine Appice got his Signature China cymbal, a very loud 18" model, and the only "professional" cymbal in nickel-silver. In 1991, 16" and 20" models were added.

There was no signature on the Power Bell Ride, with its 8" bell, and the EQ-Hats, that were designed upon a request by Mel Gaynor. The original EQ-Hats featured a flat top and a bottom cymbal with four notches, to prevent air-lock. Later models (1992) featured four holes around the perimeter of the cymbal, as drummers occasionally cut their hand on the sharp edges of the notches.

...the only professional cymbals in nickel-silver...
Carmine Appice Signature Chinas
Courtesy of Sabian

At the other end of the spectrum Sabian released the HH Classic, in the sound tradition of the old K, yet with a deviating shape and cup (1988), the Jazz Ride and the Ed Thigpen Signature Crystal Ride (Flat ride, 1992). Sabian, at that time, was the only company featuring such "signed" cymbals.

AAX

The AAX, introduced in 1992, contains three sub-series: lighter weight Studio cymbals, medium weight Stage, and heavy weight Metal cymbals. The sizes of each of these variations partly differ, party overlap. "There is a genuine difference, soundwise, between AA, AAX and HH. When comparing them, you see they all have a different color. If we would have a white line and a black one, this would be gray," says Dan Barker of Sabian.

The name AAX, at the same time, points in the direction of AA(Xtension). Both lathing and hammering are different, allowing for very thin yet "ride-able" crashes and other new sounds and possibilities.

Sabian considers the AAX Metal variations as their first entire set of cymbals for this style. The Leopards are seen more as specialty-cymbals. With the El Sabor (1992), the first specific cymbal for Latin percussionists was born. The unlathed cup produces a clear bell sound, the ride area has a limited build-up, and crashes are fast due to the "Sound Control" flange.

B8

Sabian named their B8 series simply after the material they're made from. The first series were called B8, without any suffix. They were followed by a polished and brighter sounding variation, the B8 Plus. In 1988 the B8 Rock series were introduced, featuring heavier weight and more power.

Two years later the B8 Pro series arrived, featuring AA-style hammering and lathing, and containing crashes and rides in four weights, and hi-hats in three. This variation made the B8 Rock series superfluous.

...basically a regular splash, turned inside out...
B8 Pro China Splashes
Courtesy of Sabian

The series also brought forth the China Splash, basically looking like a regular splash that has been turned inside out. The concave shape of the center of the cup made it very suitable for mounting upside down on top of other cymbals. In 1992 the B8's and the B8 Pro's were listed, each also available in pre-packed performance sets. The first Sabian B8 cymbals were made in Germany.

Other Products

In the first half of the eighties Sabian carried a line of Italian cymbals called B20, a product of the Tosco company.

Sabian's collection of Orchestral Cymbals, a love of Robert Zildjian, encompasses Viennese (AA and HH), Germanic (HH), French (AA) and Suspended (AA and HH) cymbals.

Next there are series for Concert Band, Marching Band and Drum Corps, as well as

Taiwan, Turkish and Chinese gongs. The smaller China Gongs (1992, 14" up to 22") allow drummers and percussionists to use them in their setups.

The entire staff of the Zilciler Kollektif Sirketi. Top row, 4th and 5th from the left: Agop Tomurcuk and Mehmet Tamdeger, Presidents. Bottom row, 1st and 2nd from the left: Sarkis and Arman Tomurcuk (1988)
Photo by the author

9.4. ISTANBUL

In the outskirts of Istanbul, yet just inside of the old city walls, the Zilciler Kollektif Sirketi is housed on the ground floor and the basement of a small apartment building. Notwithstanding the modern age—yet poor—looks of this building, it is here where cymbals are made the way they used to be made in the past. The piles of wood blocks for the stone oven and the soot on clothes and walls are illustrative of the company that introduced their Istanbul cymbals in the early eighties.

9.4.1. ISTANBUL: THE COMPANY

Mehmet Tamdeger (1940) and Agop Tomurcuk (1941), founders and presidents of the company, got involved in cymbal making at a very young age, living in the neighborhood of the K Zildjian company. They started fetching water for the workers when they were seven, eight years old, and got hired as workers for Mikhail Zilçan (see 9.1.2.) in the fifties.[8]

"In 1977 they lost their boss, Mikhail," says their interpreter. "After his deathness they came like fish out of water." Having no other experience than cymbal making, Tamdeger and Tomurcuk decided to establish their own company. The old tools and machines were not available, as they were either scrapped or sold by Zildjian—stories differ.

In 1981 they made their own first cymbals, in the way they were taught to. Initially these cymbals were named *Zilciler* (Cymbalsmiths). The striking similarity both in name and in style with the Zildjian logo made the Avedis Zildjian Company subpoena Zilciler. Having lost this case, but gaining a lot of publicity, Tamdeger and Tomurcuk decided to rename their products Istanbul (1984). The company itself kept the original Zilciler name, though usually it is known as Istanbul.

The cymbals that were featured at the 1984 NAMM show, shortly before, featured a logo that, due to an "Armenian" font, was sometimes read as Ziljiler.

There are a lot of different stories about how—and if—Tamdeger and Tomurcuk got hold of the Zildjian process; either they reconstructed it from what they had learned over the years, or they were given the secret by Mikhail Zilçan when the factory was closed down by Zildjian, or they simply had been in charge of melting the metal for some time. In any case, the Istanbul cymbals bear close similarities to the old K's. The late Mel Lewis, when he first heard the Istanbuls, said: "My God, they're back." He became one of their few endorsees.

Fourteen

Besides Agop Tomurcuk's brother Oksant and a few other ex-K Zildjian employees, his sons Sarkis and Arman are also working in the factory. They are to continue this non-Zildjian-branch of history when the time comes.

With a workforce of fourteen, including the aforementioned names, Zilciler produces between 10,000 and 11,000 cymbals yearly (in 1990 that was less than 1.5 % of the sum total of Paiste, Sabian and Zildjian). Contrary to most other factories, it's not the company's goal to largely expand its production. Apart from the hydraulic press for the cups and a fax machine, the only token of modern times in Istanbul is the presidents' signatures on the cymbals; it is the secretary who signs them.

9.4.2. ISTANBUL PRODUCTS

The artisan nature of the company is well reflected in the sound and the character of the Istanbul cymbals. The main series, simply called Istanbul, are quite close to the old K's. This also goes for their consistency: as implied by the manufacturing process, the differences in exact size, profile, hammering and weight between two "identical"

Istanbul Ottoman
Photo by the author

...much authentic voice...
Regular and Turk series
Courtesy of Zilciler Kollektif Sirketi

cymbals generally is considerably larger than is the case with their Trans-Atlantic counterparts.

Mehmet Tomurcuk and Agop Tamdeger acknowledge this phenomenon, saying: "Our cymbals have much authentic voice." They also state that they, like Sabian and Zildjian, have adapted their cymbals somewhat to the demands of the audience, by making them slightly brighter and giving them a larger and higher cup than the old K's.

Turk

Zilciler makes a series of unlathed, hand-hammered cymbals, called Turk. In 1991 the Ottoman series was introduced, featuring a mixture of lathed and unlathed circles at the top side and an unlathed bottom. One year later two combinations were presented: Vezir cymbals, that are lathed on the top only, and the Sultan series, that have a lathed bottom and an Ottoman pattern on top. Vezir and Sultan are Turkish for "Prime Minister" and "Emperor."

Together with the traditional Janissary (Turkish marching) and Orchestral cymbals the Istanbul catalog listed 200 different models and sizes, each one being available in extra-thin to extra-heavy weights, and most in either of the aforementioned versions.

9.5. PAISTE

If it hadn't been for the Russian Revolution of 1917, for World War II, or for a number of other historic reasons, Paiste might still have been an Estonian company. It also might have become Canadian, or Swedish. As with other Western companies whose past extends more than a few decades, world politics have played a major part in the history of the Paiste company.

Ever since the new headquarters were established in Switzerland (1957), the company has grown into a stable force in the cymbal industry. It is the only Western company that runs two factories: one in Switzerland and one in Germany.

9.5.1. THE PAISTE HISTORY

The grandfather of Robert and Toomas Paiste, presidents since 1963, established a music store in his native Estonia at the turn of the twentieth century. Estonia, having been incorporated by Russia in 1710, had first gained a considerable autonomy, but started to give in since the latter half of the 19th century.

Somewhere before 1910 Michael Paiste decided to move the company to St. Petersburg. It was expanded into selling records and record players, as well as publishing sheet music. Musical instruments were being sold as well as repaired. Possibly a very limited number of cymbals was being produced.

Toomas and Robert Paiste
Courtesy of Paiste

Different Cultures

When the Russian Revolution started, Estonia having a fair chance to regain its independence, Michael Paiste decided to move back (1917). He re-established his company in the capital, Tallinn. For the time being he decided to leave his children at boarding schools near St. Petersburg, now renamed Leningrad.

Not being safe from the consequences of the Revolution there either, the Red Cross took his son Michael, born in 1910, together with a group of fellow sufferers to a refugee camp near Moscow. From there, a very young Michael Jr. started to roam over the world, ending up in Siberia, China, Japan and, finally, New York.

At age seventeen, after seven years, he was reunited with his parents in Estonia, now being an independent state. After less fruitful attempts to finish school, not being able to suddenly fit such a "system," Michael Jr. joined the company in 1927 and took over in 1928.

Having been exposed to music in different cultures and being in the possession of some natural handcraft skills, he was mainly interested in developing the cymbal-making part. The company started to grow. The first exports were realized in the late 1920s. In 1932 Paiste's cymbals reached the USA, imported by Ludwig.

Poland, Canada, Germany, Switzerland

New developments, however, caused the Paistes to move again.

Fearing new Russian invasions—which indeed happened—the family fled to Poland in the autumn of 1939. Having neither tools nor basic materials, being housed in a internment camp, work was impossible there at first. "But whether times are good or bad, music is being played anyway," Toomas Paiste (1939), says. "There's no war without music. So somehow my father got the materials he needed and he started producing again. He even had some exports, indirectly. Most of the production went to Germany, and it was exported from there. My father never told me that. I found out when I got together with instructors from Swedish military bands, and they had cymbals from Poland from that time."

First Employee

Around 1944 all papers were signed to migrate to Canada, away from it all. Yet the convoy of ships had to interrupt their voyage to the new world in Kiel, Germany, due to risks of mines and attacks. In 1947, somewhat later pushed by the Marshall Plan funds, Paiste started making cymbals again. The first employee was hired around that time. It took another two years to be able to produce a complete series of cymbals, including some "traditional" China types. The company, established in Rendsburg, started exporting again to the USA, Scandinavia, England and many other countries.

The wish to avoid future involuntary migrations made Michael Paiste decide to move once more—to a politically neutral country this time. Having mastered the German language in the meantime, Switzerland was favored above Sweden. The plant in Germany was retained.

9.5.2. SWITZERLAND

The Swiss headquarters were established in 1957, in the small village of Nottwil, in a rural area not too far from Lucerne *(Luzern)*. Next to the original building, now housing the offices, R&D and the showroom, there is the main factory and the home of Robert Paiste.

Two years later, Paiste's first professional series, the Formula 602, was released. "My father had been looking for a place to get new materials from. That's why he went to Italy [UFIP] in the early fifties. But they were casting their cymbals; my father wanted to have the alloy rolled," Toomas Paiste recalls. "He never actually changed the way of making the cymbals that much. Lacking good quality materials since the beginning, he always had been forced to find the best methods in order to make a good sound out of inferior alloys."

...expanding the production capacity would be at the expense of the workshop atmosphere...
Courtesy of Paiste

PPS

Finally, having the right materials at his disposal, there was yet another problem to overcome. Music shops carried mostly Zildjian cymbals, and they weren't exactly looking for a new brand. Robert and Toomas therefore started to get in touch with drummers to let them hear their cymbals, making them ask for Paiste in the shops. This initiative soon led to the establishment of Paiste International Drummer Service (1959), an organization employing Paiste Percussion Specialists (PPS) throughout the world. "Our father always had been in touch with musicians also, wanting to know what they needed. What we did was a logical step beyond what he started," says Toomas Paiste.

Sounds

Since 1963, when Michael Paiste passed away, Robert and Toomas have been leading the company. Robert Paiste (1932), who started working in the factory at age seventeen, specialized in research and development. "What we are making is sounds. The cymbals and the gongs themselves are just a means to that end," says Robert Paiste, whose ideas are the basis of every new product leaving the factory.

Toomas Paiste, who at first—in spite of his Business School education—also started working in the factory, later concentrated on the administrative side. Their sons, Michael and Robert Jr. (Robert's), and Eric (Toomas'), having been involved in the company much the same way—learning cymbal making from the start—are due to take over the legacy when the present presidents retire. The sons have closely followed their respective fathers footsteps: Eric Paiste has been heading Paiste America, founded in 1981; in 1992, the first cymbals designed by Michael Paiste (III) were introduced.

The Factories

In Nottwil, where most professional series are made, production is taken care of by 40 to 50 workers. This number indicates the large amount of handwork that is involved—

contrary to the rumor that Paiste makes "pressed" or "stamped" cymbals.

The German Rendsburg plant, where originally the other, less expensive series (up to the 1000 series), gongs and percussion instruments were being fabricated, used to be smaller, employing about 30 people.

With the introduction of the Sound Formula series (1990), Paiste started making professional series in Rendsburg, too. For this purpose the German factory was largely expanded. "Expanding the production capacity in Nottwil," said Toomas Paiste some years before, "would be at the expense of the workshop atmosphere in the factory. We want to retain that. Nottwil is not going to be any bigger than it is."

9.5.3. PAISTE PRODUCTS

After setting a nearly unbreakable world record by introducing five new series in one year, Paiste had the largest number of series of all cymbal manufacturers. In 1992, having introduced four more series and discontinued three of the lower priced ones, the total number of series amounted to thirteen, including Reflector and Rude variations, containing around 400 different cymbals.

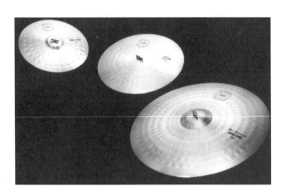

...The Paiste Sound Creation series involved a number of quite experimental individual sounds... Courtesy of Paiste

Paiste Seven Sound Set
Nr. 1 Bell, 8"
Nr. 2 Splash, 11"
Nr. 3 Bright Ride, 17"
Nr. 4 Flat Ride, 18"
Nr. 5 Ride Crash, 18"
Nr. 6 China Type, 18"
Nr. 7 Deep Ride, 20"
Paiste catalog, 1977
Courtesy of Paiste

Formula 602

The Formula 602 (Fo 602), as said above, was the first professional series of the company. Featuring "pure and controlled vibrations, making the sound delicate and crystal-clear" these cymbals clearly discerned themselves from B20-alloy series of other manufacturers. This was the first series to feature the patented Sound Edge hi-hats, with the corrugated edge on the bottom cymbals (1967). Sound Edges later became available in all other series.

Within the Fo 602 series Paiste released the Seven Sound set (1964). This set was presented as a small series of sounds, rather than cymbals. A somewhat similar collection was presented ten years later. The Sound Creations (B20), partially inspired by Jack DeJohnette, also involved a number of quite experimental individual sounds, not having a general character as a series.

The cymbals with the designation "New Dimension" were "special further developments intensifying existing sounds," according to a 1984 catalog. These series also contained the only factory-riveted cymbals Paiste made.

Another variation within the Fo 602 series was the Joe Morello Set, consisting of a pair of 14" hi-hats, and 17", 18" and 20" cymbals, bearing Morello's name. The hi-hats featured a slightly smaller top. The cymbals, that were designed in close cooperation with Morello, had shallower grooves than the regular 602's. They were listed from the late 1960s to the late 1970s.

First B8 Cymbals

With the Giant Beat and the Stambul '65 series Paiste made their first B8-material cymbals. The Giant Beats preceded the 2002 series (1971), which was to become the most widely used Paiste series in the following decades.

In those years the 2002 cymbals were, from time to time, adapted to changes in general taste and musical developments. In some cases this was indicated by a new logo (black to red, 1984), in other cases it was not given any publicity. Other series—of any manufacturer—have always been subjected to regular minor chances as well.

Rude and ColorSound 5

The unlathed and heavy Rude series (1980) were inspired by the need for high-volume output, yet they were also used by jazz players. This was the first complete series of unlathed cymbals. Many were to follow, from all manufacturers. In 1992, their use was mainly restricted to ride playing.

A new trend in cymbal looks was marked by the ColorSound 5 series, featuring cymbals in red, black, blue, and green, and other colors on special order (1984). A special series of cymbals, containing extra highs, were developed in order to compensate for the muffling effect of the colored lacquer. Like many other Paiste inventions these cymbals were imitated soon afterwards, as far as patents allowed.

One year, Five Series
In 1987 the aforementioned five new series were introduced. The 3000's, slightly heavier, louder and broader both in frequency range and dynamics than the 2002's, were the new top series. Somewhat cleaner, fresher and more melodic sounding cymbals were to be found in the new 2000 series.

The brass 200 and (B8) 400 and 1000 series replaced former low- to medium-priced series.

Besides these series Paiste also introduced the 3000 and 1000 Rude, as well as the 2000 (red, black and turquoise) and 400 (red and black) ColorSounds. All these variations involved special cymbals and production processes, not being merely unlathed or lacquered regular cymbals.

Two years later both 3000 and 2000 series became also available with bright shining surfaces (Reflector and Sound Reflection respectively). This technology, applied at lathing, does alter both looks and sound: "It results in a channelling of the cymbal's frequency mix and produces a shimmery, glassy sound...."

In spite of these developments the 2002 series, then provided with the subtitle "The Ever Classic," were not to disappear. Especially in Europe they stayed in demand. The readers of *Fachblatt,* a German music magazine, continued to name the 2002's the most popular series, up to 1992. According to Robert Paiste this also showed "how conservative the market can be."

The Paiste Line (1989): A new approach to defining the models. Mellow Ride, Full Ride, Rough Ride and others. Courtesy of Paiste

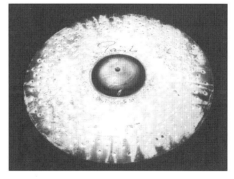

Dry Dark Ride:...the Paiste Line cymbals sound less identical to each other... Courtesy of Paiste

Paiste Sound Alloy
In the meantime Robert Paiste had secretly been working on a new alloy, feeling that "at one time the possibilities of the existing alloys would be exhausted." In early 1989 the Paiste Line, made of this Paiste Sound Alloy, were released. The series contained 71 models and sizes at that time.

In 1992 five 20" Rides were added, debuting two cymbals developed by Robert

Paiste's son, Michael: the Dry Crisp and Dark Crash Rides.

Having a considerably larger frequency range and sound potential, the Paiste Line cymbals sound less identical to each other than those of the other series. "We have always had this consistency image. Yet, what we have done, was just giving each cymbal its own set of parameters. We brought order, we organized things. That doesn't mean that one cymbal sounds exactly the same as the other. They sound similar, not exactly identical," said Robert Paiste, prior to the release of this series.

...new model names, descriptive of the cymbal's characteristics...
Paiste Sound Formula
Courtesy of Paiste

Sound Formula

The Sound Formulas, a second series of this alloy, was introduced in 1990. They were assumed to, in the coarse of time, replace the 2000 series. The introduction of the Sound Formula Reflector (1992) was expected to enhance this process.

With the Paiste Line a new set of cymbal designations was introduced as "A new approach to defining the models." Some of the names can also be found in the Sound Formula series. The new model names "are descriptive of the cymbal's sound characteristics and functions," according to the Paiste Line catalog. A scheme in which the names, the overall tonal levels of the cymbals and their sound characteristics can be traced back is included in that catalog.

Paiste in the 1990s

In 1992 a third new series, Alpha, was introduced. Made of B8, and considerably improving the quality of the 1000 series, the latter was to disappear, as well as the 400 series. The Alphas became Paiste's least expensive midrange series, followed by the 2000's.

The Brass-Tones, presented in the same year, were meant to replace the older low-budget series. The Brass-Tones also featured some new names in the field of cymbals: Tribal-Tones (rides), Shok-Tones (splash and China), Duo-Tones (hi-hats) and Rock-Tones for the crashes.

As for the 1990s Paiste planned to concentrate mainly on the latest series: Paiste Line, Sound Formula (and Reflector), Alpha and Brass-Tones. It may be the first company, at that time, to seriously cut back on the enormous—and sometimes confusing—amount of choices that the various brands offer.

The 602 and Sound Creation series disappeared from the price-lists around 1987, yet they were still available on special order for some years. As Paiste gradually diminishes the use of B20, they will eventually be discontinued.

Paiste Alpha
Courtesy of Paiste

Other Products

Besides the aforementioned drummers' series the Paiste program encompasses series of Hand, Band, Marching and Concert cymbals. Paiste also produces a large array of Tuned, Symphonic and Sound Creation gongs and other bronze percussion instruments such as Cymbal Tree Cymbals, Rotosounds, Accent Cymbals, Sound Discs and Plates, Cupchimes and Crotales.

A collection of these instruments was integrated in the Paiste Percussion Set, that has been used by drummers such as Danny Gottlieb and Paul Wertico.

9.5.4. PAISTE PRODUCTS FROM THE PAST

Dixie and Stambul (1956) were probably the first Paiste series that had specific series names. The Stambuls, bearing the name of the old city-center of Istanbul, were released in nickel silver. In 1965 they were upgraded and re-released, this time in B8.

At the same time the Giant Beat series were introduced in response to a demand for louder cymbals in "beat" music. This small series, consisting of 14" hi-hats, 18", 20", 22" and 24" cymbals without specific type designations, was discontinued in 1971.

Stanople was the name of medium-budget series in the fifties and sixties, made in the German factory. The Dixie and Stambul series were replaced by the 404 and 505's in 1978, that were in turn replaced by the 400 and 1000 series in 1987.

...Paiste also produces a large array of Tuned, Symphonic and Sound Creation gongs...
Courtesy of Paiste

9.6. MEINL

The first Meinl cymbals were cut out of large sheets of metal with a pair of metal shears, hammered, lathed and drilled by hand and, finally, transported to the railway station on the luggage carrier of Roland Meinl's bike.

Modern Secrets

Thirty five years later, in 1988, Meinl Musikinstrumente Gmbh fits every stereotype of a German manufacturer: high technology in an austere organization. When visiting Meinl terms such as efficiency, rational production and automization are constantly in the air. Reinhold Meinl, son of the founder: "There are no secrets! Whatever cymbal I get into my hands, I need just a day to get its exact formula. Our metal supplier simply takes one piece of metal and puts it in his computer. Within a few seconds you know everything—in percentages!"[9]

Yet Meinl has its secret as well. Not an ancient formula, but a sophisticated computer that does a large part of the cymbal making. A modern secret, that perfectly fits the Meinl philosophy.

9.6.1. MEINL: THE COMPANY

After an attempt to make a living by producing wind instruments, Roland Meinl decided to start making cymbals. "My grandfather had, at one time, made a few cymbals, though he never set up a real production. Hence my father hardly possessed any knowledge in that field, but he felt like he could succeed," Reinhold Meinl says. "We all assisted in packing and stamping the logos back then. It took eleven years before the first employee was hired, in 1964."

In that time about 50% of the production was exported to the USA, together with, among others, German made Tromsa drumsets. As soon as Roland Meinl found out about the first Japanese drumsets, he started to concentrate on importing these very affordable instruments. He was one of the first Pearl importers in Europe. Later he switched to Tama and Ibanez.

Meinl Musikinstrumente also started producing wind instruments again. A growing range of percussion instruments, mostly produced in the Far East, was added later. "We employ about sixty-five people. Twenty-five of them work in the cymbal factory," says Reinhold Meinl, who is mainly active in the fields of distribution and advertising. "Having a wholesale operation next to our production work gives us a wide view on the entire music industry, so we're not isolated from what's going on."

The company is established in two spacious buildings, just outside of a small town in

The first Meinl cymbals were transported on the luggage carrier of Roland Meinl's bike. Roland Meinl, founder of the company
Courtesy of Meinl

Meinl Musikinstrumente Gmbh.
Courtesy of Meinl

Bavaria, where even the smallest country roads are covered with an immaculate layer of asphalt.

The Other Way Around

From the start, Meinl's cymbal production was entirely concentrated on the low-priced market. Having the production process radically automated around 1974, this department was running well, without paying to much attention to it.

Then, in the early eighties, another European manufacturer started producing cymbals for this end of the market. "We didn't realize this until our sales went down more than 60%," Reinhold Meinl recalls. A choice had to be made: either stop making cymbals, or attempt to fight back, in a new way. Meinl decided for the second option.

In 1982 the Streamer series were re-released. Two years later Meinl set foot in the professionally oriented market with the Profile series, followed by another, more expensive top line in 1989: the Reference Class.

Contrary to most other manufacturers, that became well-known by their professional series and later on started making low-budget cymbals, Meinl did it the other way around. Reinhold Meinl: "I think it's very hard, once you have some top-of-the-line series, to make a low-budget cymbal. You'd have to improve your top cymbals to create room for a cheaper line, I guess. But how can you improve on an A Zildjian, for instance? After all, it's just a piece of metal we're talking about."

The Audience

Another striking difference with most other brands is that the number of different types within one series is very limited, even in the top series. The former Profile series contained only fifteen cymbals, and at their introduction (1989) the Reference Class collection was limited to nine types. Says Reinhold Meinl: "We only make cymbals that people want to buy. Once we made a cheap 15" hi-hat, which was not very successful. It might have been fobbed off on a fourteen-year-old beginner, because it had been on the shelf for so long. We don't want that. We'd rather make cymbals for the drummers in the audience than for the one on stage. Therefore, we're not too interested in endorsements either." (1988)

...Raker cymbals, with their highly recognizable dark-colored cup... Courtesy of Meinl

Tri-Tonal

Billy Cobham helped Meinl develop a small series of cymbals, the Tri-Tonals (1990), that carried Cobham's autograph. In combination with the Reference Class series, this event seemed to indicate that Meinl planned to adapt their philosophy and expand their position in the field of professional cymbals. Both series, as well as the Profiles, however, were discontinued around 1991. Billy Cobham stopped his cooperation with the company in that year as well. One year later Meinl indicated that they were working on a new top series.

9.6.2. MEINL PRODUCTS

The 1988 catalog of Meinl included Raker, Profile, Laser, and Dragon series. The design of the Raker cymbals, with their highly recognizable dark-colored cup, has been strongly inspired by the sound characteristics of the electronic drumset. Their sound is mainly concentrated on the higher frequencies. In 1992, the Rakers were Meinl's only professional line. The series was expanded and upgraded in 1991. Raker is the only professional series that has been available as a pre-packed set, consisting of 14" hi-hats, a 16" crash and a 20" ride, either in Heavy or Medium weights.

High compatibility for recording was, according to Meinl, the main feature of the Profile series (1984). A clean sound, in two variations: in the Profile Rock Velvet cymbals the mid-frequencies were stressed; the Volcanic Rock cymbals had a higher sound. A third variation, High Tech, was discontinued in the 1989 catalog.

*..Reference Class series, with a wider tonal range...
Courtesy of Meinl*

The brilliant finished Reference Class series (1989) had a wider tonal range than the other Meinl series. One year later the Tri-Tonal series were introduced. At the introduction three crashes, a 22" ride, a 22" China with six rivets and a pair of 14" hi-hats were presented. Special features of this series were the tone-control flange on the crashes and the strongly hammered cup of the ride. The Tri-Tonal concept, according to Meinl, gave the opportunity to "utilize different areas of the cymbal surface to get different blends of sound." For this series a new alloy was made.

The Dragon series, discontinued in 1989, were an exception in Meinl's catalog. These cymbals were made in China and, if necessary, finished off in Germany. Meinl offered both traditional Chinese models (Single Dragon) and Turkish models (Double Dragon). Similar cymbals were listed under the name Cobra.

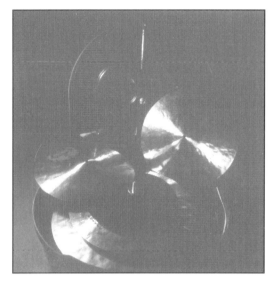

*...Dragon series, made in China, finished off in Germany...
Courtesy of Meinl*

Low-budget
In the low-budget range Meinl makes the Sterling (nickel-silver) Meteor (brass) and Marathon series. These series are all spinformed. The Laser Time is a low-cost version of the Raker series. In 1992 a new low-budget series was introduced under the name Live Sound.

The low-cost Streamer, Romen Mark 70 and Special 100 series, the predecessors of the Laser series, were discontinued.

The availability of lower-priced series has always been partly dependent on the prices of the basic materials.

Stencil Cymbals
Besides the series that are sold under the Meinl name, the German factory has long made cymbals for many other companies. Some examples are Avanti, Protec, Supreme, Headliner, Majestic, Magic, and Kent, the former USA drum company.

Contrary to other cymbal manufacturers who are active in the field of making such "stencil" cymbals, Meinl is very open about this part of their production. It forms a considerable part of their activities. The cymbal-buying companies, however, usually prefer not to have the origins of their cymbals revealed. The list above is, therefore, kept short.

*Luigi Tronci, one of the few presidents still actively making instruments
Photo courtesy of UFIP*

9.7. UFIP
Luigi Tronci is one of the few presidents who is still actively involved in the actual process of manufacturing his instruments. At UFIP the artisan tradition, stemming from a centuries-old tradition of church-bell making, is very much noticeable. "Our most important machines are our hands. The last big investment we made was that lathe, in the late 1950s. And, of course, the rotocasting machines. They're here since 1978. As far as modernization goes, that's all. The way we

UFIP, Pistoia. The offices on the left, the factory on the right.
Photo by the author

The main production hall
Photo by the author

make our cymbals doesn't allow us to go any further," said Tronci in the late eighties.

UFIP has its plants in the outskirts of Pistoia, a picturesque village in Tuscany, Italy. There are two small buildings, one housing the offices and the showroom, the other one the actual factory. Blackened walls and some broken windows can be seen.

There are about ten workers in the factory. Every one of them masters the art of making cymbals from start to finish.

Visitors are welcome, cameras and all. The word "secret" seems to be unknown in Pistoia.

Premier asking UFIP to supply "6 Pairs 15" Zinjian Cymbals" with 25% discount. "These Cymbals to be supplied with Large Cups and without Lines," dated June 21, 1934.

9.7.1. THE UFIP HISTORY

Luigi Tronci's great-grandfather started making musical instruments in the first half of the nineteenth century: Church-organs, complementing the Etruscan art of casting bronze for church bells. Slowly expanding their activities into other areas, the first Tronci cymbals were made around 1910. In the years that followed, jazz began to find its way into Europe.

Cymbals came in demand, and a few more Pistoian craftsmen started making these instruments. In 1931, after a period of intense competition, five of them decided to unite their commercial interests in the Unione Fabbricanti Italiani Piatti (UFIP), or, in English, the Association of Italian Cymbal Manufacturers.

Apart from Luigi Tronci's grandfather this Association included the cymbal makers Zanchi, Benti, Biasei and Rosati. Benti left after a couple of years. In 1947 the Zanchi Brothers started their own company, Zanki. Rosati's grandson, Buiani, was to be one of the co-founders of Tosco (1973). In 1968 the official status of UFIP was transformed to that of a production company.

Exports

According to the late Giovanni Spadacini, former consultant and export-manager of UFIP, the Italians didn't have an easy start. "Around 1930 the demand for jazz cymbals really started to grow. Italian cymbal makers could have profited from that development, if it hadn't been for Mussolini. At that time he was governing Italy, and he thought jazz to be a sin. The only style of music that was allowed was Italian folk music. I don't really dislike that kind of music, but there are hardly any cymbals involved.... After World War II things didn't improve right away. We were given space now, but the audience preferred American-made products, whether it was chewing gum, guitars or cymbals."

Later on UFIP, however, accomplished a good position, selling cymbals to various companies under various names. Some examples are Pearl, Ludwig, Premier (Zinjian, 1930s), Slingerland (UFIP and Kashian, sixties and seventies) and Rogers (Pasha; Grossman Music Corporation). Pasha cymbals, according to UFIP, were also distributed by Trophy Music, Cleveland, in the fifties and sixties.

"Gretsch (Ajiah) has been one of our major customers for quite some time as well. Unfortunately, demands increased faster than we could supply. Pearl, for instance, started importing Paiste in addition to UFIP. Later they stopped using UFIP completely. There is one old Pearl catalog that shows both brands. Nowadays [1987] we are exporting 60% to 70% of our production," says Luigi Tronci.

Zildjian and Paiste
The Italians have also had dealings with other cymbal companies. Whether Zildjian's request for "lower priced cymbals" (see 1.2.) ever had a sequel is improbable, but UFIP has certainly been buying from the Americans, back then.

Paiste's curiosity for UFIP's products is shown in a letter dated December 10, 1957, in which Paiste asks for "submitting a 36 cm cymbal, thin, for jazz," and inquires "under what conditions they could import UFIP in Germany." Earlier, in 1952, the same is asked concerning UFIP "Cinellen und Tam-Tams."

*Zinjian cymbals appraised in 1930s
Premier catalog.
Courtesy of Premier*

9.7.2. UFIP PRODUCTS
UFIP's main series, until 1990, were the Ritmo and the Solid Ride, which related to each other as A/AA and K/HH. The Solid Rides were also available in a Brilliant version, since 1986. Both series were made from B20 bronze.

Pierre Favre, the Swiss master drummer, first used the Solid Ride cymbals in 1975. Being a small company without the luxury of a full time R&D department, it took several years to officially introduce them.

Tiger
Roberto Spizzichino, who later started Spizz (see 9.8.), was involved in improving these series for some time. He also came up with the multi-colored Tiger series, which were played by Bernard Purdie, among others. The Tigers were discontinued in the mid-eighties.

In developing new cymbals and sounds, UFIP has always been assisted by a group of Italian pro-drummers, who frequently visit the factory. Also American name drummers—be they endorsers of other brands—have often supplied the company with useful feedback after having used its products.

Class
The involvement of Alex Mühlbauer, of the German company Drum Partner, led to great changes at UFIP, marketing- and productwise. In 1989 the first signs of this cooperation, aimed towards a larger share in the professional market, were released: a series of hand-hammered Class cymbals, that originally did not bear the UFIP name. They were then announced as a "special selection of handmade Italian cymbals for the German market."

*Reversed Chinas, Experience series
(Class), 1992
Courtesy of UFIP*

The Class series was included in the UFIP catalog of 1990, now as their own—internationally available—top series. At the Frankfurt Music Fair of that same year, the Solid Ride series had undergone some minor changes and was renamed Solid.

A new concept was introduced as the Experience series. All new cymbals, either single types or small series, were introduced within the Experience series first. If any of these products turned out to be successful, it was then decided whether it would be sold as Class—a series involving more handwork—or Solid.

...Rough Sound series, first released within the Experience series... Photo by Bas Westerweel

Natural and Rough

The Natural Sound and Rough Sound series were first released within the Experience series. With the Natural Sounds, featuring a very matte looking top side and a bright, regularly lathed bottom side, a new look in cymbals was introduced. The appearance of these cymbals is, according to UFIP, due to a "special tempering process that reduces surface tension in a way that naturally occurs over a period of some ten years, resulting in a soft, dark sound quality without losing strength and brilliance."

The Rough Sounds, meant for heavier drummers, feature unusually large hammermarks and a very fine type of lathing.

In 1992 the Natural and Rough Sound cymbals were extricated from the Experience series, which then became an experimental garden for newly developed individual cymbals. These cymbals may end up in the Class, Natural Sound or Rough Sound series.

Reversed and Flat Chinas and Samba Splashes were part of this collection in 1992. The Solid series had then been discontinued. Former Experience products, such as the China Splashes (regular bow, square cup) and Fast Crashes (with a flanged edge) were introduced in the Class series.

SCS

A new feature of the 1990 UFIP cymbals is the omission of the regular designations ride, crash and such. "Drummers have to decide for themselves how they want to use a certain cymbal," says UFIP. The exact weight is marked on the bottom, next to an indication of the sonic characteristics of the cymbal: Low, Medium or High.

This is known as the SCS (Sound Classification System). At the same time, the words "Handcrafted Cymbals," displayed on each cymbal, were replaced by "Earcrafted Cymbals."

Other Products

In the early nineties the B8 Kashian series (1980) were updated and renamed Kashian Pro. In 1992 experiments were going on to make this series from B12. The Brass Kashian 2000 series (1987) were renamed Kashian Standard.

Prior to the Kashians, UFIP made a series of low-budget cymbals under the name Red Sound. A series of heavier B8 cymbals, the Galaxy series, were discontinued one year after their introduction in 1989.

Apart from cymbals and gongs, UFIP also produces a large array of (Ice-, Burma- and other) bells, chimes, plates and more bronze percussion instruments, made from B20. Mastering the art of casting bronze, they have, for example, made replicas of 19th-century La Scala bells for the Florence Florentine Opera Orchestra and other, similarly unique items.

Abroad and the Past

In most countries UFIP cymbals have always been sold under the UFIP name. In the USA, UFIP cymbals used to be sold under the name Atlas. Before (until about 1988) they were also distributed by Abraxis, under the Abraxis name (On-Site). As of the early nineties the UFIP name was used internationally. Latin Percussion's Icebells also come from UFIP. The English importer has been distributing the low-budget series under the name of Percussion Plus.

In an old Premier catalog (1936), a series of Zinjian cymbals is mentioned. Contrary to what would be expected, these cymbals were made by UFIP: "Exclusive to Premier, made by hand, specially thin, for modern rhythmic playing." The series featured an 8" Sting model, and 10", 11" and 12" cymbals, "supplied THIN, unless specially ordered thick for pedal or parade work."

From 1950 up to the mid-sixties UFIP made and marketed a series of Super Constantinople cymbals for the French company Dolnet. Besides the name, also the logo of a half moon and three stars pointed in the direction of Turkey. The Super Constantinoples were a machine-hammered Ritmo type cymbal, mainly meant for marching.

The UFIP Ritmo series, introduced in 1968, was preceded by a series simply called Standard.

9.8. SPIZZICHINO

Roberto Spizzichino, originator of the Italian Spizz cymbals, started his cymbal-making career doing sound development and research for UFIP, Italy. One of his most striking results from that period was the multi colored Tiger series.

Because of non-matching philosophies, Spizzichino left UFIP in the mid-eighties. He established his own one-man cymbal factory where he started hand-hammering B20 cymbals, based on the rotocast process, yet with considerable differences in casting, tempering and heating procedures. These cymbals soon gained popularity and were used by international drummers (e.g. endorsee Joey Baron, and others who will remain unknown because of their endorsements with other companies).

USA distribution was taken care of by The Modern Drum Shop, New York, NY, that promoted them saying: "Of course they're not exactly like those old 'classics'—they just sound exactly the same."

In 1988 Spizzichino joined Bespeco International, Italy, for whom he continued producing four less-expensive series, simply called One, Two, Three and Four. The B20 cymbals were discontinued. It had turned out to be impossible to survive making such cymbals in a one-man factory, at that time.

Roberto Spizzichino
Photo by the author

Individual

According to Spizzichino, at first he produced no more than an estimated 300 cymbals of this type, about which he said: "I want these cymbals to have the looks and the sound of the old K's. Every cymbal should be an individual, each one different from the other. There's no news to the way I make them. I didn't invent anything."

In early 1991 Bespeco allowed Spizzichino to work on B20 cymbals again. As he felt that the name Spizz was to much associated with the non-professional B8 cymbals that he made for Bespeco, he named his professional series Antique, Bygone Sound.

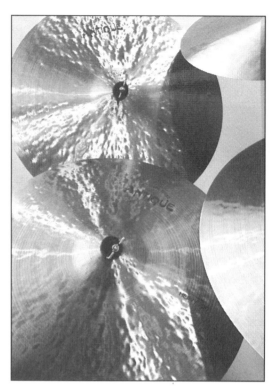

Antique, Bygone Sound cymbals by Roberto Spizzichino
Photo by the author

At the 1992 Frankfurt Music Fair these series were introduced in two versions. The Red labelled series were exclusively hand-hammered and only available in thin weights, "The sound jazz drummers are after," according to Spizz. The Black labelled series were machine-hammered in irregular patterns, and available in different weights. Shortly afterwards Spizz left Bespeco. He continued some time later, working with discs that were supplied by other companies: "The origins of the disc are not important; I can make the sound I want with any disc of the right material."

The Antique, Bygone Sound series was discontinued. The new hand-hammered cymbals, now available in all weights, were marked "Artisan cymbals by Roberto Spizzichino."

China

In 1989 Spizzichino visited the Wuhan factory in China with Wuhan distributor Paul Real.[10] Some prototypes were made at that time, resulting in a small series of Wuhan/Spizz cymbals. Spizzichino did not want to be associated with those cymbals: "I was involved in the design, but not in the production and the distribution." Paul Real stated that "A small number of Wuhan/Spizz cymbals do exist, but will not be available, except directly through our company."

Bespeco

The low- to medium-priced Two (brass) and One (B8) series were introduced in 1987. The slightly more expensive Three (hand-hammered B8) and Four series (identical to One, but with a special tempering process), came out in 1989. By that time Bespeco had provided Roberto with two more employees.

In 1992 two series of low-budget B8 cymbals were produced by Bespeco, now without Spizzichino, but according to his processes.

...a total percussion company...
Hammering cymbals at Pearl
Courtesy of Pearl

9.9. PEARL

The roots of today's Pearl Musical Instrument Company were founded in 1946, when Katsumi Yanagisawa started making music stands. During World War II the US Armed Forces had brought jazz to Japan, and this style of music was strongly gaining popularity.

The lack of instruments to perform this music on inspired Yanagisawa to start manufacturing drums. In 1950 his company was renamed in Pearl Industry Ltd. The first cymbals appear in the 1953 catalog, by then under the name Pearl Musical Instrument Company, a firm that employed thirty people.

Besides making their own series, Pearl has imported UFIP and later Paiste cymbals for quite some time. The products of the latter brand have clearly inspired the series they released in later years.

Today Pearl is the only company manufacturing both drums and cymbals. "Our goal has always been to be a total percussion company," says Mitsuo Yanagisawa, president and son of the founder.

Pearl Products

Pearl's first cymbals were low-budget brass instruments. In 1980 the CX 600 series was introduced, being their first step in the professional cymbal market. This series, made from B8, were originally meant for the domestic market only. When Pearl ceased importing Paiste they were able to distribute their own cymbals worldwide.

Pearl's other series, the low-budget brass CX 300 and CX 500 had been around for some time already. In 1985 the CX 500 series were expanded by a range of unlathed cymbals, that Pearl designated as "Wild." The CX 600 Wilds had been released before that time.

Inspired by the numerous new models and series that were presented each year by other companies, Pearl started doing extensive research for a new series. This resulted in the CX 900 cymbals, introduced in 1987. These series, featuring a notable reversed splash, replaced the 600's. Brilliant and unlathed Wild ranges were added in 1988.

...Wild and Brilliant ranges...
Photo Messe Frankfurt

Level

According to Mr. Yanagisawa's comments on these cymbals, Pearl was at that time continuing their research and development, and new, higher quality series were to be expected: "We're still not satisfied with these cymbals. More and more we need to walk again. We make first-class drums, and our cymbals have not yet reached that same level." Later that year (1989), however, the 900 series was discontinued. In 1992 Mr. Nakamura, spokesman for the company, stated that there are no plans for new professional series.

The cymbal department of Pearl, established in Japan, employed 25 people in 1989. Both B8 and Brass raw materials are made in Japan.

9.10. CHINA

The history of Chinese copper and bronze instruments dates back thousands of years. In the twentieth century old traditions and craftsmanship are combined with, be it modest, adaptations to new techniques, such as mechanical hammering and lathing. The most important and well-known Chinese cymbal company is Wuhan.

The company has two factories; one in Wuhan City, the other one in a small county town, in the province of Hubei. In the City factory—sources not coinciding—between 110 and 200 people are employed. According to Paul Real the vast majority of the Wuhan production, however, is not cymbals and gongs but brass and copper products for domestic use.[10]

Entrance of the Wuhan factory,
China, 1989
Photo by Paul Real, Paul Real
Sales/PR Percussion

Gaohongtai

This factory has been in production for 1900 years. The original name of the company was the Gaohongtai Company. It was renamed Wuhan at the time of the Cultural Revolution (1960): "All traces of the former China were to be purged, eliminated. Historical monuments were desecrated, rivers and cities changed names and the Gaohongtai factory was forced to be renamed after the city of its location," says Bruce Howard in an article on Wuhan Gongs and Cymbals.[11]

Within the next decades the original name came into use again, in combination with the name of Wuhan.

Besides Wuhan there are many other cymbal makers throughout China, such as in Peking, Tienjing (Skylark), Soochow and Canton, all having their own brand names.[12] The original labels are, in some cases, removed by importers who put their own name on the cymbals, making it impossible to trace the origins.

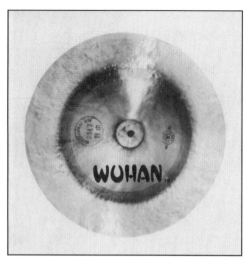

Wuhan Lion cymbal
Courtesy of Paul Real, Paul Real Sales/PR Percussion

Rancan Chinese Crash, "Turkish" cymbal from China
Photo Courtesy of Latin Percussion

Lion

The "original" China-cymbal, as it is used by many drummers, is officially called Lion. This name refers to the roaring sound that is caused by the material itself, but also by the flanged edges and the shape of the cup. The Lion cymbals, in sizes from 12" up to 27", are the main product of most Chinese cymbal manufacturers.

Jing cymbals, which stem from the Peking Opera, are quite thick and small. Therefore Western distributors also name them Bell cymbals. The sizes of these cymbals, which have a spherical cup, vary from 5" to 7.5". Chinese splash cymbals have a similar cup, be it relatively larger in width.

The Lion, Jing and Splash cymbals are just a small part of the total number of different cymbals and gongs. Bruce Howard mentioned seven categories, 64 varieties and 140 different designs being made in Wuhan (1982).[11]

Turkish

Chinese companies have been making Turkish cymbals as well for some decades. A Slingerland catalog of the 1930s lists 8" and 10" "Chinese Jazz Cymbals; Have that peculiar hiss-tone that is high, sharp and piercing."

Especially as China opened up to the Western part of the world, a demand for Turkish types of cymbals arose among drummers who started working in dinner and dance combos in tourist hotels. However, the Western-made cymbals that are needed to play this music are hardly available in China.[12] The Chinese-Turkish cymbals have a very peculiar complex, dark and dry sound, differing quite a lot from any of their Western counterparts.

9.11. OTHER MANUFACTURERS

Apart from the manufacturing companies mentioned above, there is an unknown number of other cymbal makers. Most of them produce low-budget cymbals, often without a specific brand name.

Besides Aïda in Japan there is a number—estimates vary from two to six or more— of factories in Taiwan. Presumably, cymbals are also being produced in other parts of the world. These products are mainly meant to be sold with very low-budget drumsets. In Thailand, cymbals are made according to the Chinese tradition.

Some examples of smaller companies are Weril, MZ and Adnan.

Weril

A Brazilian company, Weril Musical Instruments manufactures their cymbals mainly for the domestic market. They started cymbal making at the founding of the company in 1909. In 1940 Weril made their first cymbals for set drummers, in limited series.

Their Ziltannan cymbals used to be available in regular and Stripes finishes, the latter with a circular stripe-pattern in two shades, as a result of lathing (late eighties). Possibly these cymbals offered some inspiration for the Istanbul Ottoman series. The Ziltannan cymbals, from an alloy of 94% copper and 6% tin, were made by a combination of spinforming and (mechanical) hand-hammering.

The name Ziltannan dates from 1965. In 1991 this brand name was replaced by a small series under the name of Karachi, made of B10 "and a little phosphor." According to Weril, the name Karachi had an onomatopoeic character: "If you pronounce it beautifully, it sounds just like the cymbals."

MZ

Michael Zagrebin of St. Petersburg, Russia, lends his initials to a small series of cymbals in various sizes, well-made with relatively primitive tools. The alloy, presumably, is B8 or B12. There are no exports.

Karachi, by Weril
Photo by the author

MZ:...a small series...
Photo by Jørgen Ingmar Alofs

ADNAN

At the 1992 Frankfurt Music Fair, three small handmade Turkish cymbals were presented by Adnan Yilmaz of A&Y, Istanbul. Mr. Yilmaz indicated that, in the past, he had been cooperating with one of the presidents of the Zilciler Kollektif Sirketi (Istanbul). This statement was denied by representatives of the latter company. A larger range of Adnan cymbals, according to Yilmaz, could be expected in the future.

9.12. MANUFACTURERS OF THE PAST

Throughout the century some manufacturing companies have either disappeared completely, or stopped producing cymbals. Tosco and Zanchi belong to the first group, Ludwig (Ludwig), Premier (Zyn) and Sonor (Tyrko and Zymbor) to the latter.

Presumably there have been other, mainly small manufacturers of cymbals all over the world. The author would appreciate any additional information for future editions.

The late Giovanni Spadacini,
co-founder of Tosco
Photo by the author

9.12.1. TOSCO

A Texaco gas truck passing by inspired the late Giovanni Spadacini, co-founder of the company, to come up with the name Tosco: *Toscana Company,* after the Italian region where the factory was to be established. As with the other Tuscanian cymbal companies, the town of their choice was Pistoia.

Mr. Buiani, grandson of one of the co-founders of UFIP, was Spadacini's partner. From the early days of the company Robert Zildjian was also involved. When he left Zildjian, he brought his Tosco share with him into Sabian.

In the early eighties Robert Zildjian appointed Edmond Bauthier president of Tosco.

History and Products

The first Tosco castings were made on February 20, 1974. According to Spadacini the company never applied the rotocasting process. Tosco mainly made two series of Italian-style B20 cymbals. One series was only machine hammered, the other series was also hammered by hand.

In 1985 the dark sounding Super T series were introduced. One year later these series were redesigned, and renamed Martelato a Mano (Italian for "hand-hammered"). New casting techniques, allowing for a decrease of the thickness of the rough castings, had improved the quality of the cymbals.

One of the most striking Tosco products was the Octagonal, introduced circa 1978, which inspired the Sabian Rocktagon. A B8 series was made under the name Solaris.

Tosco has made cymbals for other companies, mainly in Europe (e.g. Royal, for Schenkelaars, Holland). According to Mr. Bauthier, Tosco cymbals were also sold to Ludwig (Ludwig) and Gretsch (Ajaha). Until the end of 1983 Tosco made Abex cymbals for the Meisel Company (USA)

Tosco "by Sabian"

In October 1986 the Tosco Company was closed. Spadacini, who had left the company three years before, later went back to UFIP. He passed away in 1991. Buiani, his co-founder, had left Tosco in 1980. Both of them sold their shares to Robert Zildjian. In its heyday there were approximately twenty people employed by Tosco. Sabian has been selling Tosco-made cymbals under the name of Sabian B20 from 1982 to 1985, clearly distinguishing them from their own Canadian cymbals. Tosco "by Sabian" cymbals have been sold in the USA by Samson.

9.12.2. ZANKI

The official name of the Italian company that produced Zanki cymbals is Zanchi, Fiorello & Figli (Fiorello Zanchi and Sons). Fiorello Zanchi, who had worked with the Tronci family since the early twenties, initiated the company. It was taken over by his sons Mariano, Roberto and Roni later. Carlo Biasei (UFIP) depicts Fiorello Zanchi as the teacher of all Pistoian cymbal makers: "He was the man with the golden hands." Fiorello died in the eighties.

The Zanchi family shares its history of Etruscan bronze craftsmanship with their fellow citizens, UFIP. In 1947 Zanchi left this Association and established his own company, also in Pistoia. In order to prevent foreigners from mispronouncing the Zanchi name they labelled their cymbals Zanki.

The story of Zanki is, of course, quite much like UFIP's, be it that Zanki always remained smaller. In April of 1992 Zanki was closed. Mariano and Roni joined UFIP; Roberto had left the company before.

Cooperation

In the company's heydays, the early fifties, there were around fourteen people involved in the production. When in the seventies the demand for Zanki cymbals suddenly increased dramatically, especially from the USA (distributed by Unicorn), the company couldn't deliver sufficiently. This, according to their spokeswoman, Grazia Zanchi, was one of the reasons that the size of the company decreased. In 1990 the entire production was taken care of by the aforementioned brothers.

They were the inventors of the rotocasting technique and made up the first machines for this process, which improved Italian cymbal making considerably. The fact that all the Zanki castings were made at the UFIP plant illustrated the close cooperation between the two companies—and the small size of Zanki.

Roni, Roberto and Mariano Zanchi (left to right)
Courtesy of Zanki

Zanki Products

The 1985 Zanki catalog mentioned 85 different cymbals in various weights. Splash cymbals, in 10" to 13", were listed both in Thin and Medium Thin, in which Zanki was

 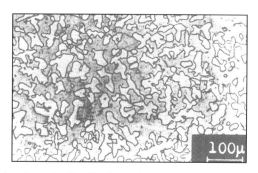

"Rotocasting represents the happy synthesis of both [traditional casting and mill-rolling] methods... In musical terms, our patented process obtains a decidedly superior response of the cymbals: a higher pitch, greater volume, longer duration."
Zanki pamphlet, 1980s. Microphotos of traditional (left) and rotocast (right) Italian cymbals.
Courtesy of Zanki

unique. An unusual feature of the catalog was that it mentioned approximate weights for each cymbal.

The bulk of Zanki's production used to be the Professional line, a series of B20 cymbals that was comparable to UFIP's former Ritmo series. They also had a small line of hand-hammered cymbals, called Super Zanki (1989). In 1991 a series of intensively hand-hammered Tuscan series was introduced, as well as the Dark Bronze series, the latter bearing close resemblance to the UFIP Natural Sound series.

A third new series, Zanki Classic, was first hammered by hand, followed by a mechanical hammering.

Vibra

Zanki's low-budget B8 cymbals were originally indicated as the Hobby series, consisting of special Rock and Jazz cymbals in a limited number of sizes. Later this series was

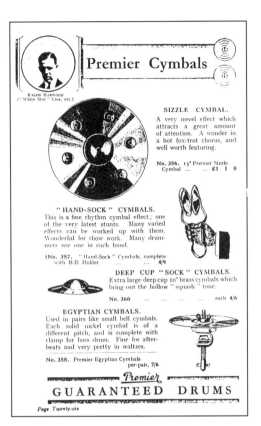

Sections of 1930's Premier catalogs Collection Classic Drum Museum, England

renamed B8 Professional. In 1989 the heavier B8 Rocks were added to this series. The B8 cymbals, again, are made in the fashion as UFIP's Kashian series. Zanki has also produced tam-tams and other bronze percussion instruments, as well as stencil cymbals for other companies.

Zanki has used the brandname Vibra for their hand-hammered cymbals since the 1950s. The name Vibra was re-introduced in England for a range of Zanki cymbals, distributed by Chalklin Percussion (1990)

9.12.3. PREMIER: ZYN

Zyn cymbals were made by Premier, England, from 1950 to 1984. The 5-Star Super Zyn series was introduced in 1968. They were featured as top-quality cymbals, be it in a limited range. The cymbals were made from the traditional B20 alloy. Premier bought this alloy as sheet metal and processed it in their Leicester factory, basically with the same kind of machines that were used by other manufacturers at that time.

The main reasons for discontinuing this series were the high cost of the material required, combined with bad supplies. Besides, Premier became the Zildjian distributor at that time.

Series

The regular Zyn series, according to Premier spokesman Roger Horrobin, were of middle price and quality, also available in a limited range. A price list of August 1981 shows that the 5-Star series cost about 10% to 15% less than the A Zildjian series.

The cheapest Premier range was the Krut series. Probably not having thought of the fact that this was pronounced similarly to "crud," Premier had tried to get a Turkish element in the name: spelling it backwards reveals that intention.

It was not only because of their image that they were renamed 2-Star Zyn in the late seventies. These cymbals were mostly sold through wholesalers and importers, to go with low-budget drumsets from the Far East.

Zyn's top series were discontinued some years before the final end of the brand in 1984. The main reason to end Zyn was the fact that in the early eighties competitors came up with large numbers of low-budget alternatives.

Premier and Imported Cymbals

Premier always used to have a large number of series of cymbals in their catalogs. Before Zyn came along, they advertised their own low-priced Premier Spun Cymbals (1936): "10" Deep Cup Cymbals for the foot pedal," that "bring out that hollow 'squash' tone."

Another notable item was the Premier Choke Cymbals: two 8" brass cymbals face to face on a holder, no muffling required. This item may well have inspired the invention the later X-Hat.

In the 1930s Premier promoted their 10" to 15" Imitation Turkish cymbals as "hand-hammered, hard and thin, and having a fine crisp tone." The same catalog lists a 13" sizzle cymbal, Hand-Sock cymbals, and Egyptian cymbals.

Furthermore, Premier distributed Zildjian, Zilco, Zinjian (see 9.7.2.), and Genuine Chinese cymbals in that period.

9.12.4. TYRKO AND ZYMBOR

Sonor produced Tyrko and Zymbor cymbals from the mid-1970s to the early eighties. The Tyrkos, mainly intended to go with Sonor's Orff educational instruments, were spinformed out of brass sheet metal. The Zymbor cymbals were sold with Sonor's low-priced Action, Ranger and Rocker drumsets.

French jazz drummer Daniel Humair is known to have frequently recorded with an unfinished Tyrko: he just had a hole drilled in one of the flat discs.

9.12.5. TROWA

In 1875, Johannes Link (1947) founded a small percussion company in Weissenfels/Saale, in former East Germany. In 1907 Link registered the Sonor trademark in Berlin. The original factory, later under the name Takton, produced Trowa cymbals.

According to Sonor, Trowa cymbals were low-budget pressed or spinformed cymbals.

Notwithstanding their limited quality, Trowa has been leading the Eastern market for quite some years. The production ceased when the Berlin wall was pulled down. Shortly afterwards Sonor attempted to buy the Takton factory in order to set up another production space for various percussion instruments. When arriving at the old factory, it turned out to be completely empty. All—reasonably advanced—machinery had disappeared.

9.12.6 LUDWIG[7]

"Tone is the chief requisite of cymbals. Ludwig own make Cymbals are 'spun' by skilled workers, and are processed to meet the exacting requirements of the drummer," so says a Ludwig catalog of the 1930s. An 8" brass cymbal cost 75 cents.

Ludwig's Nickel Silver cymbals, "polished to a satiny silver finish," were somewhat more expensive, listing an 8" for $1.20. Largest size in both series was 13". The Nickel Silver series were "practical for pedal cymbals where a clear, ringing bell-like tone is desired."

For their Sizzle Cymbals, provided with six rivets, Ludwig produced a special "notched" stick. The notches "are drawn across the cymbal's edge for a 'chattering, rasping, sizzling tone'." The Ludwig Sizzle looks remarkably like the Premier one, indicating that they may have come from outside companies after all.

Zenjian

Besides their own-make cymbals, Ludwig listed Zenjian Turkish Cymbals and K. Zildjian Constantinople Cymbals. A 10" Deep Cup Cymbal, available from all three brands, cost $1.23, $8.00, and $12.00 respectively. Before Gretsch took over, Ludwig had been the sole distributors of the K Zildjian cymbals in the USA. Ludwig also was the first company to sell Paiste cymbals in the USA (spun brass cymbals, around 1932; see 9.5.1.). In the 1950s they bought Paiste's third line of cymbals and stamped them "Ludwig Standard." "We had package deals where we would give away four 'Ludwig Standard' cymbals with every Ludwig outfit," recalls W.F. Ludwig Jr.[13]

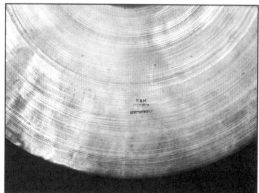

...cradle of the Turkish cymbals...
Detail of a cymbal by K&H
fabricants, Constantinople
Photo by the author
Collection British Historical Drum
Society

9.12.7. K&H

Istanbul (Constantinople), cradle of the Turkish cymbals, has presumably housed lots of small cymbal companies in the past. The British Historical Drum Society owns a cymbal of that time, labelled "K&H, fabricants Constantinople." No doubt, there are more cymbals of similar small and unknown companies around, such as those of Vram Hachikian.

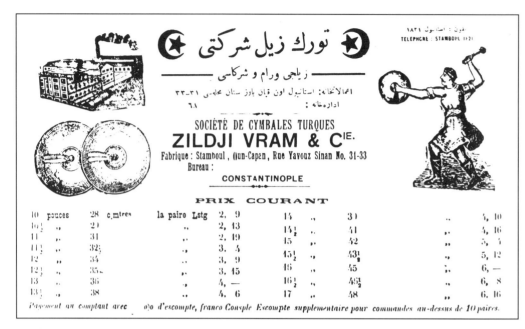

Price list of the Turkish Cymbal Company Zildji Vram, formed by Vram Hachikian
Courtesy of Dr. Pars Tuğlacı, Istanbul

9.12.8. ZILDJI VRAM[1]

According to Pars Tuğlacı's book *Turkish Bands of Past and Present*, Zildji Vram cymbals were made by a Vram Hachikian (Haçikyan), who at one time has adopted the name of Zilman. Vram was a master craftsman and foreman of the Kerope Zildjian Company.

A two-year contract, dating from September 1921, states that "At least 45 pairs of cymbals must be produced per week." For that he was to receive 30 liras per week. If he "falls ill he will be paid 30 liras per week for a period up to two months and 20 liras per month for the following two months. If his illness is further prolonged his payment will cease."

It may have been for this quite limited social security that Hachikian started making cymbals on his own. A price list of his Zildji Vram & Cie, Stamboul, Constantinople, mentions cymbals in seventeen sizes, ranging from 10" to 17", incrementally in half inches.

9.13. BRAND NAMES

The number of brands of cymbals largely surpasses the number of manufacturers. In most cases wholesale organizations—in some cases retailers—just order one or more series from one of the manufacturing companies, having the cymbals supplied with a logo and brand name of their own. Cymbals that are used for this purpose are referred to as "stencil" cymbals.

The series mentioned in this section do not always coincide with existing types and/or series of the manufacturer's own brand; the differences may involve anything from material to details of manufacturing process, according to the wishes of the distributor.

Most—but not all—of the following series are meant for starting and intermediate drummers, having low- to medium-budget price tags. This list will never be complete: you might order your own "name" cymbals tomorrow— at some of the factories.

AVANTI

In their mid-eighties catalog, Avanti (a brand name of Camber, USA) introduced the computer as an aid to design cymbals. The R&D process started off with a number of cymbals of all brands, which were divided into not-preferred and preferred groups by "musician advisors."

Avanti employed an acoustic researcher (Robert A. Berkovits of North American Digital Systems, Mass.) to analyze the sound spectrums of each cymbal within these groups. Bizarre looking computer-graphics of sound-spectrums and waves, printed in a folder with the name The Avanti Story, were to demonstrate significant differences. Avanti applied a "Newly developed computer program based on studies of human hearing." The graphics represented "'snapshots' of sound as a human listener might hear them. These measurements, therefore, reflect psycho-acoustic considerations."

The Avanti series were made according to the specifications found. The accompanying catalog listed over twenty models.

Avanti cymbals were shown at the Frankfurt Music Fair in 1985. In 1986 5000, 6000 (in red, black and blue) and 7000 series were distributed in the USA. A heavy unlathed, unfinished series, the 9000, was added later. *Modern Drummer's Equipment Annual '89/'90* mentioned just the 5000 Silver Tone series. In 1991 Avanti was not mentioned anymore. The cymbals were made in Germany.

ATLAS/UFIP
Atlas (Jim Atlas) distributed ATLAS/UFIP cymbals in the USA during the late eighties. The Italian-made range encompassed professional Pro II and hand-hammered Pro II Special series in B20 material, the Pegasus B8 and the A2000 (Kashian) series. UFIP's Tiger series was also listed. Each series contained special Symphonic and Marching/Concert Band cymbals. Atlas also distributed a number of Italian bronze percussion instruments.

BEATO
Fred Beato distributed UFIP cymbals under the Beato Turkish Sounds name from the mid- to late eighties. Beato listed both regularly hammered (Ritmo) and hand-hammered (Solid Ride) series.

COPPERHEAD
Walker, Runner and Sprinter were the illustrative names of three low- to medium-priced series of German-made cymbals, under the brand name Copperhead. They were distributed by Pustjens Percussion Products, The Netherlands, under the brand name Copperhead in the 1980s. Earlier Copperhead cymbals were produced in Taiwan. As of 1991 Copperheads, in one low-budget series only, were made in Italy.

HEADLINER
Headliner cymbals were released in 1985 in four low-budget series, the nickel-Silver 5K, and 7K, 9K Fashion Sound (colored) and the medium-priced 11K in B8 bronze. Headliner is a Meinl product.

PERCUSSION PLUS
Percussion Plus, a British wholesale company, started selling BS 700 bronze and BS 700 brass cymbals in the late 1980s, made by UFIP (Kashian and Kashian 2000 series).

PROTEC
The name Protec was launched at the end of 1986, featuring two German made series:

Protec I (nickel silver) and II (B8). Both series were made for the semi-pro market. Colin Barratt, Exports in Sound, England, later renamed the brand Magic.

RANCAN

Rancan is a brand name of Latin Percussion. Their 1988 catalog mentioned Rancan Lion Cymbals in six sizes (12" to 24"), an 18" Chinese Crash cymbal, Sheung cymbals in 6", 12" and 14" (big flange, very big cup), all made in China, and Italian made 6 1/4" and 8" Icebells (UFIP).

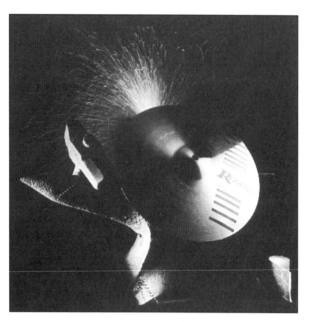

Rogers cymbals, made in Germany
Courtesy of Gary Mann

ROGERS

German-made Rogers cymbals were re-released at the Frankfurt Music Fair of 1987 in four series, all low- to medium-budget spinformed models, ranging from Red Hot for beginners and White Hot for students, to the "high energy" Black Rock and Power Rock series for pro and semi-pro drummers.

Arbiter Musical Instruments licensed the Rogers name and trademark from Fender USA for worldwide marketing. The line was developed by Gary Mann (later employed by Remo, Inc.) in cooperation with a team of professional drummers. Rogers cymbals were discontinued some years later.

VADER

Vader cymbals, made in West Germany, have been available in four series since their introduction in 1982: Invader, NuVader, Rainbow (colored, 1985) and SoundVader, all series with a low- to lower-medium pricetag. These cymbals were exported and distributed by Vader Musical GmbH, Rendsburg, West-Germany.

MISCELLANEOUS BRANDS

Mostly German-made and inexpensive cymbals have been or still are available under the following names: Adam, Biscayne, Camber, Cosmic Percussion (Cosmic and Ascend), DC 1000 Percussion, Kaman (CB Percussion, MX and Internationale, late eighties), Magic, Martin (England), Maya, Supreme, Studio 2000 tm, and Vega. This list is not complete.

Notes

1   "Inside Sabian," by Chip Stern, *Modern Drummer,* vol. 7, no. 11, Modern Drummer Publications, NJ, USA, 1983.
     The names of Yako Toledo and Salomon Covo have been spelled according to old invoices of the company.

2   *Mehterhane'den bando'ya* (Turkish Bands of Past and Present), by Dr. Pars Tuğlacı, Cem Yayinevi, Istanbul, Turkey, 1986.
     The text in this book is both in Turkish and in English.
     Pars Tuglaci also quotes from another book, *The History of Turkish Military Music* (R. Gazimihal; year not provided): "Following the death of Kerope, the cymbal workshop was taken over by his brother Karabet." Karabet was never mentioned in any other stories.

3   "The Avedis Zildjian Story," by Lennie DiMuzio, *Percussive Notes*, Vol. 28, no 2, PAS, Urbana, IL, USA, 1990.

4   "Manufacturing Secrecy: The Dueling Cymbal makers of North-America," by David H. Shayt, IA, *Journal of the Society for Industrial Archeology*, Volume 15: Number 1, Washington, D.C. (1989)

Also published in *Percussive Notes*, October 1991. The story that is referred to in this article is derived from "In Crashing World of Clang and Bang, Zildjian is the Cymbal of Excellence," by Peter Gorner, *Chicago Tribune*, May 18, 1983.

5   *Music, Musicians and Musical Instruments*, O. Commetant (1869), as quoted in the book of Pars Tuglaci (1). In the quote, the city of Istanbul is mentioned; at that time it was still called Constantinople, however.

6   *Amir* is Turkish for "Commander" or "Superior".

7   Relevant catalogs supplied by the Classic Drum Museum, by Alan Buckley, England.

8   Mikhail Zilçan is sometimes referred to as Mikhail Zildjian, which is misleading.

9   "Inside Meinl," by Donald Quade, *Modern Drummer,* vol. 9, no. 2, Modern Drummer Publications, Inc., New Jersey, USA, 1985.

10   Paul Real Sales/PR Percussion.

11   "Wuhan Gongs and Cymbals," by Bruce Howard, *Modern Drummer*, vol. 6, no. 2, Modern Drummer Publications, Inc., New Jersey, USA, 1982.

12   Information from Michael Ranta of Asian Sound, Cologne, Germany, as supplied to the author.

13   *The History of the Ludwig Drum Company*, by Paul William Schmidt, Centerstream Publishing, Fullerton, CA, USA, 1991.

...casting bronze...

SPIZZICHINO

Courtesy of Roberto Spizzichino

...entirely hand-hammered... (8.5.5.)

MEINL

Courtesy of Meinl

"Direct to disc"
Slogan for Meinl Profile series
(4.2. / 9.6.2.)

Heating the cup of a Raker cymbal (9.6.2.)

Meinl Tri-Tonal:... "utilize different areas of the cymbal surface to get different blends of sounds"... (9.6.2.)

SABIAN

Courtesy of Sabian

...taken out with long shovels... (8.3.3.)

...the assertion that "they do not know what they're going to make" is outdated...(8.3.)

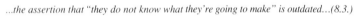

Receiving side of the rolling mill (8.3.3.)

Sizzle Hats (2.3. / 9.3.2.)

SABIAN
Courtesy of Sabian

...the tonal grooves are created, the sound opens up and the cymbal starts shining... (8.2. / 8.3.10.)

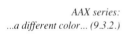

AAX series:
...a different color... (9.3.2.)

A new trend in cymbal looks; the 1984 ColorSound 5 series (5.3.5. / 9.5.3.)

PAISTE
Courtesy of Paiste

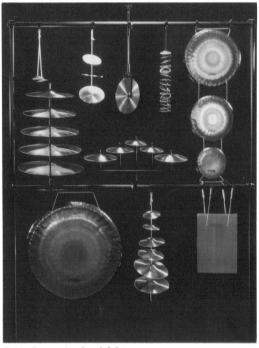

Paiste Percussion Set (9.5.3.)

...corrected by hand... (8.4.5.)

...the first series of unlathed cymbals... (9.5.3.)

...200-500 bpm, the power controlled by a footpedal... (8.4.5.)

"The Ever-Classic" (9.5.3.); note the Novo China (8.5.5.)

ISTANBUL

Photos by the author

...old-fashioned logs to heat the melting pots... (8.2.2.)

...the outskirts of Istanbul... (9.4.)

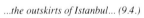

Photos by the author

...the salt eats away the tin-oxide... (8.3.5.)

...the hammerers hand the cymbals over to the lathemen, sitting right next to them... (8.3.14.)

...spectacular flames may be seen... (8.3.3.)

UFIP

Courtesy of UFIP

Natural Sound and Rough Sound Series (9.7.2.)

Preparing for rotocasting; note the rotocasting devices, with the lids opened (8.5.2.)

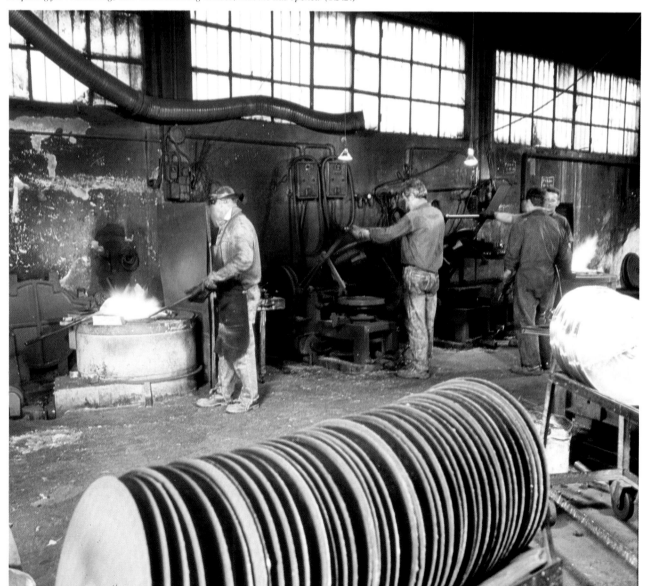

192

...the multi-colored Tiger series...
(8.5.3. / 9.7.2.)

...big jumbles of bronze-wire... (8.5.6.)

ZILDJIAN

Courtesy of Zildjian

Cast, rolled, cupped, tempered, hammered, lathed: a cymbal (8.3.)

Platinum series: ...a microscopically thin layer of metal is added... (5.3.4. / 8.3.12. / 9.3.2.)

A Custom series:...new machinery and an old style lathing pattern...
(8.3.15. / 9.2.3.)

Z series; clockwise: Closed Hex, Five Point Star (Power Smash),
Open Penta and Six Point Star (5.3.2. / 8.3.9. / 9.2.3.)

Four phases of a B8 cymbal (8.4.)

...a way of mixing copper and tin that was pioneered by Avedis Zildjian in 1623... The Zildjian alloy (8.3.1.)

HISTORICAL DATES

This list contains a collection of main events and highlights in the history of cymbals; it is not intended to be complete.

1700 BC

Beginning of the Bronze Age: tools are made from bronze, and people soon discover the acoustical qualities of this material.

1050 BC

Cymbals are mentioned in the Bible for the first time, when David returns to Israel with the Arc.

700 BC

Babylonian pictures display cymbals that clearly show similarities to contemporary instruments.

1623

The Armenian alchemist Avedis discovers a formula for mixing cymbal bronze. Based on this discovery and the cymbals he makes of it, he acquires the name Zildjian (Family of Cymbal Makers).

1680

Strungh is the first composer to have cymbal used in the Opera *(Esther)*.

1851

Avedis II introduces Zildjian cymbals at European Trade shows. Until then these cymbals were known only as "Turkish cymbals." From 1851 the name Zildjian is used as brand name.

Around this time Berlioz is the first composer to require the playing of a single "suspended" cymbal. The term suspended, as opposed to playing cymbals in pairs, is still being used today for orchestral cymbals.

1865

Avedis II passes away. Kerope Zildjian II continues manufacturing cymbals until his death in c1909. The name of the K Zildjian series is derived from this Kerope's first name.

1910

Mr. Tronci, grandfather of the present UFIP president, starts producing "Turkish" cymbals in Pistoia, Italy.

1925
The low-boy, predecessor of the hi-hat pedal, is developed, according to legend by drummer Vic Berton.

1928
Walberg & Auge start producing hi-hat pedals.

Michael Paiste takes over his father's music store and starts making his first cymbals.

1929
Aram Zildjian turns over the secret formula to his nephew Avedis III, who had moved to Boston some years earlier. The Avedis Zildjian Co. is established.

1930
The Turkish government changes the name of their capital from Constantinople to Istanbul. Cymbals bearing the name "Constantinople" date from before this period and are considered curiosities.

1931
Five small Italian cymbal companies of Mr. Tronci, Mr. Zanchi, Mr. Benti, Mr. Biasei and Mr. Rosati start cooperating in the Unione Fabbricanti Italiani Piatti (UFIP). Benti is the first one to leave. Sixty years later the sons of Mr. Tronci, Mr. Biasei (both UFIP) and Mr. Zanchi (Zanki; UFIP since 1992) are still actively involved in cymbal making.

1932
Paiste, at this time still settled in Estonia, makes its first exports to the USA. The cymbals are distributed by Ludwig. In 1929, exports to England and other countries had been realized.

1935
Mikhail Dulgaryian, grandson of Kerope Zildjian. at that time in charge of the Turkish K Zildjian factory, has to change his family name because of the Turkish government. He names himself Zilçan (Bell of the cymbal), a name that in pronunciation is hardly distinguishable from the Armenian Zildjian.

1945
Michael Paiste, father of the present Paiste presidents Robert and Toomas, settles in Rendsburg, West Germany. In the first decades the factory mainly concentrates on budget-series cymbals and gongs; later some of the professional series are also being made here.

1947
Michael Paiste hires his first employee.

Renato, Giovanni and Mariano Zanchi leave the UFIP corporation and start making Zanki cymbals.

1949
Paiste is the first Western manufacturer to make a "China Type."

1950
Pearl Industry is founded; the first cymbals are made shortly afterwards.

1951
Roland Meinl starts a factory to make wind instruments. A few years later he starts making cymbals.

1954
Paiste invests in their first mechanical hammer machines, which are only used for the initial, rudimental hammering. The final hammering is still done by hand.

1957
Paiste establishes Paiste Switzerland, the present headquarters of the firm. The prototypes of the Formula 602 series are made. This series, the first professional Paiste series, becomes available in 1959.

1964
The Paiste Seven Sound Set. This series encompassed the first Flat Ride (18") and 8" Bell cymbals.

Meinl experiments with the first spinforming machines and hires the first employee.

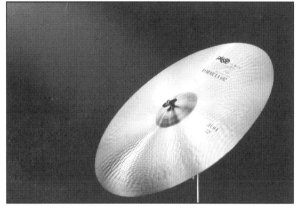

The first professional Paiste series, the Formula 602

1965
Paiste introduces the Giant Beat series, the first cymbals for which a bronze-alloy of 92% copper and 8% tin (B8) is used.

1967
Paiste Sound Edge hi-hats are introduced. In 1987 the patent ends and UFIP (Free Sound) and Meinl (Sound Wave) enter the market with similar hi-hat cymbals.

1968
The American Zildjian Company buys the K. Zildjian trademark from the Istanbul factory, and opens up the Azco. Ltd. in Meductic, Canada, as a subsidiary factory. Zilco

cymbals are made in this plant. In 1970 the first "new" K's are lathed and hammered at Azco. Melting and rolling takes place in the American plant. After the separation of brothers Armand and Robert Zildjian (1979) the latter begins Sabian in the Canadian plant.

1971

The Paiste 2002 series are introduced.

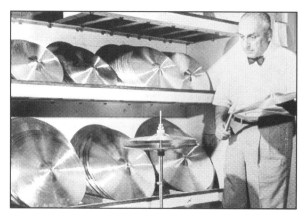

Avedis Zildjian III (1888-1979)
Courtesy of Zildjian

1972

Avedis Zildjian III moves the Zildjian plant from Boston to Norwell, Massachusetts.

1973

Buiani, one of the UFIP partners, starts Tosco with Giovanni Spadacini. This Italian factory later on (1979) is owned by Robert Zildjian, who has his Sabian B20 cymbals made there. In October 1986 Tosco is closed.

1974

The new Paiste Sound Creation cymbals are, like the older Seven Sound Set, meant as additional cymbals to a more regular setup.

Crew of the Turkish K factory,
closed around 1977
Courtesy of Zilciler Kollektif Sirketi,
Istanbul

c.1978

The Turkish Zildjian factory is closed. Sources vary as far as the exact year is concerned.

After fourteen years of experimentation, the Italian Zanchi brothers start using the rotocast system, which will also be applied by UFIP.

1979

Avedis III passes away. His sons Armand and Robert Zildjian take over. Dissentions about various subjects eventually separate them, and Robert Zildjian moves to Canada to start on his own (Sabian).

The first unlathed cymbal, the Zildjian Earth Ride, is introduced, followed by the first unlathed series (Paiste Rude) one year later.

1980

UFIP is the first Italian factory to make B8 cymbals, the UFIP Kashians.

Pearl enters the professional cymbal market with CX 600 series, which will be replaced by the CX 900 series in 1987.

...first all-American-made K series...
Courtesy of Zildjian

Zildjian Amir; the notches are intended to prevent air-lock.
Courtesy of Zildjian

1981

Zildjian introduces the first all-American-made K series.

Sabian Ltd. is founded by Robert Zildjian.

Mehmet Tamdeger and Agop Tomurcuk, two former employees of the Turkish Zildjian company, establish the Zilciler Kollektif Sirketi. In 1982 they first export cymbals under the brand name Zilciler (cymbal makers).

1982

Sabian cymbals enter the European market. Due to an agreement between Zildjian and Sabian, the Canadian cymbals may not be sold in the USA until 1983.

Zildjian introduces the Amir series, the first "European-style/sheetmetal" B8 cymbals that are made by a manufacturer with Turkish origins.

Meinl introduces a series of chrome-plated cymbals, which are sold in the USA under the name Avanti.

1983

Paiste turns a China cymbal inside-out. The Novo China is born.

1984

Paiste is the first to manufacture cymbals in various colors, The ColorSound 5 series.

Zilciler appears on the USA market. The company is sued by Zildjian, who finds the similarities in name and logo too strong. Zilciler looses and renames their products Istanbul, after the place where they are made.

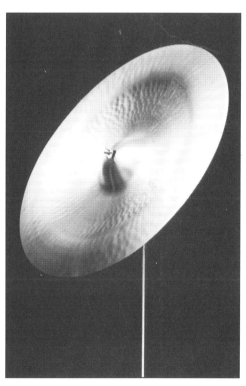

Paiste Novo China
Courtesy of Paiste

With the Profile series, Meinl steps out of the low-budget market. The Profiles are hammered by computer-controlled machines, a first in the manufacturing of cymbals.

UFIP presents the first Italian hand-hammered cymbals, the Solid Ride series, which was available in prototype versions since 1978.

Premier discontinues their Zyn cymbals, which had been in production since 1950.

1985

Meinl introduces a new look for cymbals with their Raker series, of which the dark-looking cup is unlathed. The Raker series are to become their most steady professional series.

Sabian starts producing Brilliant versions of their AA and HH series at no extra cost.

1986

Paiste presents five new series in one year: 200, 400, 1000, 2000 and 3000. The 400 and 2000 come in regular and colored versions, while the 1000 and 3000 are also available as unlathed Rude cymbals, bringing the sum total to nine.

Zildjian introduces the Z series, the first computer-hammered cymbals of Turkish origins.

Sabian makes a ride cymbal with a slight flange, appropriately called Flange Ride. This type of cymbal is the precursor of the AA and HH Sound Control series that appear in 1987.

Martellato a Mano is Italian for hand-hammered. Under this name Tosco presents a new series. Later that year, the factory is closed.

Roberto Spizzichino, former UFIP employee, starts a new cymbal company on his own. His handmade B20 cymbals are called Spizz. The name is later changed to Antique, Bygone Sound (1991). The name Spizz is then reserved for low-budget series.

1987

Zildjian introduces a line of cymbals that is automatically as well as hand-hammered, the K Custom series.

1988

Zildjian celebrates its 365th birthday and is officially declared to be America's oldest company.

1989

Paiste introduces the Paiste Line, based on a new alloy. The Paiste Line is the first series of a new Paiste program.

Zildjian introduces a cymbal with an 8" cup, the Z series 21" Mega Bell.

Jack DeJohnette has his own Signature Series made by Sabian. They are the first complete series ever that are neither lathed nor hammered.

Meinl introduces the Reference Class series, a new top line of the German brand.

1989
Pearl discontinues their only professional series, the 900.

1990
Meinl cooperates with Billy Cobham to develop the Tri-Tonal series.

The Class series, introduced by Pro Percussion Centre (Germany) in 1988, becomes part of the UFIP catalog. The cymbals lack designations such as ride, medium and thin. UFIP also introduces a new phenomena under the name Experience series, being reserved for new, experimental types of cymbals.

1991
Meinl discontinues their professional Profile, Reference Class and Tri-Tonal series

With the introduction of the Sound Formula series (Paiste Sound Alloy, 1990), the Alpha series (B8, 1991) and the Brass-Tones (Brass), Paiste's new range of series is completed.

The Istanbul Ottoman cymbals feature an unusual pattern of lathed and unlathed circles. Combinations of this pattern with regular and unlathed bottom sides follow in 1992, under the names of Sultan and Vezir.

Zildjian's A Custom series are hammered with a new type of "rotary" hammering machine.

1992
Sabian introduces the first cymbal that is specifically designed for Latin percussionists: the 18" El Sabor. The Sabian AAX series consists of three sub-series: Stage, Studio and Metal, each with their own range of sizes and weights.

Sabian El Sabor
Courtesy of Sabian

Adnan Yilnaz, from Turkey, features three small handmade cymbals at the Frankfurt Fair, under the name Adnan. Expansion of the brand is planned.

The Italian Zanki factory is closed. Mariano and Roni Zanchi join UFIP.

INDEX OF NAMES

The lists of names of groups and artists that drummers have performed with are not intended to be complete. Names of companies refer to the actual situation in 1992.

(q) = Quote
(n) = Notes
(s) = Setup

GENERAL INDEX

SOURCE MATERIAL / RECOMMENDED LITERATURE

BOOKS
- *Percussion Instruments and Their History*, James Blades, first published in 1970;
  Revised and updated 4th edition: Bold Strummer Ltd, Westport, CT, USA, 1992.
- *Max on "Swing"*, Max Bacon, The Premier Drum Co., Ltd., London 1934
- *The Art of Playing the Cymbals*, Sam Denov, Belwin-Mills Publishing Company, New York, 1966
- *The Selection, Care and Use of Cymbals in the Stage and Dance Band*, Roy Burns,
  Belwin Mills Publishing Company, New York, 1966
- *Mehterhane' den bando' ya* (Turkish Bands of Past and Present),
  by Dr. Pars Tuğlacı, Cem Yayinevi, Istanbul, Turkey, 1986.

MODERN DRUMMER ARTICLES
Articles from *Modern Drummer*, Modern Drummer Publications, Inc., New Jersey, USA:
- "The Care & Feeding of Cymbals," by Frank Kofsky, *Modern Drummer*, vol. 5, no. 6, 1981
- "Cymbals: Tips and Myths," by Roy Burns, *Modern Drummer*, vol. 5, no. 8, 1981
- "Wuhan Gongs and Cymbals," by Bruce Howard, *Modern Drummer*, vol. 6, no. 2, 1982
- "Tips on Cleaning Cymbals," by Chris King, *Modern Drummer*, vol. 7, no. 1, 1983
- "Inside Sabian," by Chip Stern, *Modern Drummer*, vol. 7, no. 11, 1983
- "Cymbals for Club Drummers," by Rick Van Horn, *Modern Drummer*, vol. 8, no. 2, 1984
- "Inside Meinl," by Donald Quade, *Modern Drummer*, vol. 9, no. 2, 1985
- "Inside Paiste," by Robyn Flans and Simon Goodwin, *Modern Drummer*, vol. 9, no. 11, 1985
- "Getting the Right Sound in the Studio," by T. Bruce Wittet, *Modern Drummer*, vol 13. no. 5, 1989
- "Cymbal Rivets," by Colin Schofield, *Modern Drummer*, vol. 13, no. 9, 1989
- "Inside Paiste," by Rick Van Horn, *Modern Drummer*, vol. 16, no. 6, 1992
- "Inside Sabian," by Rick van Horn, *Modern Drummer*, vol. 18, no. 8, 1992

OTHER ARTICLES AND PUBLICATIONS
- Zildjian White Papers no.'s 1-4, Avedis Zildjian Company, Norwell, Mass., USA, 1984
- "Cymbal Acoustics, Selection, and Care," by Larry C. Jones, April 1979, reprinted in *Percussion Anthology*
  (a compendium of percussion articles from *The Instrumentalist*, Evanston, IL, USA.)
- "Manufacturing Secrecy: The Dueling Cymbalmakers of North-America," by David H. Shayt, IA, *Journal of the
  Society for Industrial Archeology*, Volume 15: Number 1, Washington, D.C. (1989) Also published in *Percussive Notes*,
  October 1991.
- *Percussive Notes*, Vol. 28, no 2, PAS, Urbana, 1990: Featuring cymbals, with "The Avedis Zildjian Story" and
  "Cymbal Maintenance" by Lennie DiMuzio, "Cymbal Miking" by Colin Schofield and other articles.
- *Modern Drummer Equipment Annuals*, Modern Drummer Publications, Inc., New Jersey, USA, 1986 and onward.
- Catalogs, folders, and newsletters from Istanbul, Meinl, Paiste, Pearl, UFIP, Sabian, Spizz, Tosco, Zanki, Zildjian and
  other companies.

...and articles, interviews and sections from: *Modern Drummer*, USA; *Drums & Percussion*, Germany; *Percussive Notes*,
USA; *Rhythm*, England; *Slagwerkkrant*, The Netherlands.

PHYSICAL STUDIES OF CYMBALS
- "Vibrations of Plates, Gongs and Cymbals," by Thomas D. Rossing and Richard W. Peterson, *Percussive Notes*, vol 19
  no 3, Percussive Arts Society, Illinois 1982
- "Chladni's Law for Vibrating Plates," by T.D. Rossing, *American Journal of Physics*, 50, 271, 1982
- "Vibrational Modes of Plates and Cymbals," by T.D. Rossing, R.B. Shepherd, R.W. Peterson and C.A. Anderson, Proc.
  1st International Modal Analysis Conference. (Union College, Schenectady, NY, 1982)
- "Modes of Vibration and Decay Times in Cymbals," by R.B. Shepherd and T.D. Rossing, *Journal of the Acoustical
  Society of America*, 71, S64, 1982
- "*The Physics of Musical Instruments*," N.H. Fletcher and T.D. Rossing, Springer-Verlag, 1991
- "Some Acoustical Properties of Cymbals," reprinted from "Some Acoustical Properties of Triangles and Cymbals and
  Their Relation to Performance Practices," by Dr. John Baldwin, *Percussive Notes*, vol. 12, no. 1, PAS, Indiana, 1974.

RELATED ARTICLES BY THE AUTHOR
- "Visit to Zildjian," *Slagwerkkrant* 22, vol. 5, Stichting Slagwerkkrant, Amsterdam, The Netherlands, 1987
- "Visit to Meinl," *Slagwerkkrant* 27, vol. 6, Stichting Slagwerkkrant, Amsterdam, The Netherlands, 1988
- "Visit to Paiste," *Backstage Music Magazine*, vol. 6, nr. 57 / nr. 58, Stage Productions, Antwerp, Belgium, 1987
- "Visit to UFIP," *Music Maker*, vol. 11, May 1988, Audet, Nijmegen, The Netherlands
- "Visit to Sabian," *Music Maker*, vol. 12, January 1989, Audet, Nijmegen, The Netherlands
- "Visit to Istanbul," *Slagwerkkrant* 30, vol. 6, Stichting Slagwerkkrant, Amsterdam, The Netherlands, 1989 / *Rimshot
  Publication*, 2. Quartal 1991, Nieswand, Germany
- and reviews of all new cymbal series since 1983

SOURCES OF QUOTES AND SETUP STATEMENTS

DaD: *Drums and Drumming*, Miller Freeman Publications, San Fransisco, CA, USA (discontinued)
DP: *Drums & Percussion*, SZV Spezial Zeitschriftengesellschaft mbH & Co. Verlag KG, München, Germany
MD: *Modern Drummer*, Modern Drummer Publications, Inc., New Jersey, USA.
OTT: *One Two Testing*, IPC Magazines Ltd, London, England (discontinued)
R: *Rhythm,* Music Maker Publications, Ely, Cambridge, England
SN: *Sabian NewsBeat*, Sabian Ltd., Meductic, New Brunswick, Canada
ZT: *Zildjian Time*, Avedis Zildjian Company, Mass, USA
ZWP: *Zildjian White Paper*, Avedis Zildjian Company, Mass, USA

All quotes and statements not accounted for, were taken from interviews by the author. Most of these quotes were published in *Slagwerkkrant*, published by Keijser 18 Mediaprodukties, Amsterdam, The Netherlands. This also goes for quotes and statements within the text.

SETUPS (Chapter 4)
Some of these statements have been added to by the author